MEDITATION, YOGA AND SADHNA

MEDITATION, YOGA AND SADHNA

Editor-in-Chief
Swami Chidatman Jee Maharaj

ANMOL PUBLICATIONS PVT. LTD.
NEW DELHI - 110 002 (INDIA)

ANMOL PUBLICATIONS PVT. LTD.
H.O.: 4374/4B, Ansari Road, Daryaganj,
New Delhi-110 002 (India)
Ph.: 23278000, 23261597
B.O.: No. 1015, Ist Main Road, BSK IIIrd Stage
IIIrd Phase, IIIrd Block,
Bangalore - 560 085 (India)
Visit us at: www.anmolpublications.com

Meditation, Yoga and Sadhna

First Published, 2009
ISBN 978-81-261-3629-2

PRINTED IN INDIA

Printed at Mehra Offset Press, Delhi.

Contents

Preface

India colourful and vibrant, a land as diverse as its people. A mosaic of faiths, cultures, customs and languages that blend harmoniously to form a composite whole. One of the world's oldest living civilizations—which gave to the world—the concept of zero, the primordial sound Aum..., Yoga and Buddhism.

She is old. She is young. The two diametrically opposite, different yet unique and dynamic faces of India coexist even at this turn of the millennium. With a history of heritage, learning and civilisation dating back to almost 5000 years or perhaps even more, the modern India presents itself as an ideal country. From snow clad mountains to breezy sparkling blue sea side. From arid deserts with shifting sand dunes to lush green country sides. From ancient relics and architectural ruins dating back into antiquity to modern cities, India has it all.

To the north it is bordered by the world's highest mountain chain, where focthill valleys cover the northernmost of the country's maximum states. Further south, plateaus, tropical rain forests and sandy deserts are bordered by palm fringed beaches. Its southernmost tip is the meeting point of three Oceans.

India is a land of staggering contrast with a mingling of the tradition and modernity that is an unique experience to be in India. One will forever remember the stay in this wonderful Homeland-a land truly of mystery and enchantment. Only India can offer such an astonishing variety of contrasts.

She has given birth to numerous spiritual leaders and founders of some of the popular religions of the present day world. India probably has the most religious diversity in any country. It's the birthplace of Hinduism, Buddhism, Sikhism and Jainism and is among the few places to have a resident

Zoroastrian population. India with her veritable treasure trove of culture, mysticism, philosophy, art, music and architecture to name a few. Much of India's classical music is devotional and the North Indian Hindustani and South Indian Carnatic streams are distinct and both have a complex 'raga' framework. The legacy of dance in India is tremendous. The classical dances of India are numerous such as Kathakali of Kerala, Bharatnatyam of Tamil Nadu, Kuchipudi of Andhra Pradesh, Manipuri and Odissi from Orissa are the prominent dance forms in this country that sways to an altogether novel beat. The Yakshagana, nautanki and puppetry are ancient folk forms that live on till date. The earliest specimens of Indian painting are the ones on the walls of the Ajanta Caves dating back to 2nd century BC. The Mughals had a huge impact on Indian art. The influence of Persian art brought placid garden scenes, illustrations from myths, legends and history into Indian art. Word craft, handicrafts, architecture and sculpture all contribute to this rich and varied domain. Indian literature, both in English and in the vernacular, is ever more popular around the world.

The book aims at presenting perspectives of different aspects of Indian culture. It has topics on Indian classical music and dance, painting, ayurveda and yoga which are traditional and indigenous system of physical and mental wellbeing, language, philosophy and excellence achievements by Indian in the different branches of science and social sciences. It also includes our ancient religious and classic literature.

It is hoped that this book will be welcomed by the general readers as also scholars who are interested in the Indian heritage.

—*Editors*

1

Ancient India Meditation

Contemporary Hindu culture originated primarily with the Aryans who invaded India about 1500 B.C. bringing with them the Sanskrit language and the Vedic religion. However, for at least 1000 years prior to this invasion, there existed a culture in India about which we know very little.

The cities of the Indus river valley left no large monuments and although they did have a written language, it has not yet been translated. From some fragmentary evidence that does remain, scholars conclude this early culture contained within it many elements that were later incorporated into the Hindu religion.

The Language of Consciousness

The exploration of consciousness has developed to a remarkable degree in the Hindu culture. In fact, the Sanskrit language has shown itself to be sufficiently precise in describing the subtleties of consciousness exploration that many Sanskrit words, with no adequate English equivalents, have become commonplace in our own contemporary culture. Consider for example these terms:

Asanas: Postures used to stimulate flow of life-force through the body and to aid meditation.

Atman: The human soul or spirit—the essence of the inner being.

Ahimsa: The doctrine of nonviolence toward sentient beings.

Akasha: The ether; primordial substance that pervades the entire universe; the substratum of both mind and matter. All thoughts, feelings, or actions are recorded within it.

Brahman: Hindu god who represents the highest principle in the universe; the essence that permeates all existence. Brahman is the same as atman in the philosophy of the Upanishads.

Dharma: One's personal path in life, the fulfilment of which leads to a higher state of consciousness.

Dhyana: The focusing of attention on a particular spiritual idea in continuous meditation.

Guna: A cosmic force or quality. Hindu cosmology maintains that the universe is composed of three such qualities: satvic, meaning pure or truthful; rajasic, meaning rich or royal; and tomasic meaning rancid or decaying.

Ishwara: Personal manifestation of the supreme; the cosmic self; cosmic consciousness.

Karma: The principle by which all of our actions will effect our future circumstances, either in the present or in future lifetimes.

Mantras: Syllables, inaudible or vocalized, that are repeated during meditation.

Maya: The illusions the physical world generates to ensnare our consciousness.

Moksha: The attainment of liberation from the worldly life.

Mandala: Images used to meditate upon.

Nirvana: The transcendental state that is beyond the possibility of full comprehension or expression by the ordinary being enmeshed in the concept of selfhood.

Ojas: Energy developed by certain yogic practices that stimulates endocrine activity within the body.

Prana: Life energy that permeates the atmosphere, enters the human being through the breath, and can be directed by thought.

Pranayama: Yogic exercises for the regulation of the breath flow.

Samadhi: State of enlightenment of superconsciousness. The union of the individual consciousness with cosmic consciousness.

Sadhanas: Spiritual disciplines. Practical means for the attainment of a spiritual goal.

Samsara: The phenomena of the senses. Attachment to samsara leads to further rebirth.

Siddhis: Powers of the soul and spirit that are the fruits of yogic disciplines.

Soma: A plant, probably with psychedelic properties, that was prepared and used in ritual fashion to enable men to communicate with the gods.

Tantras: Books dealing with the worship of the female deities and specifying certain practices to attain liberation through sensuality, particularly through the heightened union of male and female energies.

Yoga: This is the Sanskrit word meaning union and refers to various practices designed to attain a state of perfect union between the self and the infinite.

The Discipline of Yoga

The Yoga Sutras of Patanjali prescribe a system of eight stages, or limbs for one's higher development. The first two limbs are known as yama and niyama. They involve a highly ethical and disciplined lifestyle—control, indifference, detachment, renunciation, charity, celibacy, vegetarianism, cleanliness, and nonviolence. The third step involves the development and care of the body through the use of exercises and postures called Asanas. The fourth stage involves pranayama breathing exercises. The next stage, pratyahara, involves meditation, by means of which one withdraws consciousness from the senses.

The fifth limb of yoga is called dharana which means concentration. An object of contemplation is held fixedly in the mind; it must not be allowed to waver or change its form or colour—as it will have a tendency to do. Often the yogi will concentrate on different chakras or focal points within the body. Self-analysis is used to observe breaks in concentration. Often he will carry a string of beads and one is pulled over the finger every time a break begins.

The next stage of dhyana occurs when the sense of separateness of the self from the object of concentration disappears and one experiences a union or oneness with that object. In the final stage, samadhi, one experiences an absolute, ecstatic cosmic consciousness. This does not, as some suppose, entail a loss of individuality. "The drop is not poured into the Ocean; the Ocean is poured into the Drop." The self and the entire universe are simultaneously experienced.

In the past decades, Western scientists have begun to study the abilities yogi practitioners can achieved. Body functions such as heartbeat, temperature, and brainwaves, that which had been previously thought of as totally autonomic, have been shown to be under the conscious control of some yogis. This research has paved the way for the newly emerging science of consciousness which will be discussed in Sections III and IV.

A Journey to Yoga-meditation: A Balance Path (a win-win solution)

"Life is full of contradiction and surprises, that it is infact, full of paradox like success or failure, happiness or distress etc. So always one question arises in the mind, how we can balance our life in paradox (duality in nature).

Definitely Yoga-Mediation is a third alternative for overcome such dualities, balance the mind and for living the life with totality. Yoga is a remedy for doubt, confusion and intellectual dissatisfaction.

A basic principle of yoga is that practising mental equilibrium neutralized the effects of delusion. Yoga-Meditation is a scientific process of neutralization of duality of Mental Speculation and Emotional stimulation from Successes & failure, Strength & Weakness, Discrimination and self sense-mind,

Spirits and matter, Soul & Body, Knowledge & ignorance, health and diseases, Changeless and transistorizes, Light & darkness, Divine self & False Ego, Self-control and temptation, Life and death.

"It is the Holistic universe where everything is fundamentally interconnected by a common background".

So In simple Term, Yoga means integration, unification, addition of positive elements in our bodies, minds, hearts and souls for harmonization of our all thoughts, actions and deeds for wellness of humanity.

Lord Krishna in Bhagavad Gita has described different yoga system for different types of people according to their way of living, nature and their conditional mind. All type of yoga-bhakti yoga (Devotion oriented), karma yoga (action oriented), Raja yoga (Patanjali Yoga system-scientific method of meditation) and janan Yoga (wisdom oriented) reach every body on path of self-realization.

Patanjali, the father of Yoga, is famous for his ancient eightfold path of yoga. The idea is to follow a path of positive mind control that leads one to the living understanding of being that is so effective that for the greatest students and masters of yoga-this goal is the ONLY GOAL. Pantajali called it Samadhi. It is also known as Nirvana,Union with the Divine Intelligence, Cosmic Consciousness, and Ultimate Bliss.

Patanjali Yoga system is a systematically method for attaining Ultimate bliss. The sequesnce of patanjali Yoga system is reprented in following way.

1. Yama (Moral conduct)
2. Niyama (Religious observance),
3. Asana (Right posture to still bodily restlessness),
4. Pranayama (control of Prana, Subtle life control),
5. Pratayahar (Interiorization),
6. Dharana (concentration),
7. Dhyana (Meditation),
8. Samadhi (superconscious experience-Ultimate Bliss).

The Ultimate aim of yoga to understand true nature of self (consciousness) and integrate with cosmic consciousness for attaining ultimate bliss which is described in this line beautifully.

The Four Great Vedic statements: 'That Thou Art,' 'I am Brahman', 'This self is Brahman', and 'Brahman is Consciousness (Mind).'

Every Sage has said, "Know Thyself"

Concentration = Definite : Meditation = Infinite

Yoga = Definite + Infinite = Ultimate Bliss

Yoga = Self Consciousness + Cosmic consciousness = Ultimate Bliss

Basically Yoga provides a sets of experience based techniques so that we can aware our whole mind (Left Brain-logical, analytical, Fact based, sequential and right brain-synergetic, intuitive, Emotional, synthesizing, holistic) for integration of our thinking pattern and how it work effectively when it is driven by the soul. It brings us towards centre (root) which is infinite powerful, infinite creative and infinite bliss. So let's go ahead-It is your choice but remember it is win-win deals for all human being.

I am sharing following divine songs of Bhagavad Gita for better understanding of Yoga-meditation.

"The uncontrolled mind does not guess that the Atman (soul) is present:

How Can it Mediate?

Without meditation, where is peace

Without peace, where is happiness?"

"For one who has conquered the mind, the super soul is already reached, for he has attained tranquillity to such a man: success & failure, happiness and distress, honour and dishonour are all the same".

"Performed your duty equipoise, abandoning all attachment to success or failure. Such equanimity is called Yoga".

"You have a right to perform your prescribed duty, but you are not entitled to the fruit of action. Never consider yourself the cause of the result of your activities and never be attached to not doing your duty".

"Now the Atman (Soul) as the lord and the master of the chariot, which is the body. The intellectual you should know as the charioteer. The mind should be known as (merely) the rein. The one whose mind is not harnessed properly, who's is devoid of proper knowledge and wisdom, his sense organs go beyond the control of the intellect as vicious horse go beyond the control of charioteer".

"Those who are beyond the dualities that arise from doubts, whose minds are engaged With in, who are always busy working for the welfare of all living being and who are free from all sins achieve liberation in the supreme".

"He is perfect yogi who, compare to his ownself, see the true equality of all being, in both their happiness and their distress".

Yoga (Integration or unification) is a vision of all sciences or arts & religion. Yoga resonance with psychology and quantum mechanics in a very scientific manner and bring us from happiness to Bliss. Yoga-Meditation moves yourself for understanding thoughts, feeling and experiences effectively. Yoga-Meditation active our consciousness who integrates body, mind and heart. Yoga-Meditation is about true taste which you can feel in last continuously.

So Just drinks (experience or feel it) this timeless wisdom from mind with complete devotion & faith in the heart and integrates your consciousness with cosmic consciousness for attaining ultimate bliss.

It is a first step for understanding of this cosmic wisdom because Our Journey begins from Zero to Infinite. So at this balance path try to walk few steps with devotion & faith then you automatically can disclose mystery of complete happiness. It is your journey, only you can experience & feel it because true knowledge is just medium (a vehicle) for reaching ultimate goal (perfect happiness).

Vipassana Meditation

The technique of Vipassana is a simple, practical way to achieve real peace of mind and to lead a happy, useful life. Vipassana means "to see things as they really are"; it is a logical process of mental purification through self-observation.

From time to time, we all experience agitation, frustration and disharmony. When we suffer, we do not keep our misery limited to ourselves; instead, we keep distributing it to others. Certainly this is not a proper way to live. We all long to live at peace within ourselves, and with those around us. After all, human beings are social beings: we have to live and interact with others. How, then, can we live peacefully? How can we remain harmonious ourselves, and maintain peace and harmony around us?

Vipassana enables us to experience peace and harmony: it purifies the mind, freeing it from suffering and the deep-seated causes of suffering. The practice leads step-by-step to the highest spiritual goal of full liberation from all mental defilements.

Historical Background

Vipassana is one of India's most ancient meditation techniques. It was rediscovered 2500 years ago by Gotama the Buddha, and is the essence of what he practised and taught during his forty-five year ministry. During the Buddha's time, large numbers of people in northern India were freed from the bonds of suffering by practising Vipassana, allowing them to attain high levels of achievement in all spheres of life. Over time, the technique spread to the neighbouring countries of Myanmar (Burma), Sri Lanka, Thailand and others, where it had the same ennobling effect.

Five centuries after the Buddha, the noble heritage of Vipassana had disappeared from India. The purity of the teaching was lost elsewhere as well. In the country of Myanmar, however, it was preserved by a chain of devoted teachers. From generation to generation, over two thousand years, this dedicated lineage transmitted the technique in its pristine purity.

In our time, Vipassana has been reintroduced to India, as well as to citizens from more than eighty other countries, by S.N. Goenka. He was authorized to teach Vipassana by the renowned Burmese Vipassana teacher, Sayagyi U Ba Khin. Before he died in 1971, Sayagyi was able to see one of his most cherished dreams realized. He had the strong wish that Vipassana should return to India, the land of its origin, to help it come out of its manifold problems. From India, he felt sure it would then spread throughout the world for the benefit of all mankind.

S.N. Goenka began conducting Vipassana courses in India in 1969; after ten years, he began to teach in foreign countries as well. In the thirty-five years since he started teaching, S.N. Goenka has conducted many ten-day Vipassana courses, and trained over 800 assistant teachers who have conducted many courses worldwide. In addition, many Centres have been established in India for the exclusive practice of Vipassana. Centres for exclusive practice have been established across the world as well. The invaluable gem of Vipassana, long preserved in the small country of Myanmar, can now be practised in many places throughout the world. Today ever-increasing numbers of people have the opportunity to learn this art of living which brings lasting peace and happiness.

In the past, India had the distinction of being regarded as a World Teacher. In our time, the Ganges of Truth is once again flowing out from India to a thirsty world.

The Practice

To learn Vipassana it is necessary to take a ten-day residential course under the guidance of a qualified teacher. The courses are conducted at established Vipassana Centres and other places.For the duration of the retreat, students remain within the course site, having no contact with the outside world. They refrain from reading and writing, and suspend any religious practices or other disciplines. They follow a demanding daily schedule which includes about ten hours of sitting meditation. They also observe silence, not communicating with fellow students; however, they are free to discuss meditation questions with the teacher and material problems with the management.

There are three steps to the training. First, the students practice abstinence from actions which cause harm. They undertake five moral precepts, practising abstention from killing, stealing, lying, sexual misconduct and the use of intoxicants. The observation of these precepts allows the mind to calm down sufficiently to proceed with the task at hand. Second, for the first three-and-a-half days, students practice Anapana meditation, focusing attention on the breath. This practice helps to develop control over the unruly mind.

These first two steps of living a wholesome life and developing control of the mind are necessary and beneficial, but are incomplete unless the third step is taken: purifying the mind of underlying negativities. The third step, undertaken for the last six-and-a-half days, is the practice of Vipassana: one penetrates one's entire physical and mental structure with the clarity of insight.

Students receive systematic meditation instructions several times a day, and each day's progress is explained during a taped evening discourse by S.N. Goenka. Complete silence is observed for the first nine days. On the tenth day, students resume speaking, making the transition back to a more extroverted way of life. The course concludes on the morning of the eleventh day. The retreat closes with the practice of metta-bhavana (loving-kindness or good will towards all), a meditation technique in which the purity developed during the course is shared with all beings. Pictorial representation of a 10 day retreat at Dhammagiri

The Courses

Vipassana courses are held regularly at permanent centres and rented sites in different countries. In addition to frequent ten-day courses, special courses and long courses of 20, 30, 45 and 60 days are offered for advanced students at long course centres like Dhamma Tapovan established for this purpose.

Short, courses in Anapana, the introductory part of the Vipassana technique, are courses offered for children in India and in other countries. The courses last for one to three days and serve children in two age groups: eight to eleven, and twelve to fifteen years.

All courses throughout the world are run solely on the basis of freely-offered donations. No fee charged: the courses are financed totally by donations from students who have completed a prior course and wish to share the benefits they themselves received by giving donation for the students who come after them.

Neither the Teacher nor the assistant teachers receive remuneration; they and those who serve the courses volunteer their time. This practice is consistent with the pure tradition, whereby the teaching is to be offered freely, free from any taint of commercialism, and supported solely by donations stemming from the wholesome volitions of gratitude and generosity.

A Non-Sectarian Technique

Although Vipassana is a part of Buddha's teaching, it contains nothing of a sectarian nature, and can be accepted and applied by people of any background. The Buddha himself taught Dhamma (the way, the truth, the path). He did not call his followers "Buddhists"; he referred to them as "Dhammists" (those who follow the truth). The technique works on the basis that all human beings share the same problems, and a pragmatic method which can eradicate these problems can be universally practised.

Vipassana courses are open to anyone sincerely wishing to learn the technique, irrespective of race, caste, faith or nationality. Hindus, Jains, Muslims, Sikhs, Buddhists, Christians, Jews as well as members of other religions have all successfully practised Vipassana. The malady is universal; therefore, the remedy has to be universal. For example, when we experience anger, this anger is not Hindu anger or Christian anger, Chinese anger or American anger. Similarly, love and compassion are not the strict province of any community or creed: they are universal human qualities resulting from purity of mind. People from all backgrounds who practice Vipassana find that they become better human beings.

The Present-day World Environment

Developments in the fields of science and technology, in transportation, communications, agriculture and medicine, have revolutionized human life at the material level. But, in actuality, this progress is only superficial: underneath, modern men and women are living in conditions of great mental and emotional stress, even in developed and affluent countries.

The problems and conflicts arising out of racial, ethnic, sectarian and caste prejudices affect the citizens of every country. Poverty, warfare, weapons of mass destruction, disease, drug addiction, the threat of terrorism, epidemic, environmental devastation and the general decline of moral values-all cast a dark shadow on the future of civilization. One need only glance at the front page of a daily newspaper to be reminded of the acute suffering and deep despair which afflict the inhabitants of our planet.

Is there a way out of these seemingly insolvable problems? The answer is unequivocally, yes. All over the world today, the winds of change are readily apparent. People everywhere are eager to find a method which can bring peace and harmony; restore confidence in the efficacy of wholesome human qualities; and create an environment of freedom and security from all types of exploitation-social, religious and economic. Vipassana can be such a method.

Vipassana and Social Change

The technique of Vipassana is a path leading to freedom from all suffering; it eradicates the craving, aversion and ignorance which are responsible for all our miseries. Those who practice it remove, little by little, the root causes of their suffering and steadily emerge from the darkness of former tensions to lead happy, healthy, productive lives. There are many examples bearing testimony to this fact.

Several experiments have been conducted at prisons in India. In 1975, S.N. Goenka conducted a historic course for 120 inmates at the Central Jail in Jaipur, the first such experiment in Indian penal history. This course was followed in 1976 by a course for senior police officers at the Government Police

Academy in Jaipur. In 1977, a second course was held at the Jaipur Central Jail. These courses were the subject of several sociological studies conducted by the University of Rajasthan. In 1990 another course was organized in Jaipur Central Jail in which forty life-term convicts and ten jail officials participated with very positive results.

In 1991, a course for life-sentence prisoners was held at the Sabaramati Central Jail, Ahmedabad, and was the subject of a research project by the Dept. of Education, Gujarat Vidyapeeth.

The Rajasthan and Gujarat studies and indicated definite positive changes of attitude and behaviour in the participants, and demonstrate that Vipassana is a positive reform measure enabling criminals to become wholesome members of society.

In 1995, a massive course was organised for 1000 prisoners in Tihar jail with far-reaching effects. Vipassana was adopted as a prison reform technique in the largest jails of India. A detailed report of the scientific studies carried out to assess the impact of Vipassana meditation on the prisoner's mental health proves that Vipassana is capable of transforming criminals into better human beings.

The civil service career of S.N. Goenka's meditation teacher, Sayagyi U Ba Khin, is an example of the transformative effect of Vipassana on government administration. Sayagyi was the head of several government departments. He succeeded in instilling a heightened sense of duty, discipline and morality in the officials working under him by teaching them Vipassana meditation. As a result, efficiency dramatically increased, and corruption was eliminated. Similarly, in the Home Department of the Government of Rajasthan, after several key officials attended Vipassana courses, decision-making and the disposal of cases were accelerated, and staff relations improved.

The Vipassana Research Institute has documented other examples of the positive impact of Vipassana in such fields as health, education, drug addiction, government, prisons and business management.

These experiments underscore the point that societal change must start with the individual. Social change cannot be brought about by mere sermons; discipline and virtuous conduct cannot be instilled in students simply through textbook lectures. Criminals will not become good citizens out of fear of punishment; neither can caste and sectarian discord be eliminated by punitive measures. History is replete with the failures of such attempts.

The individual is the key: he or she must be treated with love and compassion; he must be trained to improve himself-not by exhortations to follow moral precepts, but by being instilled with the authentic desire to change. He must be taught to explore himself, to initiate a process which can bring about transformation and lead to purification of mind. This is the only change which will be enduring.

Vipassana has the capacity to transform the human mind and character. It is an opportunity awaiting all who sincerely wish to make the effort.

Types of Meditation

Before we begin the study of different types of meditation it is necessary to keep in mind two important points. One is that meditation is not just ordinary concentration but a special type of internal concentration.

The second point is that meditation is not an entirely independent discipline but a stage in concentration common to almost all spiritual paths. Each path of sadhana or spiritual discipline begins in a different way. But every path has a stage which corresponds to meditation. The name given to this common stage varies from path to path. But whatever be the name given, it means some form of meditative awareness.

Patanjali's Yoga begins with purification of the mind, posture and breath control followed by withdrawal of the mind from external objects (pratyahara) and fixing the mind (dharana) at a particular center. Then comes meditation (dhyana). The path of jnana begins with hearing scripture (sravana) and reflection (manana). This leads to inquiry (nididhyasana) which corresponds to meditation. In the path of bhakti, the aspirant moves from prayer, singing of hymns and worship to meditation which is known under different names like abhyasa (Ramanuja), smarana and bhavana. Even in the path of karma one finds the need to maintain self-awareness in the midst of work. In fact the Zen masters speak of "action meditation," "walking meditation," etc. Buddhism gives more importance to meditation than any other religion does. In Christianity the main spiritual discipline is called prayer. It consists of several stages or "degrees." First comes vocal prayer, then discursive prayer (which corresponds to manana or reflection in Vedanta), then affective prayer (prayer proper, done with intense longing). Then follows the fourth degree of prayer which is variously called prayer of simplicity, prayer of the heart, etc. This fourth degree corresponds to Hindu meditation or dhyana. In Islamic mysticism (Sufism) also meditation, known under different names, plays a central role.

In every path the aspirant begins with a large number of thoughts in the mind. These gradually become reduced, and the aspirant reaches a stage when there exists only a single pratyaya or thought in the mind. This is the state of meditative awareness. It is the common highway which every aspirant has to travel in order to realize God or the Supreme Self. Beyond this common path lies the luminous realm of the Spirit.

Then why are there so many different techniques of meditation? These are really techniques of dharana or fixing the mind. They are like different gates which open to the same highway. These techniques only teach you how to begin meditation, they only open different doors to meditative awareness. But they do not teach you how to maintain meditation, which is something you have to learn through practice.

This does not, however, mean that the goal of meditation is the same for all. The goal is determined by the beginning, that is by the dharana technique that you follow. Each technique of dharana leads you through meditation to a certain experience. The beginnings and ends of meditation are different. But the process of meditation itself is the same in so far as a single thought is maintained. The nature of this single thought (pratyaya or vritti) may also vary from person to person. For instance, one may meditate on Siva or Krishna or Jesus or an impersonal object like light or the sky or the sun. Nevertheless, the essential meditative process-the maintenance of a single pratyaya or vritti-is the same whatever be the object meditated upon.

Meditation thus acts as a great junction where all spiritual paths converge, meet, go together for a short distance-and then diverge again to their respective goals. Meditation may also be compared to a broad road having several tracks or "lanes" marked on them for the guidance of motorists. Each meditator keeps to his or her own "lane" but all the lanes are parts of one great highway.

Meditation-Subjective and Objective

Meditation is of two types: subjective and objective. Objective meditation is concentration of the mind on an object. The object may be the form of a deity, light, sky, etc. or some qualities like love, compassion, strength or one's own self objectified. Consciousness is focused on the object by an effort of will. Objective meditation is called upasana.

Subjective meditation is called nididhyasana or atmavicara. Here there is no focusing of consciousness or effort of will. It is rather an attempt to seek the source of consciousness, to trace one's "I" back to its roots. It is a process in which the ego, instead of rushing towards objects as it constantly does, withdraws into its own original source-the Atman.

The majority of spiritual aspirants find nididhyasana, subjective meditation, difficult to practice. They succeed in tracing their "I" back only up to a certain point. To penetrate further backward is possible only for a mind which is properly sharpened through training and strengthened by the observance of continence. Upasana or objective meditation gives the mind the necessary training. After practising upasana for some time it becomes easier to practice nididhyasana. In fact, Madhusudana Sarasvati in his Advaita Siddhi classifies aspirants for jnana into two groups: kritopasti (those who have attained proficiency in upasana) and akritopasti (those who go directly to inquiry without practising upasana).

According to Mandana and some of the earlier schools of Advaitins, upasana can give rise to direct realization of Nirguna Brahman (the Absolute without attributes). But Sri Sankara and his followers hold the view that upasana will lead only to the realization of Saguna Brahman (Reality with attributes). Sankara states that the benefit derived from upasana is either worldly prosperity (abhyudaya) or "gradual liberation" (kramamukti). In other words, upasana is only a preparation for nididhyasana. On the other hand, Sri Ramanuja holds the view that upasana can lead to full liberation. He even identifies it with bhakti.

The difference between upasana and nididhyasana as two different disciplines has also been clearly pointed out by Ramatirtha in his well-known commentary on the Vedanta Sara. Vidyaranya too has made this distinction by describing upasana as vastu-tantra (object-oriented) and nididhyasana as kartri-tantra (subject-oriented).

A similar distinction is found in Buddhism. Buddhist meditations are of two types: One is samatha (samadhi in Sanskrit) or mental concentration of various kinds leading to different mystic experiences. Tibetan Buddhists are specialists in this kind of meditation. These meditation techniques existed even before Buddha who himself practised them. But he was not satisfied with them because they did not lead to total liberation. He regarded these mystic states only as "happy living in this existence" (dittha-dhamma-sukha-vihara) and nothing more. According to him mystic experiences are created or conditioned by the mind. He therefore went further and discovered the other form of meditation known as vipassana (vipasyanam in Sanskrit) or "insight."

It is an analytic method which involves constant mindfulness and awareness of all experiences, good and bad. It is not a withdrawal from life but an attempt to understand life and thus enlarge one's self-awareness. The most authoritative scripture for vipassana is the Satipatthana-Sutta included in the Buddhist Tripitaka. (The "choiceless awareness" technique of the well-known contemporary teacher J. Krishnamurthy comes close to this method.) It was more or less a similar distinction between objective and subjective meditations that gave rise to the two schools of Japanese Zen: Soto and Rinzai.

What is common to both subjective and objective meditation is a distinct awareness of a higher center of consciousness, the higher Self. In both, awareness is not allowed to move too far away from this center. But whereas in objective meditation a circle of consciousness is created around the center and there is a struggle to shut out distracting thoughts from this inner circle, in subjective meditation there is no such struggle: the aspirant just holds on to the "I" center. Strictly speaking, nididhyasana is not meditation though it is translated that way. It is more correctly called "self-inquiry" and belongs to the path of knowledge (jnana marga). Here we are concerned only with upasana.

Need for Combining Subjective and Objective Meditations

It is, however, important to keep in mind that these two types of meditation are not mutually contradictory. They actually complement each other and can be practised together. Most of the meditation techniques taught to aspirants are upasanas. Spiritual initiation (diksa or upadesa) usually means initiation into some form of upasana. In the path of bhakti this is the only type of meditation practised. Even those who study books on Advaita seldom attempt self-inquiry in practice and remain satisfied with objective meditations. But though nididhyasana is mainly followed in the path of jnana, there is nothing wrong in following it in the path of bhakti also. Indeed it is better or even necessary to combine self-inquiry with upasana.

One of the aims of upasana is to establish a living relationship with God, "an eternal relationship between the eternal soul and the eternal God," as Swami Vivekananda puts it. The ordinary ego of which we are all so painfully aware is not eternal but is constantly undergoing change. Only the Atman, our true higher self, is unchanging and eternal. This means that, in order to establish a truly loving relationship with God, it is necessary to be aware of one's higher self. Self-inquiry leads the aspirant away from the ego towards the true self.

There is a second reason why a combination of objective and subjective forms of meditation is desirable. Meditation is usually done at a definite center of consciousness, by which is meant the point where the aspirant is able to feel the higher self or Atman. It is there that the mind is to be fixed first, and it is there that the chosen deity is to be worshipped. What most aspirants attempt is to visualize a point of light or a lotus in the region of the heart or the head.

But many people find this too unreal or abstract. A little nididhyasana or self-inquiry will, however, greatly help in locating the center of the true self and make the lotus or light meaningful and real. Before the aspirant starts actual meditation, if he or she spends a few minutes in tracing the "I" back to its source, the aspirant will find it easier to fix the mind at the right center of consciousness.

And every time the mind wanders away from this center, the aspirant may apply the same method. Once the mind is tied down to the true center of consciousness, meditation on one's chosen deity becomes easy. This is a much better form of mind control than the conventional ones. Those who do not feel intense devotion will find this combination of nididhyasana and upasana helpful.

Then there is a third point in favour of such a combination. Upasana increases one's power of concentration but does not necessarily increase one's power of self-control to an equal degree. As a result the aspirant may find it difficult to remain unaffected by the contact of other people and the cares and distractions of daily work. Nididhyasana enables the aspirant to abide in the real abode within and remain calm and unaffected by the environment.

Further, it prevents the aspirant from mistaking strong imaginations and hallucinations for genuine spiritual experience, as often happens in those who practice only objective meditation. A true spiritual experience transforms one's consciousness and produces some knowledge of the higher self. Self-inquiry is necessary to recognize this. Lastly, combining nididhyasana and upasana satisfies both the head and the heart.

Upasana in the Vedic Period

It is possible that even during the early Vedic period there were independent thinkers and groups of people who practised meditation as their chief spiritual discipline. That was perhaps how the Samkhya and Yoga systems developed independently of the Vedas.

In Vedic literature upasana first appears as a part of rituals in the Brahmanas (the part of the Veda which deals with rituals). The emphasis then was on sacrificial rites (yajna). In the Brahmanas we find a few meditations prescribed along with these rites. The sacrifice was regarded as most important and sufficient in itself to produce the desired results. The meditation that was practised along with it was only an auxiliary part of it and had no independent existence. The purpose of such meditations was to gain some additional merit and their omission in no way affected the sacrifices. This kind of upasana was called angavabaddha meaning "connected to parts (of the sacrifice)."

Gradually, upasana became separated from the rituals. In the Aranyakas we find meditations replacing actual sacrifices. But the meditations still resembled the sacrifices. They were mostly symbolic representations of external rituals. The whole external rite was, as it were, transferred to the mind. These upasanas may therefore be called "substitution-meditations." A well-known example is found in the very beginning of the Brihadaranyaka Upanisad which is an Aranyaka as well as an Upanisad. Here the sacrificial horse is to be meditated upon as identified with the Cosmic Being (Virat or Prajapati), the horse's head standing for the dawn, its eye for the sun, its prana for the air and so on.

The next stage in the evolution of upasana is found in the Upanishads. Here meditations are in no way connected to rituals nor even symbolically resemble them. They directly deal with Brahman, the ultimate Reality. But Brahman is a transcendent principle which cannot be known through the ordinary senses and mind. So the great sages of the Upanishads used various familiar objects of the phenomenal universe like the sun, akasa (space), vayu (air), water, prana (the vital energy), manas (mind), words, etc. to represent Brahman. However, what the sages attempted was not mere concentration of mind on one of these symbols. In that case it would have become only a form of the yogic exercise known as dharana. What they actually did was to connect each symbol to a certain framework of meaning-a spiritual formula. Upasana in the Upanishads are meditations on these spiritual formulas. These formulas are devices to guide the mind from the symbol to Reality. When a mind which is sufficiently purified meditates on such a formula, its true meaning-the ultimate Reality-will be revealed to it. These meditation formulas were called vidyas.

So then, angavabaddhas (in the Brahmanas), substitution-meditations (in the Aranyakas) and vidyas (in the Upanishads): these were the three stages in the evolution of upasana during the Vedic period. Sri Sankara says that lower upasanas do not deserve to be called vidyas.

Therefore, vidyas represent the highest forms of upasana. The entire knowledge of the Upanishads came out of the meditations of the great rishis on these vidyas. It was through these meditations that they discovered the great truths that underlie the phenomenal universe. A scientist tries to understand the ultimate truth through a series of steps, meticulously analyzing each step. But in ancient India the sages went straight to the Reality with the help of certain mental paradigms. Says Deussen: "That India more than any other country is the land of symbols is owing to the nature of Indian thought, which applied itself to the most abstruse problems before it was even remotely in a position to treat them intelligently."

Vidyas are paradigms of Brahman. In ancient India each teacher developed his or her own concept model of Brahman and taught it as a meditation technique to his or her disciples. That was how so many vidyas came into existence. Some of the Upanishads, especially the Brihadaranyaka, Chandogya and Taittiriya, are a rich storehouse of these vidyas. The importance attached to the vidyas was so great that the Brahma-Sutra has a whole section dealing exclusively with them. The vidyas really hold the key to the Upanishads, and no one can properly understand the Upanishads without understanding the vidyas. The vidyas are said to be thirty-two in number, but many more must have been known to the ancient sages. Among these gayatri-vidya, antaraditya-vidya, madhu-vidya, sandilya-vidya and dahara-vidya are well known. It is beyond the scope of the present article to deal with these vidyas in detail. They are to be learnt directly from competent teachers who have attained illumination through them. But long before the beginning of the Christian era the lineage of Vedic rishis had ended. And in the absence of a living tradition, the vidyas ceased to be practised and their true inner meaning was soon forgotten.

One major cause for the neglect of the vidyas was the rise of Buddhism and its influence on Hindu thought. A second reason was the crystallization of Hindu philosophy into six schools or darsanas and the triumph of the Advaita system. Nondual experience was originally sought through a gradual expansion of consciousness attained by the practice of vidyas. But gradually the goal became more important than the means. Vedanta neglected its mystical roots, became more speculative and polemical, and thus moved farther away from life and experience. A third reason for the neglect of the vidyas was the popularity of Yoga and, later on, of the Tantras.

Under the influence of Yoga and Tantra new techniques of meditation were developed during the Middle Ages which survive to this day. Meditation techniques in modern times are strongly influenced by Yoga and Tantra. We are now witnessing a great revival of mysticism, and ancient methods are being adjusted to suit the needs of modern aspirants. Some enterprising people are experimenting with new techniques of meditation.

We shall next discuss the traditional methods of meditation which are still surviving and are suitable for modern times.

Upasana and Dhyana

Concentration can be practised on any object. In fact, in our daily life we are concentrating on something or other most of the time. This kind of concentration is more or less unconscious and is done under the compulsion of desires. True meditation differs from it in being a conscious process involving the detachment of the will from lower desires and its focusing at a higher center of consciousness.

We have seen that meditation is a stage in concentration common to all spiritual paths. We have also seen that meditation is of two types: subjective and objective. Subjective meditation is of the nature of an inquiry into the Atman and is called nididhyasana. Objective meditation is concentrating the mind on an object. Objective meditation is known under different names. Patanjali calls it dhyana. In Vedanta a more common term is upasana. Both these terms are, however, met with in the Upanishads.

In ancient India meditation was a subject of deep study, research and experiment. The followers of the Samkhya philosophy developed it into an independent science of mental life. When properly concentrated on an object, the mind undergoes certain changes. These changes are the same for a particular degree of concentration whatever be the object chosen. In other words, concentration follows certain universal laws. These laws were discovered by the great yogis of ancient India. Patanjali codified and compiled them in his famous Yoga Aphorisms. These laws form the basis of upasana also. So Sankaracarya defines meditation as "a process of unwavering application of the same thought on some object, such as a deity prescribed by the scriptures, without being interrupted by any alien thought." However, there are some important differences between Yogic meditation and Vedantic meditation.

The immediate aim of Yogic dhyana is to discover the functions of mind at higher levels of consciousness. Its ultimate aim is the separation or isolation of Purusa from prakriti. As Bhoja points out, Yoga is really viyoga, disunion. On the contrary, upasana aims at union. Its immediate aim may be to unite the meditator with a deity. But its ultimate aim is to unite the individual self (jivatman) with the Supreme Self (Paramatman).

Another difference is that in Yogic meditation the choice of God is optional. According to Patanjali, meditation can be practised on any object one likes. Bhoja in his commentary points out that in Yoga the object of meditation (bhavyam) is of two types: God and the tattvas [elements of the differentiated universe-ed.]. The tattvas again are of two types: Purusa and the twenty-four categories of prakriti. Dhyana may be practised on any of the tattvas. But in upasana God alone is the object of meditation, and not the tattvas.

The third difference is that in order to practice yogic meditation it is not necessary to have any preconceived ideas about Reality. But upasana is based on the Vedantic conception of Reality and operates within a definite conceptual framework. What upasana does is to convert the conceptual or indirect (paroksa) knowledge into intuition or direct (aparoksa) experience.

Development of Upasana in the Post-Vedic Period

These two types of meditation-Yogic dhyana and Vedantic upasana-became united in the post-Vedic period. It was shown last month how upasana evolved in the Vedic period from ritual-bound meditations (angavabaddha) into substitution meditations and finally into the vidyas. In the meantime the Yoga system was getting perfected. It was then that the Tantras arose, probably a few centuries after the Vedic period had ended. The Tantras combined the monism of the Upanishads with the theism of the puranas. Secondly, they united Yogic meditation with Vedantic upasana. Apart from this, the Tantras made independent discoveries about mantras, kundalini, etc. The all-round harmony and synthesis effected by the Tantras opened a new era in the history of spirituality in India. This continues to this day. The meditation techniques now prevalent show the strong influence of the Tantras.

Form, Name and the Self

One of the important changes that the Tantras introduced was in the field of symbols. The images of different gods and goddesses have completely replaced the Vedic images of fire, sun, air, etc. In the Vedic period the approach to ultimate Reality was direct. The Tantras made it indirect: the aspirant first attains the vision of a god or goddess and then through him or her realizes the ultimate Reality. Again, in the Vedic period words were used primarily for their meaning (abhidhana). The Tantras have, however, shown that certain mystic words have an intrinsic power to produce changes in consciousness.

Symbols play an important part in human life. Other than pure consciousness, all our thinking is based on symbols. These symbols can be divided into two groups: rupa (form) and nama (name). These, along with the self, constitute the knowing process. Emotions are also of course a part of mental life. But they are not essential to knowledge. In fact, they very often distort the knowing process. A person overcome by anger, envy, fear and other emotions has a distorted view of other people. That is why Patanjali regards emotions as "false knowledge" (viparyaya). They are great obstacles in spiritual life, and the aspirant is advised to rid himself or herself of them before attempting real meditation. True knowledge arises only when the mind is freed from emotional disturbances. It is, however, important to note here that bhakti, love of God, which is a great help in upasana, is not an emotion and is therefore never regarded as an obstacle. True devotion is a property of the self, its longing for union with the Supreme Self.

When the mind is freed from the hold of instincts and emotions, there remain in it only three elements of pure cognition: form, name and the self. These are the only factors that constitute the meditative act. Spiritual aspirants show great variation in their ability to manipulate these three factors. When we speak of differences among people we usually mean their emotional make-up. Some people are more loving and kind, some cruel and harsh. Some are arrogant, some humble. And so on. One of the important tasks in spiritual life is to level up these differences and make every aspirant pure, virtuous, calm.

However, these are not the only differences among aspirants. The very structure of the mind and the way names, forms and the self influence it vary from person to person. Some people find visualization of images very easy but find it difficult to manipulate abstract ideas, especially mathematics. Their thinking is a kind of inner seeing and they have what is called a "photographic memory." The minds of these people are form-oriented. Some others find it difficult or even impossible to visualize forms and do their thinking mostly through sound symbols. These are the people who benefit most from listening to talks and lectures. Their minds are name-oriented. There are yet others who find both names and forms a great botheration and prefer to hold on to the self without any visual or ideational support. Their minds are self-oriented.

To meet the needs of these three different mental types, three kinds of upasana have been developed: pratikopasana (meditation on visual images), namopasana (meditation on sound symbols) and ahamgrahopasana (meditation on the self). Each aspirant should know which type of mind his or hers is: form-oriented, name-oriented or self-oriented. This the aspirant can easily find out by a little self-analysis and practice in meditation. The aspirant must then choose that type of upasana which suits him or her most. It may be surprising to know that there are some people who are totally incapable of visualizing forms. Such people find it very difficult to meditate on the image of a deity. When they close their eyes they only feel a blank with various ideas moving somewhere inside. It is like listening to the gurgling of a stream in the dark. They, however, find repetition of a mantra very easy and producing great harmony in them. Whereas there are others who find such repetition difficult, distracting and unrelated to their basic spiritual urge.

Fortunately, however, most people have a mixed type of mind. They can make their minds form-oriented, name-oriented or self-oriented as they wish. So they can easily combine all the three types of upasana in their practice. Nevertheless, during the early stages of spiritual life even they may find it easier and more beneficial to give more emphasis on one type of upasana according to their individual temperaments, while not neglecting the other two. Meditation is a difficult task for beginners but they can make it a bit easier by following the line of least resistance, their own natural orientation of mind. Once the aspirant acquires proficiency in any one method, he or she will find it easy to practice all the other methods.

Pratika Upasana

Pratika means a symbol-literally, "going towards," something upon which the mind is focused. Though words are also symbols, pratika is generally used to mean visual symbols-images, pictures and natural objects used as symbols. During the Vedic period fire, the sun, the air, the mind, etc. were treated as pratikas to represent Brahman. How were the pratikas related to Brahman? There were two ways of doing this, and accordingly Vedic pratikopasana was of two types: sampad and adhyasa.

In sampad upasana an inferior object is used as a symbol to represent superior Reality. The symbol is unimportant, the attributes of the higher reality dominate the meditative field. (To give a modern example, when a stone idol or salagrama is worshipped as Vishnu / Vishnu, the worshipper forgets the stone and thinks only of the luminous splendour of Vishnu. This may be regarded as a modern form of sampad upasana.

In adhyasa upasana the symbol chosen is itself a superior object and dominates the meditative field. Upon this symbol the attributes of the Reality are superimposed, but the symbol is as important as the attributes. Meditation on the sun (one of the most beautiful meditations ever conceived) is an instance of this. The Upanisad teaches, "The sun is Brahman, this is the instruction." The sun with its dazzling brightness has a striking resemblance to Brahman and can itself be directly meditated upon as Brahman. All that one has to do is to superimpose upon the sun the attributes of Brahman like infinity, consciousness, bliss, ultimate causality, etc.

With the disappearance of the Vedic tradition these ancient pratika meditations are no longer in vogue. There is at present a great need to revive them.

In modern times the images of various deities and the symbols connected with them have almost wholly replaced the Vedic pratikas. Not only that. The conception of the connection between the symbols and the Reality has also changed. Vedic symbols directly connect the meditator with the ultimate Reality. But in Tantric symbols this connection is indirect. First of all, the deity behind the symbol is to be realized, and then through the deity the ultimate Reality is to be attained.

Pratikas used in modern times may be divided into two groups: aniconic and iconic. The former group includes yantras (mystic diagrams), mandalas (psychic diagrams), salagrama, Siva / Shiva linga, water pot, etc. These are used more in ritualistic worship than in meditation. The lotus symbolizing a chakra or center of consciousness, the flame symbolizing the self, the sky symbolizing space and similar impersonal symbols which are often used in meditation may also be included in this group.

The second group of pratikas includes the anthropomorphic images of gods and goddesses which are called pratimas. A pratima may be a picture drawn on paper or cloth (pata) or a three-dimensional idol (vigraha) made of stone or metal. The Brahma-Sutra clearly teaches that the pratika is to be looked upon only as a symbol of Brahman. God should not bc lowered to symbols, but symbols are to be exalted to God. In other words, the purpose of a pratima is to serve only as a visual aid (dristi saukaryam) to concentration. This may be true in the case of meditation but not necessarily so in the case of worship. The widely accepted belief is that a properly consecrated pratima which is daily worshipped, acquires a special sanctity and power and becomes a center of divine grace. According to Sri Ramanuja there is a special manifestation of God known as arca in the idol.

In this context two points are to be kept in mind. The statement that pratikas are only symbols of God does not imply that the gods and goddesses of Hinduism are only symbols. Hundreds of illumined souls have directly realized these divinities. Even the great Sankaracarya has not denied their existence. Each deity represents a particular aspect of Saguna Brahman, the Personal God, and is at least as real as a human being, if not more.

The other point to note is that though pratikas are mainly used as aids to concentration, the purpose of upasana is not mere concentration of mind but the direct vision of the deity represented by the pratika. The pratika may be a picture or idol made by an artist. Upasana does not mean simply transferring the artist's imagination to our own minds. It is not merely an exercise in memory, trying to remember the picture we have seen outside. Upasana is an attempt to go beyond the symbol and meet the real god or goddess in the depths of consciousness. It is a search for the soul's eternal Beloved. For this a living image must first of all be implanted deep inside the heart. It is the continuous interior gazing at this living image in the depths of consciousness that really deserves to be called pratikopasana. As concentration deepens, the image sinks into consciousness drawing the mind with it deeper, deeper... until it touches the undercurrent of pure consciousness and bursts into ethereal phosphorescence.

True pratikopasana, then, is a process of converting imagination into Reality. It is a technique for the transformation of consciousness. How does this transformation take place? Three principles are involved in it: the principle of khyati [knowledge-ed.], the yatha-kratu principle ["As is one's will, so does one become." Chandogya Upanisad-ed.] and the theory of mantra.

Nama Upasana

If in pratikopasana meditation is practised on a visual symbol, in namopasana it is done on a sound symbol-the name of a deity or a mantra. This, however, is not the only difference between the two. There are much deeper differences based on certain basic properties of the human mind.

Here we wish to mention only two or three points. The repetition of a mantra or a name of God is called japa. When the words used are many, it may take the form of stuti (hymnody), bhajan (singing of songs set to music) or samkirtana (group singing). These are better regarded as forms of worship though, when properly done, they produce a meditative effect.

It should be kept in mind that mere mechanical repetition of a mantra hardly deserves to be called upasana. As true pratikopasana is visualizing a "living image," so true namopasana is the repetition of an "awakened mantra." The mantra becomes awakened (chetana) when it becomes connected to the basic rhythm of consciousness in the depths of the heart. Another point should be noted here.

In popular usage only pratikopasana is known as meditation, while namopasana is known as japa. As a matter of fact, both come under meditation. To make the distinction between these two types of meditation more clear it is better to describe pratikopasana as bhavana (visualization), a term more commonly used in the Tantras and Buddhist scriptures. As a general rule japa is accompanied by bhavana (visualization) of a god or goddess. But several sects in Hinduism and especially the Sikhs practice japa without visualizing the form of any deity. They are pure namopasakas. In their case japa itself becomes meditation.

Ahamgraha Upasana

Ahamgraha literally means "self-grasping," that is "self-identification." Unlike the two types of meditation described above which are purely objective techniques, ahamgraha-upsana is a subjective-objective meditation technique. It is a meditation on the self as the object. But it is not mere concentration of mind on the object as the other two meditations are. It means the "grasping" of a vaster whole by the Self. It is an attempt of the self to identify itself with the Supreme Self.

Since the pure Atman cannot be an "object" of meditation, various symbols are used to enable the self to "grasp" the supreme Self. Thus like the other two upasanas described above, ahamgrahopasana is also a kind of symbolic meditation.

Objectivity and the use of symbols, these are precisely the two points which distinguish ahamgrahopasana and nididhyasana or subjective meditation. In nididhyasana no symbols are used, nor is the self objectified. It is a negative process of neti, neti ("not this, not this") by which the self cuts asunder all identifications and withdraws into its own locus. The distinction between these two techniques is important though it may not be so obvious to an untrained mind.

The simplest form of ahamgrahopasana is to visualize the Atman as a point of light and meditate on it thinking "I am this light." However, as the individual self is part of the infinite

Supreme Self, ahamgrahopasana usually means meditation on the union of the individual self with the supreme Self. Again, as the Supreme Self is all-pervading, this meditation necessarily involves an awareness of divine immanence in creation. Thus ahamgrahopasana actually takes the form of double meditation: meditation on the self as a part of God and meditation on God as present in all beings.

It is now clear that some of the vidyas, if not all, discussed in the Upanishads are really ahamgraha meditations. In fact this is the only way contemporary humanity can understand and practice the vidyas, for their original esoteric tradition has been lost. One of the most famous of these meditations is the antaryami vidya. Uddalaka, the son of Aruna asks the sage Yajnavalkya about the Inner Controller. In reply the latter describes the immanence of Brahman in the earth, in the sky, in the sun etc.

He who dwells in the earth, but is within it, whom the earth does not know, whose body is the earth, and who controls the earth from within, is the Inner Ruler, your own immortal self.

He who dwells in water ...

He who dwells in fire ...

He who dwells in the sky ...

He who dwells in the sun .... etc.

Another important meditation is Sandilya Vidya, which runs as follows:

These passages are not meant to be understood theoretically. They are meant for actual practice. It is not possible to have the experience of Advaita all of a sudden. For this our consciousness must be gradually expanded. These meditations are meant to expand our consciousness. It is only when we try to practice them shall we understand how difficult they are. Those who have reduced Advaita to talking and writing will find these meditations a lesson in humility.

Apart from the vidyas there are many other splendid passages in the Upanishads which may be used in meditation. The four mahavakyas, "That thou art," "I am Brahman," etc. (which are supposed to produce direct intuition of Brahman in highly qualified aspirants) may also be used for this purpose. It should be noted that these mahavakyas are not meant for repetition, for that would be a kind of namopasana. They are actually meant for the practice of ahamgrahopasana. Some of the great sannyasa mantras into which Hindu monastics are initiated also belong to this category. Apart from these, some of the well-known verses of Sankaracarya like the "Morning Remembrance Hymn," "Six Stanzas on Nirvana," etc. may also be used for the practice of ahamgrahopasana for which they are really intended.

Need for Synthesis

The three types of upasana discussed above could be practised independently. But they are not contradictory to one another. Each stands for a particular aspect of cognition and develops a particular faculty of the mind. A combination of the three types of meditation will lead to all-round development of consciousness.

There is especially a great need to include ahamgrahopasana in our daily spiritual practice. It reminds us of our real nature as the Atman. It is only when we understand that we are potentially divine can we establish a loving spiritual relationship with the Deity. Moreover, awareness of our higher self enables us to remain unaffected by the external influences and maintain constant remembrance of our chosen Deity and mantra. Even a devotee who worships an idol can practice ahamgrahopasana. He or she may think that the Deity dwelling in the idol dwells also in his or her own self and meditate on the union of the two. In fact, this kind of meditation is an essential part of Tantric worship.

To conclude: all preliminary spiritual disciplines end in some form of meditative awareness, and all meditation paths lead to spiritual illumination of some kind or other.

Yoga and Meditation in India

Modern age life has given too many news things to us. It has made our lives easier in many ways. But more than that, it has also increased the stress levels, the complexities and mental pressure under which we keep going on. What we immediately do not realize is the impact of living such a lifestyle on our health.

But those who do care about their lives and want to live it the healthy way, what could be a better way to de-stress from the distresses of life than to relax in the soothing and therapeutic balm of India's Yogic and Meditational practices. India is internationally renowned for its ancient healing practices and alternative therapies. For more than thousands of years now, we have followed our own indigenous healing systems and medicinal practices such as Ayurveda, Naturopathy, and Pranic Healing to name just a few. It is no wonder then that people from all over the world are turning to the Indian sub continent for guidance towards a more spiritually satisfying way of life.

Yoga and Meditation are just such indigenous twin techniques of self-realization and purification. One incomplete without the other, they help an individual to develop a sense of physical, mental, emotional as well as spiritual well being. Yoga in all its forms tries to create harmony of the body with the mind and soul. It is a very general term that encompasses many different disciplines ranging from the purely physical to the purely spiritual, and is a truly original Indian concept.

Many people believe that yoga and meditation are mystic arts that demand complete devotion to the exclusion of everything else. However, the truth is that Yoga and Meditation are not the hard taskmasters they are often made out to be. Yoga and Meditation can easily be incorporated into our daily lives, requiring no more than a few minutes, if not more, everyday. Their benefits on the other hand are wide-ranging and restorative. For instance, meditation has proven to be highly effective in treating psychological conditions, such as obsessive-compulsive disorder, depression, and anxiety, and Yoga is known to increase levels of self-confidence and memory.

We have designed special Yoga and Meditation tour packages that will allow you to combine your holiday and travel to India with a truly uplifting and revitalizing experience. What could be better way to spend a vacation than to go on an inspiring health holiday that will leave you physically, mentally and spiritually refresh

All about Yoga

When everything else fails to ease and calm your mind, a therapeutic session of Yoga is sure to relax you and fill you with peace and serenity. Travel to India to discover Yoga, a 5,000 year old scientific technique for spiritual development, that at the very least will soothe your agitated senses and fill you with a sense of wellbeing, and at the most, help you to attain nirvana or Moksha, the ultimate unification of the body, mind and soul with the entire universe, as one interconnected whole. Yoga is an originally Indian concept that was propounded by the ancient Indian sage Patanjali and is derived from the Sanskrit word Yog which means 'union,' presumably union with the divine being or God.

Yoga is Not a Religion: It is a secular and scientific methodology of the experience and integration of the mind-body-spirit. It consists of a large body of varied techniques through a balanced practice of Astanga or the eight limbs of yoga. Some of the most often practised types of Yoga are:

Karma Yoga: The way of right action that propounds selfless serving without the motivation of obtaining results of labour.

Bhakti Yoga: The way of devotion thorough devotion to a supreme being to submerge emotion and self in pure love.

Jnana Yoga: The way of knowledge through studying divinity and learning to discriminate between illusion and reality.

Hatha Yoga: The physical path that trains the body to control the mind and senses through asana and pranayama.

Tantric Yoga: The feminine path that worships the goddess of energy and sees the body as the temple of the divine.

Kundalini Yoga: The path of energy that arouses the energy stored in the chakras through breathing and movement.

Raja Yoga: The path of meditation that controls the mind from wandering and helps to obtain mastery over thought.

Yoga essentially seeks to utilize the energy present in every human being to regulate the heart rate, clear confusion and provide peace of mind. It provides long lasting results, and is perhaps the only discipline that works as a deterrent to the development of any further disease, without the help of any orally administered medicine. It has also been known to retard the ageing process.

According to the philosophy of Yoga, at the deepest (or highest) level of our existence on this earth, we are all perfectly free. However, this is not our everyday experience for in our ordinary state of consciousness, we are subject to all kinds of limitations, and most significantly, experience suffering (duhkha). The practice of Yoga can help us discover our innate freedom, through an extensive process of self-purification and cleansing of the mind.

Yoga detoxifies the body through purification of bowel, enemas, cleansing of the nasal passage and eyes. The breathing exercise 'Pranayama' enables one to get rid of blockages in the nadis. These harmful blockages are caused by various factors such as stress, toxins and improper diet and, impede the flow of prana throughout the body. According to proponents of Yoga, the interrupted flow of prana leads to adversities in mental, physical and emotional health of an individual. Regular practice of Yoga can rid us of these injurious blockages.

Our tours allow you to travel around India and delve into your latent spirituality at the same time. Our exclusive holidays combine sightseeing either with rejuvenating Ayurvedic Health Treatments in Madras (Chennai), Yoga and Meditational Holidays in Rishikesh, magical Sanjeevanam therapeutic massages in Kerala, a stay at the famous Bihar School of Yoga or Yogic instruction at the Ananda Spa Resort in the Himalayas.

So get ready to revive yourself with travel and a Yoga and Meditation holiday in India. You will be refreshed and rejuvenated in the beautiful environs of nature within no time and experience your spirituality like never before. Travel in India is sure to be a truly refreshing experience this time around!

Meditation

Meditation and Yoga are synonymous with India and Indian spirituality. You can now make travel to India a truly blissful and spiritual experience that will far exceed any holiday or vacation you have experienced so far.

Meditation is one of the most important components of Yoga, which is a mind-body therapy involving a series of exercises. The word 'meditation' covers many disparate practices from visualizing situations, focusing on objects or images, thinking through a complex idea, or even getting lost in a provocative book, all qualifying as meditation in the broad sense. However in Yoga, meditation generally refers to the more formal practice of focusing the mind and observing oneself in the moment.

Simply put, meditation is designed to carry us beyond the illusions created by our thoughts and senses so that we are able to experience everything in its truest form. Therefore, it is a focusing of the mind on a single object so as to create a cessation of all thought. As thoughts dissipate, the mind becomes quiet and devoid of all distractions, and we are able to exist completely in the present moment. Practised to its advanced stages, meditation is contended to be the means of achieving the exalted state of enlightenment or supreme self-realization.

The techniques of meditation are simple and easy to learn, though the ability to keep the mind focused takes time, patience and practice. And while few reach the exalted state, meditation confers many benefits along the way. The benefits of practising meditation regularly include reduction of stress, tension, anxiety and frustration, as well as improved memory, concentration, inner peace and physical wellbeing. Meditation has also proven to be highly effective in treating psychological conditions such as obsessive-compulsive disorders, depression, schizophrenia and anxiety.

That is why we have developed special Yoga and Meditational holiday package tours that allow you to combine travel in India with a glimpse at its inherent spirituality. Our exclusive Yoga India tours combine sightseeing either with rejuvenating Ayurvedic Health Treatments in Madras (Chennai), Yoga and Meditational Holidays in Rishikesh, magical Sanjeevanam therapeutic massages in Kerala, a stay at the famous Bihar School of Yoga or Yogic instruction at the Ananda Spa Resort in the Himalayas. Not only that, we also offer you complete travel services and hotel bookings, and assume responsibility for ensuring that you keep to your schedule.

So now that you know that an enriching and uplifting vacation is just a mouse click away, get ready to experience a spiritual travel in India. You will, for the first time, realize what true peace of mind really is.

Popular Destinations

India is a land of inherent spirituality and people have been known to travel here to find solace in its ancient wisdom since time immemorial. India is also the birthplace of the concept of Yoga and Meditation, practices that are becoming increasingly relevant and popular in the context of today's spiritual aridity. Developed by the ancient sage Patanjali in his search for the ultimate unification of the mind, body and spirit with the divine being, or God, Yoga and Meditation are a combination of a series of exercises and mind focusing techniques. They are believed to be the means of achieving 'enlightenment' and 'nirvana.' The verdant valleys and pristine Himalayas of India are the perfect environs for furthering your quest for spirituality.

Some of the most popular Yoga and Meditation tourist destinations in India are the picturesque and peaceful state of Kerala, the spiritual land of Buddha-Bihar, the pilgrim center of Rishikesh or the quiet and serene town of Dharamshala on the shores of the holy Ganga.

Kerala

Kerela is famous for its beautiful backwaters, Ayurvedic Healing Centers and practice of alternate therapies. It offers you a wide range of therapeutic Ayurvedic and herbal oil massages from experienced professionals. These massages and naturopathic regimes leave you feeling truly refreshed and energized. A stay at Kareeleyam for a magical Sanjeevanam massage is an extremely popular and rejuvenating tourist preference. In fact, it would be very correct to say that a trip to Kerala is incomplete without opting for a stint at an Ayurvedic Resort.

Uttaranchal

A tour to the northern part of India, on the other hand, involves visiting some of the most holy Indian pilgrimage sites like etc. Rishikesh is widely considered the Yoga capital of India. Tourists and travellers attend the International Yoga Week that is organized here, in hordes every year. Numerous travellers searching quietude and inner peace also stop to practice Yoga and meditation in this serene town nestled in the lap of the Himalayas.

Bihar

Another favourite tourist destination for those seeking a cultural heritage tour combined with Yogic instruction is the state of Bihar. Bihar was the home state of the Lord Gautam Buddha, and numerous places associated with different stages of his life, such as Bodhgaya, Sarnath, Kushinagar, Gaya, Nalanda, etc. are located here. The renowned Bihar School of Yoga at Munger in Bihar offers meditation and yoga sessions for tourists.

The Kairali Ayurvedic Health Resort set amid 50 acres of lush greenery in Chennai, the monastries of Dharamshala and the idyllic Ananda Spa in the foothills of the Himalayas are some of the other popular travel and tourist destinations that have a tradition of Yoga, Meditation and spirituality attached to them. With us you can always be sure of a unique travel experience that not just takes you to new places, but also gives you blessedness and peace of mind.

Yoga and Meditation Tours

At Indian visit, it is our aim to provide you with a wide range of travel and tour services that take care of all your travel needs. We also try to anticipate your requirements and design special holidays that offer you more than just a travelling or sightseeing tour. Our Yoga and Meditation in India tour packages are one such effort that combines sightseeing with Yoga and Meditation sessions at some of the best Yoga and Meditation Centers in India.

Our Yoga and Meditation travel holidays give you an unmatched opportunity to explore your latent spirituality. We offer you the chance of actually being instructed in Yoga techniques and Meditation practices by some of India's best-known Yoga Masters. Not only that, you will also be living in some of the most beautiful ashrams and health spas in India for the entire duration of the Meditation and Yoga session.

Some of the exclusive Yoga and Meditation Tours of India that are offered by us are:

"*Rejuvenation and Meditation*

"*Keraleeyam Magic*

"*Yoga and Meditation*

Please remember that these itineraries can be tailor-made to your requirements and adjusted to your specific needs. We hope you will find our tours uniquely rejuvenating and relaxing experiences. We also hope that they will give you a deeper insight into how Yoga and Meditation can be helpful in reducing stress-levels and creating a sense of healthy wellbeing in our daily lives.

The Ananda Spa Resort or Ananda in the Himalayas is a Rafael Resort and Spa. Located in the summer destination of Narendra Nagar, Ananda is housed in the palace of the erstwhile Maharaja of Tehri Garhwal. Ananda is an exclusive spa where you'll find, royalty, film stars and exclusive leisure and business travellers.

Ananda, which means happiness in Sanskrit, offers its guests the opportunity to relax, de-stress and reuvenate. The Ananda Resort and Spa offers its guests a luxurious retreat from the stresses of life. Stay in sylvan surroundings, treat yourself to a range of therapies on offer and indulge at the tea lounge or enjoy a quiet read in the library. The rooms are furnished in teakwood and silk, and are decorated with tantric art and local handicrafts to provide an elegant, opulent and relaxing ambience.

The therapies on offer at the Ananda Resort and Spa include Ayurveda, Panchakarma, Yoga and Hydotherapy. There is a fitness center and swimming pool, where you can work out and tone your muscles. Other facilities include a jacuzzi and a sauna. Treatments such as Thai Massage, Swedish Massage, Aroma Therapy, Reiki, and Reflexology, are offered to guests at the spa. The cuisine offered at the spa is in keeping with holistic nutritional principles. Organically grown fresh food is served flavoured with locally grown herbs and spices. Packages offered by the Ananda Spa Resort include the Ananda Wellness Bliss Package, Ananda Sanjeevni Packages and Ananda Ayurvedic Rejuvenation Package. Relax at Ananda in the Himalayas on your summer vacation and return feeling, younger fresher and totally rejuvenated. Enjoy a spa holiday in India at the Indian summer destination of the Ananda Spa Resort.

Mantra Meditation

Peace is not made in documents; it is made in the hearts of individuals. Tragically though, we tend to look for peace outside. We seek joy in the world of objects. A mind that is only extrovert is caught up in the myth of security. Can there be an enlightened approach to security? We live in a universe and the universe lives within us. The art of looking within is the mantra of wise living.

Mantras help draw energy from both external and internal universes. The nature of our thoughts is largely compulsive. We are conscious beings but we live like machines. Our likes and dislikes are programmed. Addictive thoughts take away from the soul of the individual as a conscious being. By chanting mantras with understanding, compulsive thoughts are transformed. The mind becomes calm and our perception will be wise with respect to both the external and internal universes.

If we look at life in silence, the world becomes a divine university. Just by observing, one can learn so much. The lotus, for instance, grows from muddy waters; yet, it gives out fragrance. Despite the many bad things happening around us we should strive to be as fragrant as the lotus.

Unless there is a commitment to grow, no growth can happen. The commitment to excel should be the way of life. Creativity is not doing something new and different; it is about bringing a new energy of love and joy in whatever one does. We should connect the universe within us to the one outside us. Mantras give a mystic dimension to connect. Mantras are like a ladder. Climb it with love and trust.

History of Mantra Meditation

Handed down since ancient times by religious seers who had attained self-realization by chanting them, mantras are words or syllables in Sanskrit which when repeated in meditation helps you transcend into a higher state of consciousness.

As sound energies that have always existed the universe, they cannot be created or destroyed and command the power to heal you physically and spiritually. At the very basic level mantras help you to concentrate in meditation. And once you enter its auspicious circle, the mind instantly gets focused and you discover a new realm of peace and tranquillity.

Mantras are words or phrases that are chanted out loud or internally as objects of meditation. Often these mantras are associated with particular Buddhist figures, whose qualities can be cultivated by the repetition of the relevant mantra.

Mantra meditation predates Buddhism, probably by hundreds of years. The origins of mantras go back at least to the Vedic tradition that preceded the Buddha, where mantras were used as incantations to influence, or even to control, the gods.

Throughout history, cultures have believed in the sacred power of words, and have believed that uttering certain words or names could control the external world, or control the unseen forces, like gods or spirits, that they believed acted upon the world. We can see that in the English word "spell", which can mean simply to put letters together to make words, or to use words in order to control the world. The words grammar and glamour have the same original meanings. Gramma-techne was the Greek term for the science or art of letters. This came into English as the word grammar, but also came in Scots (as "glammer") to mean "to cast a spell upon". The word glammer was anglicized as glamour, and came to have its more contemporary romantic and aesthetic associations. So the English language contains fossilized notions that words can have magical powers.

This was particularly so for the words that we call "names". In ancient India it was believed that if you knew the true names of the gods, then you could call upon them and compel them to do your bidding. If this sounds primitive, then imagine how you would feel if you discovered that someone had written your name of a piece of paper, put it in the toilet bowl before using the bathroom, and then flushed your name away. Most of us still, it seems, have a lingering belief in the special nature of names.

Although early Buddhism used chanting as a means of practice, and used the recitation of verses as a way of cultivating an awareness of the qualities of the Buddha (Buddhanusati), the use of mantras doesn't seem to have come into Buddhism until the rise of the Mahayana traditions, which incorporated elements of the non-Buddhist approach to spirituality known as "Tantra."

Tantra made extensive use of mantras as ways of communing with and influencing the gods, and Buddhism co-opted this methodology as a way of getting in touch with the qualities of enlightenment. The Mahayana had already developed a "pantheon" of symbolical figures in human form to represent the diversity of the enlightened state. Given the close contact with the Tantric traditions, it was natural that these archetypal Buddhas and Bodhisattvas came to be associated with particular syllables and mantras.

Defining Mantra Meditation

The word mantra is said to come from a root meaning "that which protects the mind".

In Buddhist meditation, many things can be used as objects of concentration, as "mind protectors". The breath is used in anapanasati (mindfulness of breathing), the sensations of walking are used in walking meditation, the emotions are used as a focus in metta bhavana (development of lovingkindness), and visual images are used in visualization. Mantras are sounds, words or phrases, that are used as an object of concentration.

The sounds may be chanted out loud, or may be heard internally. Mantras can be associated with particular historical or archetypal figures, or may have no such associations. For example, there are mantras associated with the historical Buddha (Om muni muni maha muni Shakyamuni svaha), and the mythical figure Avalokiteshvara (Om mani padme hum). The Prajnaparamita mantra (Gate gate paragate parasamgate bodhi svaha) is associated not with an enlightened figure, but with a body of texts known as the Perfection of Wisdom (Prajnaparamita) sutras. The mantra Om shanti shanti shanti (Om peace peace peace) is not, as far as I'm aware, associated with any figure, and the Pali phrase Sabbe Satta Sukhi Hontu (May All Beings Be Happy) is chanted as a mantra, again without being associated with any particular figure.

How does Mantra Meditation Work?

Mantras are rather mysterious. They are said to be "sound symbols", sounds that in some way correspond to and evoke the spiritual forces that can be represented in visual form as Tara, Avalokiteshvara, etc. We can easily see how an image of a particular figure can have symbolic value, but quite how a sound does this it is not possible to explain rationally. Perhaps it's best to think of mantras as being a cross between poetry and magical incantations.

Many mantras don't make any real, rational, sense, even in Sanskrit, and so they can't really be translated in the same way that a normal sentence can. The mantra of Tara, for example, Om tare tuttare ture svaha, is a play on her name, which means "savioress" or "star" or "she who ferries across." But it doesn't make any kind of statement about Tara, beyond giving us some rather evocative sounds.

Mantras often contain syllables like Om, Ah, and Hum (approximately pronounced hoong), which have no literal meaning whatsoever. There are various "understandings" or interpretations of what these might mean, and the three syllables have been correlated with (respectively) body, speech, and mind; or (again respectively) the Dharmakaya, Sambhogakaya, and Nirmanakaya. They are also correlated with the Buddhas of the mandala, with Om being the seed syllable of Vairochana, the central Buddha, Ah with Amoghasiddhi, the northern Buddha, and Hum with Akshobya, the Buddha of the east. These kinds of associations can become important as we become familiar with Buddhism.

Some words in mantras give rise to more definite associations. The "mani" in the Avalokiteshvara mantra (Om mani padme hum) means "jewel," while "padme" means "lotus". The mantra is sometimes taken to mean, "Hail to the Jewel in the Lotus" although the grammar is rather obscure. I see the mantra as being more poetic and symbolic. The jewel is symbolic of the clarity of wisdom, while the lotus is a symbol both of purity and compassion. So the Avalokitesvara mantra brings together wisdom and compassion. In reciting the mantra, one is calling those qualities to mind.

But trying to understand mantras intellectually is probably a bit like deconstructing a joke, you can do it, but by the time you have finished the task you've completely lost the point of the joke in the first place. Some people hold that mantras have an inherent "spiritual meaning"-that is that someone chanting the mantra of Avalokiteshvara will develop a connection with the compassion of Avalokiteshvara, even without knowing anything of the meaning (in as much as there is one) of the mantra, and without knowing anything about the bodhisattva himself. Others hold that the one develops associations with the mantra as one chants it and begins to learn more about the bodhisattva. Certainly, it is possible to benefit from a mantra while knowing nothing about it.

As an object of concentration, like any other, a mantra can help to still the mind. While you are reciting a mantra out loud or internally, there tends to be less mental chatter. Even if there is a parallel stream of internal discourse going on at the same time as the mantra, the chanting creates more of a sense of continuity, which will grow with practice. The word Mantra is said to mean, "that which protects the mind."

Mantra Meditation in Practice

Mantras may be used on their own or as part of a visualization practice. In a typical visualization practice there is a communication from the "deity" to the practitioner (in the form of blessings, or rays of light, or even speech), and there is a communication from the practitioner to the deity, in the form of mantra.

Mantras can also be used as "mind protectors" while walking, or even in sitting meditation. Often, Buddhists will count the mantras they are chanting by telling beads on a "mala." The physical action of counting round the mala helps to keep the mind focused. A mala usually has 108 beads, this number having a mystical significance in ancient India. The mala can be worn round the neck so that it can be accessed when needed. Some malas have 21 beads and are worn round the wrist. But the use of a mala is not essential.

To use mantras in formal meditation, chanted out loud or internally, first of all make yourself comfortable and upright, and spend a few minutes following your breathing and letting your mind settle. You may want to slow your breathing, directing it into the belly, and deepen it. This will help to still your mind, although you don't need to have an absolutely quiet mind before you start the mantra.

If you're saying the mantra out loud, then let the sound resonate in your chest.

It will help if you take a deep breath into your belly before each mantra. Generally, mantras sound better if you can do each mantra with a single exhalation. But if you can't manage that, then that's okay.

Let the last note of each mantra linger before starting the next mantra. You'll find that the mantra naturally falls into rhythm with your breathing. Make sure that the mantra follows your breathing and not the other way round, otherwise you may become breathless.

Don't actively think about the meaning of the mantra (if it even has one!). If you know what some of the words mean, then they will have associations for you. These associations will have an effect on your mind, and will deepen in significance over time as you explore them outside of meditation.

Let go of any concerns that may arise about whether you are doing the mantra properly. It doesn't matter if your pronunciation is a little off, it's the spirit that counts.

To bring the mantra to a close, gradually let your chanting decrease in volume until it fades away as an external sound and can only be heard internally. Then let the internal sound fade away into silence.

At the conclusion of the practice, sit in the resonant silence, letting the vibrant quietness have a refreshing effect on your mind and emotions.

2

Ancient Yoga

Yoga is a group of ancient spiritual practices originating in India. As a general term in Hinduism it has been defined as referring to "technologies or disciplines of asceticism and meditation which are thought to lead to spiritual experience and profound understanding or insight into the nature of existence." Yoga is also intimately connected to the religious beliefs and practices of the other Indian religions.

Outside India, Yoga is mostly associated with the practice of Asanas (postures) of Hatha Yoga or as a form of exercise, although it has influenced the entire Indian religions family and other spiritual practices throughout the world.

Hindu texts discussing different aspects of yoga include the Upanishads, the Bhagavad Gita, the Yoga Sutras of Patanjali, the Hatha Yoga Pradipika, the Shiva Samhita, and many others.

Major branches of Yoga include: Hatha Yoga, Karma Yoga, Jnana Yoga, Bhakti Yoga, and Raja Yoga. Raja Yoga, known simply as Yoga in the context of Hindu philosophy, is one of the six orthodox (astika) schools of thought, established by the Yoga Sutras of Patanjali.

Etymology

The Sanskrit term yoga has a wide range of different meanings. It is derived from the Sanskrit root yuj, "to control", "to yoke", or "to unite". Common meanings include "joining" or "uniting", and related ideas such as "union" and "conjunction". Another conceptual definition is that of "mode, manner, means" or "expedient, means in general".

History of Yoga

Indus Valley Seals: Several seals discovered at Indus Valley Civilization (c. 3300-1700 BC) sites depict figures in a yoga or meditation like posture. The most widely known of these was named the "Pashupati seal" by its discoverer, John Marshall, who believed that it represented a "proto-Shiva" figure. Many modern authorities discount the idea that this "Pashupati" (Lord of Animals, Sanskrit pashupati) represents a Shiva or Rudra figure.

There is considerable evidence to support the idea that the image's posture "is a form of ritual discipline, suggesting a precursor to yoga" according to archaeologist Gregory Possehl (who also questions the proto-Shiva theory). He points to sixteen other specific "yogi glyptics" in the corpus of Mature Harappan artifacts as pointing to Harappan devotion to "ritual discipline and concentration". These images show that the yoga pose "may have been used by deities and humans alike". He suggests that yoga goes back to the Indus Valley Civilization.

Gavin Flood characterizes these views as "speculative", saying that it is not clear from the 'Pashupati' seal that the figure is seated in a yoga posture, or even that the shape is intended to represent a human figure, though it is nevertheless possible that there are echoes of Shaiva iconographic themes, such as half-moon shapes resembling the horns of a bull. Other authorities do support the idea that the 'Pashupati' figure shows a figure in a yoga or meditation posture. They include Archaeologist Jonathan Mark Kenoyer, current Co-director of the Harappa Archaeological Research Project in Pakistan and Indologist Heinrich Zimmer.

In 2007, terracota seals were discovered in the Cholistan Desert in Pakistan. Punjab University Archaeology Department Chairman Dr. Farzand Masih described one of the seals as similar to the previously discovered Mohenjodaro seals, with three pictographs on one side and a "yogi" on the other side.]

Literary Sources

Ascetic practices (tapas) are referenced in the Brahmanas (900 BC and 500 BC), early commentaries on the vedas. In the

Upanishads, an early reference to meditation is made in Brihadaranyaka Upanishad, one of the earliest Upanishads (approx. 900 BC). The main textual sources for the evolving concept of Yoga are the middle Upanishads, (ca. 400 BC), the Mahabharata (5th c. BC) including the Bhagavad Gita (ca. 200 BC), and the Yoga Sutras of Patanjali (200 BCE-300 CE).

Bhagavad Gita

The Bhagavad Gita ('Song of the Lord'), thought to have been composed in roughly the 2nd century BC, uses the term yoga extensively in a variety of senses. Of many possible meanings given to the term in the Gita, most emphasis is given to these three:

- Karma yoga: The yoga of action
- Bhakti yoga: The yoga of devotion
- Jnana yoga: The yoga of knowledge

The influential commentator Madhusudana Sarasvati (b. circa 1490) divided the Gita's eighteen chapters into three sections, each of six chapters. According to his method of division the first six chapters deal with Karma yoga, the middle six deal with Bhakti yoga, and the last six deal with Jnana (knowledge). This interpretation has been adopted by some later commentators and rejected by others.

Yoga Sutras of Patanjali

In Indian philosophy, Yoga is the name of one of the six orthodox philosophical schools. The Yoga philosophical system is closely allied with the Samkhya school. The Yoga school as expounded by Patanjali accepts the Samkhya psychology and metaphysics, but is more theistic than the Samkhya, as evidenced by the addition of a divine entity to the Samkhya's twenty-five elements of reality.

The parallels between Yoga and Samkhya were so close that Max Muller says that "the two philosophies were in popular parlance distinguished from each other as Samkhya with and Samkhya without a Lord...." The intimate relationship between Samkhya and Yoga is explained by Heinrich Zimmer:

These two are regarded in India as twins, the two aspects of a single discipline. Sankhya provides a basic theoretical exposition of human nature, enumerating and defining its elements, analyzing their manner of cooperation in a state of bondage (bandha), and describing their state of disentanglement or separation in release (moksa), while Yoga treats specifically of the dynamics of the process for the disentanglement, and outlines practical techniques for the gaining of release, or 'isolation-integration' (kaivalya).

The sage Patanjali is regarded as the founder of the formal Yoga philosophy. The Yoga Sutras of Patanjali are ascribed to Patanjali, who, may have been, as Max Muller explains, "the author or representative of the Yoga-philosophy without being necessarily the author of the Sutras." Indologist Axel Michaels is dismissive of claims that the work was written by Patanjali, characterizing it instead as a collection of fragments and traditions of texts stemming from the second or third century. Gavin Flood cites a wider period of uncertainty for the composition, between 100 BC and 500 CE.

Patanjali's yoga is known as Raja yoga, which is a system for control of the mind. Patanjali defines the word "yoga" in his second sutra, which is the definitional sutra for his entire work:

yogas citta-vitti-nirodha?-Yoga Sutras 1.2

This terse definition hinges on the meaning of three Sanskrit terms. I. K. Taimni translates it as "Yoga is the inhibition (nirodha?) of the modifications (v?tti) of the mind (citta)". Swami Vivekananda translates the sutra as "Yoga is restraining the mind-stuff (Citta) from taking various forms (Vrittis)." Gavin Flood translates the sutra as "yoga is the cessation of mental fluctuations".

Patanjali's writing also became the basis for a system referred to it as "Ashtanga Yoga" ("Eight-Limbed Yoga"). This eight-limbed concept derived from the 29th Sutra of the 2nd book became a feature of Raja yoga, and is a core characteristic of practically every Raja yoga variation taught today. The Eight Limbs of yoga practice are:

(1) Yama (The five "abstentions"): violence, lying, theft, (illicit) sex, and possessions

(2) Niyama (The five "observances"): purity, contentment, austerities, study, and surrender to god

(3) Asana: Literally means "seat", and in Patanjali's Sutras refers to seated positions used for meditation. Later, with the rise of Hatha yoga, asana came to refer to all the "postures"

(4) Pranayama ("Life Force Control"): Control of prana, life force, or vital energy, particularly, the breath

(5) Pratyahara ("Abstraction"): Reversal of the sense organs

(6) Dharana ("Concentration"): Fixing the attention on a single object

(7) Dhyana ("Meditation"): Intense contemplation of the nature of the object of meditation

(8) Samadhi ("Liberation"): merging consciousness with the object of meditation

It details every aspect of the meditative process, and the preparation for it. The book is available in as many as 40 English translations, both in-print and on-line.

Hatha Yoga Pradipika

Hatha Yoga is a particular system of Yoga described by Yogi Swatmarama, a yogic sage of the 15th century in India, and compiler of the Hatha Yoga Pradipika. Hatha Yoga is a development of-but also differs substantially from-the Raja Yoga of Patanjali, in that it focuses on shatkarma, the purification of the physical as leading to the purification of the mind (ha) and prana, or vital energy (tha).

In contrast, the Raja Yoga posited by Patanjali begins with a purification of the mind (yamas) and spirit (niyamas), then comes to the body via asana (body postures) and pranayama (breath). Hatha yoga contains substantial tantric influence, and marks the first point at which chakras and kundalini were introduced into the yogic canon. Compared to the seated Asanas of Patanjali's Raja yoga which were seen largely as a means of preparing for meditation, it also marks the development of

Asanas as full body 'postures' in the modern sense. Hatha Yoga in its many modern variations is the style that most people actually associate with the word "Yoga" today. Because its emphasis is on the body through asana and pranayama practice, many western students are satisfied with the physical health and vitality it develops and are not interested in the other six limbs of the complete Hatha yoga teaching, or with the even older Raja Yoga tradition it is based on.

Yoga in other Traditions

Yoga and Buddhism: Yoga is intimately connected to the religious beliefs and practices of the Indian religions. The influence of Yoga is also visible in Buddhism, which is distinguished by its austerities, spiritual exercises, and trance states.

Yogacara Buddhism

Yogacara also spelled yogachara, is a school of philosophy and psychology that developed in India during the 4th to 5th centuries.

Yogacara received the name as it provided a yoga, a framework for engaging in the practices that lead to the path of the bodhisattva. The Yogacara sect teaches yoga in order to reach enlightenment.

Zen (Ch`an) Buddhism

Zen (the name of which derives from the Sanskrit "dhyana" via the Chinese "ch'an") is a form of Mahayana Buddhism. The Mahayana school of Buddhism is noted for its proximity with Yoga. In the west, Zen is often set alongside Yoga; the two schools of meditation display obvious family resemblances. This phenomenon merits special attention since the Zen Buddhist school of meditation has some of its roots in yogic practices. Certain essential elements of Yoga are important both for Buddhism in general and for Zen in particular.

Tibetan Buddhism

Yoga is central to Tibetan Buddhism. In the Nyingma tradition, practitioners progress to increasingly profound levels of yoga, starting with Maha yoga, continuing to Anu yoga and ultimately undertaking the highest practice, Ati yoga. In the Sarma traditions, the Anuttara yoga class is equivalent. Other tantra yoga practices include a system of 108 bodily postures practised with breath and heart rhythm. Timing in movement exercises is known as Trul khor or union of moon and sun (channel) prajna energies. The body postures of Tibetan ancient yogis are depicted on the walls of the Dalai Lama's summer temple of Lukhang.

Yoga and Tantra

Tantrism, is a practice that is supposed to alter the relation of the individual practitioner of Tantrism to the ordinary social, religious, and logical reality in which he or she lives. Through Tantric practice an individual perceives reality as maya, illusion, and the individual achieves liberation from it.

This particular path to salvation among the several offered by Hinduism, links Tantrism to those practices of Indian religions, such as yoga, meditation, and social renunciation, which are based on temporary or permanent withdrawal from social relationships and modes.

During tantric practices and studies, the student is instructed further in meditation technique, particularly chakra meditation. This is often in a limited form in comparison with the way this kind of meditation is known and used by Tantric practitioners and yogis elsewhere, but is more elaborate than the initiate's previous meditation. It is considered to be a kind of Kundalini Yoga for the purpose of moving the Goddess into the chakra located in the "heart," for meditation and worship.

Goal of Yoga

There are numerous opinions on what the goal of Yoga may be, although generally they involve some kind of union, either of a personal or a non-personal nature.

Within the monist schools of Advaita Vedanta and Shaivism this perfection takes the form of Moksha, which is a liberation from all worldly suffering and the cycle of birth and death (Samsara) at which point there is a cessation of thought and an experience of blissful union with the Supreme Brahman. For the dualistic bhakti schools of Vaishnavism, bhakti itself is the ultimate goal of the yoga process, wherein perfection culminates in an eternal relationship with Vishnu or one of his associated avatars such as Krishna or Rama.

Bhakti yoga

Bhakti yoga is a term within Hinduism which denotes the spiritual practice of fostering loving devotion to God, called bhakti. Traditionally there are nine forms of bhaktiyoga. Bhakti yoga is generally considered the easiest of the four general paths to liberation, or moksha (the others being Karma, Raja and Jnana Yoga), and especially so within the current age of Kali yuga (according to the Hindu cycle of time). In scriptures such as the Bhagavata Purana, bhakti is described as a perfectional stage in itself which surpasses even moksha as a level of spiritual realisation. Hindu movements in which bhakti yoga is the main practice are called bhakti movements.

Philosophy

Bhakti is the Sanskrit term that signifies a blissful, selfless and overwhelming love of God as the beloved Father, Mother, Child, Friend or whichever relationship or personal aspect of God that finds appeal in the devotee's heart. Bhakti incorporates a number of universal principles, also common in other world religions.

The 'Bhakti-rasamrita-sindhu' (written by Rupa Gosvami) gives the following as the nine primary activities of bhakti, with the instruction that by following all, or just one, of these activities perfectly the aspiring devotee can achieve pure love of God:

1. Hearing about the Lord-singing & chanting God's names (japa), hearing stories from scripture.
2. Glorifying the Lord-describing God's all-attractive features.
3. Remembering the Lord-internal meditation on the Lord's form, activities, names or personality.

4. Serving the lotus feet of the Lord-providing a form of physical service.
5. Worshipping the Lord-deity worship (puja) is a popular form of this within India.
6. Offering prayers to the Lord-any form of prayer offered to please God.
7. Serving the Lord-offering a service for Lord's pleasure, such as preaching activity.
8. Building a friendship with the Lord-having an internal, loving relationship with God.
9. Surrendering everything unto the Lord-surrendering one's thoughts, actions and deeds to God.

The scriptural source of these nine primary forms of bhakti is a verse in the Bhagavata Purana, spoken by Prahlada:

"Prahlada Maharaja said: Hearing and chanting about the transcendental holy name, form, qualities, paraphernalia and pastimes of Lord Vishnu, remembering them, serving the lotus feet of the Lord, offering the Lord respectful worship with sixteen types of paraphernalia, offering prayers to the Lord, becoming His servant, considering the Lord one's best friend, and surrendering everything unto Him (in other words, serving Him with the body, mind and words)-these nine processes are accepted as pure devotional service. One who has dedicated his life to the service of Katha through these nine methods should be understood to be the most learned person, for he has acquired complete knowledge."

These nine principles of devotional service are described as helping the devotee remain constantly in touch with God. The processes of japa and internal meditation on the aspirant devotees's chosen deity form (ishta deva) are especially popular in most bhakti schools. Bhakti is a yoga path, in that its aim is a form of divine, loving union with the Supreme Lord. The exact form of the Lord, or type of union varies between the different schools, but the essence of each process is very similar.

The Bhagavad Gita

While it has an extensive list of philosophical and religious associations, the Bhagavad Gita is also seen as a cornerstone for Hindu Bhakti theism, especially within Vaishnavism. However, it has been interpreted by many as being a manual not limited just for devotees of Krishna. Whatever be the case, it is adamant, in Krishna's words, that love and innocent pure intention is the most powerful motive force in a devotee's spiritual life. It is a very succinct and comprehensive statement on the mindset of the Bhakta (loving devotee), regardless of the form of God chosen:

Engage your mind always in thinking of Me, become My devotee, offer obeisances to Me and worship Me. Being completely absorbed in Me, surely you will come to Me. (B-Gita 9.34)

One can understand Me as I am, as the Supreme Personality of Godhead, only by devotional service. And when one is in full consciousness of Me by such devotion, he can enter into the kingdom of God. (B-Gita 18.55)

Branches

The various bhakti movements are monotheistic in their aim, being primarily devoted to worship of either Vishnu, Krishna or Shiva as the Supreme God or His personal energy, known as Shakti. These movements, which followed the establishment of the three Vedanta systems, rejuvenated Hinduism through their intense expression of faith and responsiveness to the emotional and philosophical needs of India, illustrated by Bharatanatyam, and can rightly be said to have affected the greatest wave of change in Hindu prayer and ritual since the advent of Adi Shankaracharya. There have been bhakti movements right through Indian history.

The philosophical schools changed the way people thought, but Bhakti was immediately accessible to all, calling to the instinctual emotion of love and redirecting it to the highest pursuit of God and self-realization. In general a liberal movement, its denouncement of caste offered recourse for Hindus from the orthodox Brahaminical systems. Of course, however, Bhakti's message of tolerance and love was not often heeded by those ensconced in the societal construct of caste.

Altogether, bhakti resulted in a mass of devotional literature, music, dance and art that has enriched the world and gave India renewed spiritual impetus, one eschewing unnecessary ritual and artificial social boundaries.

Karma Yoga

Karma yoga, (also known as Buddhi Yoga) or the "discipline of action" is based on the teachings of the Bhagavad Gita, a sacred Sanskrit scripture of Hinduism. One of the four pillars of yoga, Karma yoga focuses on the adherence to duty (dharma) while remaining detached from the reward. It states that one can attain Moksha (salvation) or love of God (bhakti) by performing their duties in an unselfish manner for the pleasure of the Supreme. Karma Yoga is an intrinsic part of many derivative types of yoga, such as Natya Yoga.

Background

The Bhagavad Gita gives a summary of the Karma Yoga process. The Gita itself is a chapter from a larger work known as Mahabharata, wherein a dialogue takes place between the prince Arjuna, and his friend and chariot driver, Krishna, on the brink of a great dynastic war. Their conversation is prompted by Arjuna as he is engulfed by sorrow and misgivings regarding the oncoming fight in which he has friends and relatives on both sides. In reply, Krishna then elucidates upon a number of philosophical yoga systems and practices (including Karma Yoga) by/through which he should indeed continue with the fight on righteous principles.

Concept

The word Karma is derived from the Sanskrit Kri, meaning 'to do', in its most basic sense karma simply means action, and yoga translates to union. Thus Karma yoga literally translates to the path of union through action. It is described as a way of acting, thinking and willing by which one acts in accordance with one's duty (dharma) without consideration of personal selfish desires, likes or dislikes. Acting without being attached to the fruits of one's deeds.

Therefore, without being attached to the fruits of activities, one should act as a matter of duty, for by working without attachment one attains the Supreme.

In the case of Arjuna in the Gita this translated to his fighting in the oncoming war to uphold the righteous cause in accordance with his duty as a warrior; even if out of compassion he did not want to fight with his relatives and teachers on the other side.

Krishna then goes on to describe how Arjuna should surrender the fruits of his actions (good or bad) to himself (as the Supreme Person or avatara) :

Therefore, — Arjuna, surrendering all your works unto Me, with full knowledge of Me, without desires for profit, with no claims to proprietorship, and free from lethargy, fight.

Krishna describes that allocated work done without expectations, motives, or anticipation of its outcome purifies one's mind and gradually makes an individual fit to see the value of reason. He states that it is not necessary to remain in external solitude, or actionless, in order to practice a spiritual life, with the state of action or inaction is primarily determined in the mind.

In order to achieve the perfection of life, Krishna describes it is important to control all mental desires and tendencies to enjoy pleasures of the senses. The practice of Karma Yoga in daily life makes an individual fit through action, meditation and devotion to sharpen his reasoning, develop intuitive power of acquiring knowledge and to transcend the mind itself.

Karma

As with a number of other philosophies in Hinduism, Karma yoga is based on the general understandings of karma and reincarnation (samsara). It is believed that a man is born with certain Samskars (karma's), both positive and negative, from his past lives which push him towards performing certain actions in his present one. This process continues until the individual attains a zero balance, (no karma remains) wherein one achieves liberation.

Schools of Thought

Shankaracharya says by practising Karma, one's mind gets purified. Thus, he describes Karma yoga as a path to Jnana yoga, with Jnana yoga ultimately leading to a state of Moksha or realisation.

Some consider personalities such as the Buddha to have been karma yogis. Buddha is the ideal karma yogi... acting entirely without motive, and the history of humanity shows him to have been the greatest man ever born, beyond compare, the greatest combination of Head & Heart that ever existed.- Swami Vivekananda

The Hindu Saint Mata Amritanandamayi says, "The beauty and charm of selfless love and service should not die away from the face of the earth. The world should know that a life of dedication is possible, that a life inspired by love and service to humanity is possible. Meditation and studying the scriptures are like two sides of a coin. The engraving on that coin is selfless service, and that is what gives it its real value. Our compassion and acts of selflessness take us to the deeper truths. Through selfless action we can eradicate the ego that conceals the Self. Detached, selfless action leads to liberation. Such action is not just work; it is karma yoga."

Jnana Yoga

Jnana yoga or "path of knowledge" is one of the types of yoga mentioned in Hindu philosophies. Jnana in Sanskrit means "knowledge".

As used in the Bhagavad Gita, the monist philosopher Adi Shankara gave primary importance to jnana yoga as "knowledge of the absolute" (Brahman), while the Vaishnava commentator Ramanuja regarded knowledge only as a condition of devotion. In the Bhagavad Gita (13.3) Krishna says that jnana consists of properly understanding kshetra (the field of activity—that is, the body) and kshetra-jna (the knower of the body—that is, the soul). Later in the Gita (13.35) Krishna emphasizes that a transcendentalist must understand the difference between these two.

Jnana yoga teaches that there are four means to salvation:

- Viveka-Discrimination: The ability to differentiate between what is real/eternal (Brahman) and what is unreal/temporal (everything else in the universe.)
- Vairagya-Dispassion: After practice one should be able to "detach" her/himself from everything that is "temporary."
- Shad-sampat-The 6 Virtues: Tranquillity (control of the mind), Dama (control of the senses), Uparati (renunciation of activities that are not duties), Titiksha (endurance), Shraddha (faith), Samadhana (perfect concentration).
- Mumukshutva-Intense longing for liberation from temporal limitations.

Raja Yoga

Raja Yoga ("royal yoga", "royal union", also known as Classical Yoga or simply Yoga) is one of the six orthodox (astika) schools of Hindu philosophy, outlined by Patanjali in his Yoga Sutras. It is also sometimes referred to as Ashanga (eight-limbed) yoga because there are eight aspects to the path to which one must attend. Raja yoga is concerned principally with the cultivation of the mind using meditation (dhyana) to further one's acquaintance with reality and finally achieve liberation.

The term Raja Yoga is a retronym, introduced in the 15th century Hatha Yoga Pradipika to distinguish the school based on the Yoga Sutras from the new current of Hatha Yoga.

Concept

Raja Yoga is so-called because it is primarily concerned with the mind. The mind is traditionally conceived as the "king" of the psycho-physical structure which does its bidding (whether or not one has realized this). Because of the relationship between the mind and the body, the body must be first "tamed" through self-discipline and purified by various means (see Hatha Yoga). A good level of overall health and psychological integration must be attained before the deeper aspects of yoga can be pursued. Humans have all sorts of addictions and obsessions and these preclude the attainment of tranquil abiding (meditation). Through restraint (yama) such as celibacy, abstaining from drugs and alcohol and careful attention to one's actions of body, speech and mind, the human being becomes fit to practise meditation. This yoke that one puts upon oneself (discipline) is another meaning of the word yoga. Every thought, feeling, perception, or memory you may have causes a modification, or ripple, in the mind. It distorts and colours the mental mirror. If you can restrain the mind from forming into modifications, there will be no distortion, and you will experience your true Self.-Swami Satchidananda

Patanjali's Yoga Sutras begin with the statement yogas citta-vitti-nirodha? (1.2), "Yoga limits the oscillations of the mind". They go on to detail the ways in which mind can create false ideations and advocate meditation on real objects, which process, it is said, will lead to a spontaneous state of quiet mind, the "Nirbija" or "seedless state", in which there is no mental object of focus. Practices that serve to maintain for the individual the ability to access this state may be considered Raja Yoga practices. Thus Raja Yoga encompasses and differentiates itself from other forms of Yoga by encouraging the mind to avoid the sort of absorption in obsessional practice (including other traditional yogic practices) that can create false mental objects.

In this sense Raja Yoga is "king of yogas": all yogic practices are seen as potential tools for obtaining the seedless state, itself considered to be the starting point in the quest to cleanse Karma and obtain Moksha or Nirvana. Historically, schools of yoga that label themselves "Raja" offer students a mix of yogic practices and (hopefully or ideally) this philosophical viewpoint.

Practice

Raja Yoga aims at controlling all thought-waves or mental modifications. While a Hatha Yogi starts his Sadhana with Asanas (postures) and Pranayama, a Raja Yogi starts his Sadhana with the mind, although a certain minimum of Asanas and pranayamas are usually included as a preparation for the meditation and concentration.

Eight Limbs of Ashtanga Yoga

The eight limbs of Ashtanga Yoga are:

- Yama-Code of conduct-self-restraint
- Niyama-religious observances-commitments to practice, such as study and devotion
- Asana-integration of mind and body through physical activity
- Pranayama-regulation of breath leading to integration of mind and body
- Pratyahara-abstraction of the senses, withdrawal of the senses of perception from their objects
- Dharana-concentration, one-pointedness of mind
- Dhyana-meditation (quiet activity that leads to samadhi)
- Samadhi-the quiet state of blissful awareness, superconscious state

Yama

Yama consists of five parts: Ahimsa (nonviolence), Satya (truthfulness), Asteya (not stealing), Brahmacharya (celibacy), and Aparigraha (non-covetousness). Ahimsa is perfect harmlessness and positive love also. This removes the brutal nature in man and strengthens the will.

Niyama

Niyama is observance of five canons: Saucha (internal and external purity), Santosha (contentment), Tapas (Sanskrit) (austerity), Svadhyaya (study of religious books and repetitions of Mantras), and Ishvarapranidhana (self-surrender to God, and His worship). He who practises meditation without ethical perfection, without the practice of Yama-Niyama cannot obtain the fruits of meditation. Purify your mind first through the practice of Yama-Niyama. Then practice regular meditation. Then you will attain illumination.

Asana

Any easy, steady, comfortable pose is Asana. Asanas steady the body. Posture is mastered by releasing tension and meditation on the unlimited.

Pranayama

Pranayama checks the outgoing tendencies of the mind. It is often misunderstood for breathing exercises. Prana means life force, while yama means to gain control

Pratyahara

Pratyahara gives inner spiritual strength. It removes all sorts of distractions. It develops willpower.

Dharana

Real Yoga starts from concentration. Concentration merges into meditation. Meditation ends in Samadhi. Retention of breath, Brahmacharya, Satvic (pure) food, seclusion, silence, Satsanga (being in the company of a guru), and not mixing much with people are all aids to concentration. Concentrate on Trikuti (the space between the two eyebrows) with closed eyes is preferred. The mind can be easily controlled, as this is the seat for the mind.

Dhyana

Sleep, tossing of mind, attachment to objects, subtle desires and cravings, laziness, lack of Brahmacharya, gluttony are all obstacles in meditation. Reduce your wants. Cultivate dispassion. You will have progress in Yoga. Vairagya thins out the mind. Do not mix much. Do not talk much. Do not walk much. Do not eat much. Do not sleep much. Do not exert much. Never wrestle with the mind during meditation. Do not use any violent efforts at concentration. If evil thoughts enter your mind, do not use your will force in driving them. You will tax your will. You will lose your energy. You will fatigue yourself. The greater the efforts you make, the more the evil thoughts will return with redoubled force. Be indifferent. Become a witness of those thoughts. Substitute divine thoughts. They will pass away. Never miss a day in meditation. Regularity is of paramount importance. When the mind is tired, do not concentrate. Do not take heavy food at night.

The mind passes into many conditions or states as it is made up of three qualities-Sattva, Rajas and Tamas. Kshipta (wandering), Vikshipta (gathering), Mudha (ignorant), Ekagra (one-pointed), and Nirodha (contrary) are the five states of the mind.

By controlling the thoughts the Sadhaka attains great Siddhis. He becomes an adept. He attains Asamprajnata Samadhi or Kaivalya. Do not run after Siddhis. Siddhis are great temptations. They will bring about your downfall. A Raja Yogi practices Samyama or the combined practice of Dharana, Dhyana and Samadhi at one and the same time and gets detailed knowledge of an object.

Control the mind by Abhyasa (practice) and Vairagya (dispassion). Any practice which steadies the mind and makes it one-pointed is Abhyasa. Dull Vairagya will not help you in attaining perfection in Yoga. You must have Para Vairagya or Theevra Vairagya, intense dispassion.

Samadhi

Meditation on OM with Bhava and its meaning removes obstacles in Sadhana and helps to attain Samadhi. Avidya (ignorance), Asmita (egoism), Raga-Dvesha (likes and dislikes), Abhinivesha (clinging to mundane life) are the five Kleshas or afflictions. Destroy these afflictions. You will attain Samadhi.

Samadhi is of two kinds:

- Savikalpa, Samprajnata or Sabija; and
- Nirvikalpa, Asamprajnata or Nirbija.

In Savikalpa or Sabija, there is Triputi or the triad (knower, known and knowledge). The samskaras are not burnt or freed. Savitarka, Nirvitarka, Savichara, Nirvichara, Sasmita and Saananda are the different forms of Savikalpa Samadhi. In Nirbija Samadhi or Asamprajnata Samadhi there is no triad.

A Bhakta gets Bhava-Samadhi, a Jnani gets Badha-Samadhi, a Raja Yogi gets Nirodha Samadhi.

Results

Practice of these precepts is said to result in a state in which one's behaviour spontaneously follows the five ethical precepts (Yamas):

- Ahimsa-refraining from injury (non-life supporting action)
- satya-truthfulness
- asteya-freedom from stealing
- brahmacarya-living within the Self (moderation; abstinence)
- aparigraha-freedom from attachment to possessions

Yamas

A yama (Sanskrit), literally a "restraint", is a rule or code of conduct for living virtuously. The yamas comprise the "shall-nots" in our dealings with the external world.

Ten Yamas are codified as "the restraints" in numerous scriptures including the Shandilya and Varaha Upanishads, the Hatha Yoga Pradipika by Gorakshanatha, and the Tirumantiram of Tirumular. Patanjali lists only five yamas in his Yoga Sutras.

Ten Traditional Yamas

The ten traditional yamas are:

1. *Ahimsa:* Nonviolence. Abstinence from injury, harmlessness, the not causing of pain to any living creature in thought, word, or deed at any time. This is the "main" yama. The other nine are there in support of its accomplishment.
2. *Satya:* truthfulness, word and thought in conformity with the facts.
3. *Asteya:* non-stealing, non-coveting, non-entering into debt.
4. *Brahmacharya:* divine conduct, continence, celibate when single, faithful when married.
5. *Kshama:* patience, releasing time, functioning in the now.
6. *Dhriti:* steadfastness, overcoming non-perseverance, fear, and indecision; seeing each task through to completion.

7. *Daya:* compassion; conquering callous, cruel and insensitive feelings toward all beings.
8. *Arjava:* honesty, straightforwardness, renouncing deception and wrongdoing.
9. *Mitahara*: moderate appetite, neither eating too much nor to little; nor consuming meat, fish, shellfish, fowl or eggs.
10. *Shaucha:* purity, avoidance of impurity in body, mind and speech. (Note: Patanjali's Yoga Sutras list Shaucha as the first of the Niyamas.)

Alternate Meaning of Yama

Yama is also the name of the ruler of the underworld in hindu folklore. An example of this is in the hindu story of Nachiketas.

Five Yamas of Patanjali

In the Yoga Sutras of Patanjali, the yamas are the first limb of the eight limbs of Raja Yoga.

They are found in the Sadhana Pada Verse 30 as:

1. Ahimsa
2. Satya
3. Asteya
4. Brahmacharya
5. Aparigraha: absence of avariciousness, non-appropriation of things not one's own.

Niyama

Niyama is a set of behaviours codified as "the observances" in numerous scriptures including the Shandilya and Varuha Upanishads, Hatha Yoga Pradipika by Gorakshanatha, the Tirumantiram of Tirumular and the Yoga Sutras of Patanjali. All the above texts list ten Niyamas, with the exception of Patanjali's work, which lists only five. They comprise the "shall-do" in our dealings with the inner world, and Swami Vivekananda describes them as the second step of Raja yoga.

The ten traditional Niyamas are:

1. *Hri:* remorse, being modest and showing shame for misdeeds;
2. *Santosha:* contentment; being satisfied with the resources at hand-therefore not desiring more;
3. *Dana:* giving, without thought of reward;
4. *Astikya:* faith, believing firmly in the teacher, the teachings and the path to enlightenment;
5. *Ishvarapujana:* worship of the Lord, the cultivation of devotion through daily worship and meditation, the return to the source;
6. *Siddhanta shravana:* scriptural listening, studying the teachings and listening to the wise of one's lineage;
7. *Mati:* cognition, developing a spiritual will and intellect with the guru's guidance;
8. *Vrata:* sacred vows, fulfilling religious vows, rules and observances faithfully;
9. *Japa:* recitation, chanting mantras daily;
10. *Tapas:* the endurance of the opposites; hunger and thirst, heat and cold, standing and sitting etc.

In Patanjali's Yoga Sutras, the Niyamas are the second limb of the eight limbs of Raja Yoga.

They are found in the Sadhana Pada Verse 32 as:

1. *Shaucha:* in the traditional codification, this item is listed under Yamas; this word means purity.
2. *Santosha:* contentment.
3. *Tapas:* austerity.
4. *Svadhyaya:* self-study or study of spiritual scriptures.
5. *Ishvarapranidhana:* self-surrender.

Asana

Asana, Sanskrit for "sitting posture" (asanam is 'sitting' or 'ass' / aste is 'he sits'), is a body position, typically associated with the practice of Yoga, intended primarily to restore and maintain a practioner's wellbeing, improve the body's flexibility and vitality, and promote the ability to remain in seated meditation for extended periods. In the context of Yoga practice, asana refers to two things: the place where a practitioner (yogin (general usage); yogi (male); yogini (female)) sits and the manner (posture) in which she/he sits. In the Yoga sutras, Patanjali suggests that asana is "to be seated in a position that is firm, but relaxed". As the repertoire of postures has expanded and moved beyond the simple sitting posture over the centuries, modern usage has come to include variations from lying on the back and standing on the head, to a variety of other positions. In the Yoga sutras, Patanjali mentions the execution of an asana as the third of the eight limbs of Classical or Raja (royal) yoga.

The word asana in Sanskrit does appear in many contexts denoting physical position, although, as noted, traditional usage is specific to the practice of yoga. Traditional usage defines asana as both singular and plural. In English, plural for asana is defined as Asanas. In addition, English usage within the context of yoga practice sometimes specifies yogasana or yoga asana, particularly with regard to the system of the Ashtanga Vinyasa Yoga. That said, it should be noted that yogasana is also the name of a particular posture that is not specifically associated with the Vinyasa system, and that while "ashtanga" (small 'a') refers to the eight limbs of Yoga delineated below, Ashtanga (capital 'A') refers to the specific system of Yoga developed by Sri Krishnamikurti at the Mysore Palace.

The Eight Limbs of Yoga

In the Yoga sutras, Patanjali describes asana as the third of the 8 limbs of classical yoga (raja yoga). These eight limbs are the yamas (restrictions), niyamas (observances), Asanas (postures), pranayama (breath work), pratyahara (sense withdrawal or non-attachment), dharana (concentration), dhyana (meditation), and samadhi (realization of the true self and/or unity with god).

Asanas are the physical movements in a yoga practice. In combination with pranayama or breathing techniques, it constitutes hatha yoga. In the Yoga sutras, Patanjali describes "asana" simply as sitting meditation, suggesting meditation to be the path of samadhi, or self-realization.

Variety of Asanas

An important publication of a rather large number of Asanas, has been presented in 1959 by Swami Vishnu-devananda. In his book The Complete Illustrated Book of Yoga his published 66 136 variations of Asanas, which found their basis at 66 different Asanas. In his book Vishnu-devananda enlarges on other subjects relating to hatha yoga, like pranayama and the filosofy and aim of yoga.

Sri Dharma Mittra, composer of the Master Yoga Chart of 908 Postures, states that there are an infinite number of Asanas. In 1975, as an offering of devotion to his guru, Swami Kailashananda Maharaj, Dharma set out to catalogue the vast number of Asanas. All together he compiled 1300 variations, that he derived from gurus, yogis, and ancient and contemporary texts. Although it will not be possible in any way to establish an exact set of postures, this work is considered a leading collection by students and yogis alike.

Common Practices

In the Yoga sutras, Patanjali suggests that the only requirement for practising Asanas is to be "steady and comfortable". The body should be held firm yet relaxed, and the practitioner should not experience discomfort of any kind. Tightness or tension observed within the body should be consciously relaxed.

According to yoga practitioners, when bodily control is mastered, they are free from what they call the "pairs of opposites", such as heat and cold, hunger and thirst, joy and grief. This non-dualistic perspective comes from the Sankya school of the Himalayan Masters.

Listed below are traditional practices for performing asana:

- A glass of fresh water should be taken before performing Asanas.
- The stomach should be relatively empty.

- Force or pressure should not be used while performing Asanas.
- Lower the head and other parts of the body slowly; in particular, raised heels should be lowered slowly.
- The breathing should be controlled. The benefits of Asanas increase if the specific pranayama to the yoga type is performed.
- If the body is stressed, perform Corpse Pose or Child Pose
- Some claim that Asanas, especially inverted poses, are to be avoided during menstruation. Others deny this view.
- Nowadays, Asanas are generally not performed on floor, but on Yoga mats instead.

Pranayama

Pranayama is the breath control in yoga and is an integral part when performing the asanas.

Patanjali discusses his specific approach to pranayama in verses 2.49 through 2.51, and devotes verses 2.52 and 2.53 to explaining the benefits of the practice. Patanjali refers to pranayama as the control of life force that comes as a result of practising the various breathing techniques, rather than the numerous breathing exercises themselves.

Surya Namaskara

Surya Namaskara ("Salute to the Sun"), is a form of worshipping God by concentrating on the Sun, for self vitalization. Surya namaskara gives equal weightage to both exercise and posture.

The physical base of the practice links together twelve asanas in a dynamically performed series. A full round of Surya namaskara is considered to be two sets of the twelve poses with a change in the second set to moving the opposite leg first through the series. Generally Surya namaskara is performed before performing "asanas".

Benefits of Practice

The physical aspect of yoga, the asanas, has been much popularized in the West, and devoted celebrity practitioners like Madonna and Sting have contributed to the increased visibility of the practice. Physically, of the practice of asanas is considered that it promotes:

- muscle flexibility
- tendon strength.
- internal massage of internal body functions.

The emphasis on the physical part has given rise to the perception that yoga consists only of asana practice. A more esoteric intention is to facilitate the flow of prana (vital energy; qi in Chinese; ki in Japanese) to aid in balancing the koshas (sheaths) of the physical and metaphysical body.

Pranayama

Pranayama is a Sanskrit word often translated as control of the life force (prana). When used as a technical term in yoga, it is often translated more specifically as "breath control". Literal translations include A. A. Macdonell's "suspension of breath" and I. K. Taimni's "regulation of breath".

Etymology

Pranayama is a Sanskrit compound.

V. S. Apte provides fourteen different meanings for the word prana including these:

- Breath, respiration
- The breath of life, vital air, principle of life (usually plural in this sense, there being five such vital airs generally assumed, but three, six, seven, nine, and even ten are also spoken of)
- Energy, vigour
- The spirit or soul

Of these meanings, the concept of "vital air" is used by Bhattacharyya to describe the concept as used in Sanskrit texts dealing with pranayama. Thomas McEvilley translates "prana" as "spirit-energy".

Monier-Williams defines the compound pranayama as (m., also pl.) "N. of the three 'breath-exercises' performed during Sandhya (See puraka, recaka, kumbhaka" This technical definition refers to a particular system of breath control with three processes as explained by Bhattacharyya: puraka (to take the breath inside), kumbhaka (to retain it), and recaka (to discharge it). There are also other processes of pranayama in addition to this three-step model.

Macdonell gives the etymology as prana + ayama and defines it as "m. suspension of breath (sts. pl.)".

Apte's definition of ayaman derives it from a + yam and provides several variant meanings for it when used in compounds. The first three meanings have to do with "length", "expansion, extension", and "stretching, extending", but in the specific case of use in the compound pranayama he defines ayaman as meaning "restrain, control, stopping".

An alternative etymology for the compound is cited by Ramamurti Mishra, who says that:

"Expansion of individual energy into cosmic energy is called pranayama (prana, energy + ayam, expansion)."

The word "yama" means "cessation" or more generally "control" or "restraint".

Bhagavad Gita

Pranayama is mentioned in verse 4.29 of the Bhagavad Gita.

Quotes: "Prana is a subtle invisible force. It is the life-force that pervades the body. It is the factor that connects the body and the mind, because it is connected on one side with the body and on the other side with the mind. It is the connecting link between the body and the mind. The body and the mind have no direct connection. They are connected through Prana only and this Prana is different from the breathing you have in your physical body."-Swami Chidananda Saraswati

"Yoga works primarily with the energy in the body, through the science of pranayama, or energy-control. Prana means also 'breath.' Yoga teaches how, through breath-control, to still the mind and attain higher states of awareness. The higher teachings of yoga take one beyond techniques, and show the yogi, or yoga practitioner, how to direct his concentration in such a way as not only to harmonize human with divine consciousness, but to merge his consciousness in the Infinite."- Paramahansa Yogananda

Yoga Sutras of Patanjali

Pranayama is the fourth 'limb' of the eight limbs of Raja Yoga mentioned in verse 2.29 in the Yoga Sutras of Patanjali. Patanjali discusses his specific approach to pranayama in verses 2.49 through 2.51, and devotes verses 2.52 and 2.53 to explaining the benefits of the practice. Patanjali refers to pranayama as the control of life force that comes as a result of practising the various breathing techniques, rather than the numerous breathing exercises themselves. Many yoga teachers advise that pranayama should be part of an overall practice that includes the other limbs of Patanjali's Raja Yoga teachings, especially Yama, Niyama, and Asana.

Medical Claims

Several researchers have reported that pranayama techniques are beneficial in treating a range of stress related disorders, improving autonomic functions, relieving symptoms of asthma, and reducing signs of oxidative stress. Practitioners report that the practice of pranayama develops a steady mind, strong willpower, and sound judgement, and also claim that sustained pranayama practice extends life and enhances perception.

Cautions and Contraindications

Many yoga teachers recommend that pranayama techniques be practised with care, and that advanced pranayama techniques should be practised under the guidance of a teacher. These cautions are also made in traditional Hindu literature.

Pratyahara

Pratyahara is the fifth element among the Eight stages of Patanjali's Ashtanga Yoga. At this stage, the consciousness of the individual is internalized in order that the sensations from the senses of taste, touch, sight, hearing and smell don't reach their respective centres in the brain. With this, the Sadhaka, or disciple, is free to meditate without distractions.

At the advanced levels, the electrical currents which pulsate through the nerves and even the involuntary muscles are turned off by the practitioners. This is accomplished through Pranayama or breath-control. Apart from Pranayama, another device that is used to aid in the development of Pratyahara is to concentrate on the point between the eyebrows. This location is known as Ajna Chakra or the third eye.

Dharana

Dharana is a Sanskrit term from the verbal root dhri to hold, carry, maintain, resolve; and it is the sixth stage, step or limb of eight elucidated by Patanjali's Ashtanga Yoga or Raja Yoga. For a detailed account of the Eight Limbs, refer to the Yoga Sutras of Patanjali.

Dharana may be translated as "holding", "holding steady", "concentration" or "single focus". The prior limb Pratyahara invoves withdrawing the senses from external phenomena. Dharana builds further upon this by refining it further to ekagrata or ekagra chitta, that is single-pointed concentration and focus, which is in this context cognate with shamata. Maehle (2006: p.234) defines Dharana as: "The mind thinks about one object and avoids other thoughts; awareness of the object is still interrupted."

Dharana is the initial step of deep concentrative meditation, where the object being focused upon is held in the mind without consciousness wavering from it. The difference between Dharana, Dhyana, and Samadhi is that in the former, the object of meditation, the meditator, and the act of meditation itself remain separate. That is, the meditator or the meditator's meta-awareness is conscious of meditating (that is, is conscious of the act of meditation) on an object, and of his or her own self, which is concentrating on the object. In the subsequent stage of Dhyana, as the meditator becomes more advanced, consciousness of the act of meditation disappears, and only the consciousness of being/existing and the object of concentration exist (in the mind).

Dhyana

Dhyana in Sanskrit or Jhana in Pali refers to a type or aspect of meditation. It is a key concept in Hinduism and Buddhism. Equivalent terms are "Chan" in modern Chinese, "Zen" in Japanese, "Seon" in Korea, and Samten in Tibetan.

Dhyana in Hinduism

In Hinduism, dhyana is considered to be an instrument to gain self knowledge, separating maya from reality to help attain the ultimate goal of Moksha.

The Bhagavad Gita, thought to have been written some time between 400 and 100 BC, talks of four branches of yoga:

- *Karma yoga:* The yoga of action in the world
- *Jnana yoga:* The yoga of Wisdom and intellectual endeavour
- *Bhakti yoga:* The yoga of devotion to God
- *Dhyana yoga*: The yoga of meditation

Dhyana in Raja Yoga is also found in Patanjali's Yoga Sutras. Depictions of Hindu yogis performing dhyana are found in ancient texts and in statues and frescoes of ancient India temples.

Dhyana in Buddhism

In the Theravada Tradition: In the Pali Canon the Buddha describes four progressive states of absorption meditation or jhana. The jhanas are said by the Buddha to be conducive to detachment but they must not be mistaken for the final goal of nibbana. The jhanas are states of meditation where the mind is free from the five hindrances (craving, aversion, sloth, agitation, doubt) and incapable of discursive thinking. The deeper jhanas can last for many hours. When a meditator emerges from jhana, his/her mind is empowered and able to penetrate into the deepest truths of existence.

There are four deeper states of meditative absorption called the immaterial attainments. Sometimes these are also referred to as the "formless" jhanas, or arupajhana (distinguished from the first four jhanas, rupajhana). In the Buddhist canonical texts, the word jhana is never explicitly used to denote them, but they are always mentioned in sequence after the first four jhanas.

Jhanas are normally described according to the nature of the mental factors which are present in these states

1. Movement of the mind onto the object, Vitakka (Sanskrit: Vitarka)
2. Retention of the mind on the object, Vicara
3. Joy, Piti (Sanskrit: Priti)
4. Happiness, Sukha
5. Equanimity, Upekkha (Sanskrit: Upekna)
6. One-pointedness, Ekaggata (Sanskrit: Ekagrata)

First Jhana (Vitakka, Vicara, Piti, Sukha, Ekaggata)

The five hindrances have completely disappeared and intense unified bliss remains. Only the subtlest of mental movement remains-perceivable in its absence by those who have entered the second jhana. The ability to form unwholesome intentions ceases.

Second Jhana (Piti, Sukha, Ekaggata)

All mental movement utterly ceases. There is only bliss. The ability to form wholesome intentions cease as well.

Third Jhana (Sukha, Ekaggata)

One half of bliss disappears (joy).

Fourth Jhana (Upekkha, Ekaggata)

The other half of bliss (happiness) disappears, leading to a state with neither pleasure nor pain, which the Buddha said is actually a subtle form of happiness (more sublime than piti and sukha). The Buddha described the jhanas as "the footsteps of the tathagata". The breath is said to cease temporarily in this state.

Traditionally, this fourth jhana is seen as the beginning of attaining psychic powers (abhigna).

The scriptures state that one should not seek to attain ever higher jhanas but master one first, then move on to the next. 'Mastery of jhana' involves being able to enter a jhana at will, stay as long as one likes, leave at will and experience each of the jhana factors as required. They also seem to suggest that lower jhana factors may manifest themselves in higher jhanas, if the jhanas have not been properly developed. The Buddha is seen to advise his disciples to concentrate and steady the jhana further.

In Mahayana traditions

In the Mahayana tradition, dhyana is the fifth of six paramitas (perfections). It is usually translated as "concentration" or "meditative stability."

In East Asia, several schools of Buddhism were founded that focused on dhyana, under the names Chan, Zen, and Seon. According to tradition, Bodhidharma brought Dhyana to the Shaolin Temple in China, where it came to be transliterated as "chan" ("seon" in Korea, and then "zen" in Japan).

Dhyana in Jainism is called Samayika.

Samadhi

Samadhi is a Hindu and Buddhist term that describes a non-dualistic state of consciousness in which the consciousness of the experiencing subject becomes one with the experienced object, and in which the mind becomes still (one-pointed or concentrated) though the person remains conscious. Sahaj samadhi is the effortless and continual state of perfection of a satguru. It varies from technical terms used to describe the higher levels of concentrated meditation, or dhyana (alt. "jhana"), in Yogic schools, and is considered a precursor for enlightenment, or Nirvana, in Buddhism. It is the eighth and final limb of the Yoga Sutra of Patanjali, and comprises the pinnacle of achievements in Samyama, the three-tiered practice of meditation including also dharana and dhyana.

Samadhi is also the Hindi word for a structure commemorating the dead (similar to a mausoleum), which may or may not contain the body of the deceased. Samadhis are often built in this way to honour people regarded as saints or gurus in Hindu religious traditions wherein such souls are said to have passed into (or were already in) samadhi at the time of death.

Etymology

Samadhi is a Sanskrit term for the state of consciousness induced by complete meditation. Its etymology comes from sam (together or integrated), a (towards), and dha (to get, to hold). Thus the result might be seen to be to acquire integration or wholeness, or truth (samapatti).

Samadhi in Hinduism

Samadhi is the main subject of the first part of the Yoga Sutras called Samadhi-pada. According to Vyasa, a major figure in Hinduism and one of the traditional authors of the Mahabharata, "yoga is samadhi." This is generally interpreted to mean that Samadhi is a state of complete control (samadhana) over the functions and distractions of consciousness.

In practice Samadhi is said to be the state of being aware of one's Existence without thinking, in a state of undifferentiated "Beingness." Three intensities (depths) of Samadhi are usually understood in Hinduism.

1. Laja Samadhi
2. Savikalpa Samadhi
3. Nirvikalpa Samadhi (or Sahaja Samadhi)

Laja Samadhi is a latent ("laja"), potential level of samadhi. It begins in deep meditation or trance-even with movement, such as dancing. This kind of samadhi is a state of joy, deep and general wellbeing, and peaceful meditation.

Savikalpa Samadhi refers to the initial temporary state of full-valued samadhi. The conscious mind is still active, as is the kalpa, meaning imagination. One should compare this meaning to that of sankalpa, which is "wish." Kalpa takes on a different, but related, meaning to sankalpa because one must use imagination or consciousness (kalpa) to envision a wish or desire (sankalpa). Conversely, vikalpa means "against imagination." At this final level of samadhi, the mind has become quiet and given up its desires and attendant. Vikalpa leads to the Truth, releasing one from any binds of mind (which are mostly imaginations). In Savikalpa Samadhi, we get the taste of Bliss and Beingness, but are still attached to our erroneous identification with the body as well as to our numerous worldly attractions.

Nirvikalpa Samadhi is the end result. There are no more kalpas (imaginings, wishes or other products from work of the mind), because the mind is finally under control. Upon entering Nirvikalpa Samadhi, the differences we saw before have faded and we can see everything as one. In this condition nothing but pure Awareness remains and nothing is missing to take away from Wholeness and Perfection.

Entering samadhi in the beginning takes effort and holding on to a state of samadhi takes even more effort. The beginning stages of samadhi (Laja and Savikalpa Samadhi) are only temporary. By "effort" it is not meant that the mind has to work more. Instead, it means work to control the mind and release the self. Note that normal levels of meditation (mostly the lower levels) can be held automatically, as in "being in the state of meditation" rather than overtly "meditating." The ability to obtain positive results from meditation is much more difficult than simply meditating. It is recommended to find a qualified spiritual master (guru or yogi) who can teach a meditator about the workings of the mind.

Samadhi is the only stable unchanging reality; all else is ever-changing and does not bring everlasting peace or happiness.

Staying in Nirvikalpa Samadhi is effortless but even from this condition one must eventually return to ego-consciousness. Otherwise, this highest level of Samadhi leads to Nirvana, which means total Unity and the logical end of individual identity (and also death of the body). However, it is entirely possible to stay in Nirvikalpa Samadhi and yet be fully functional in this world. This condition is known as Sahaja Nirvikalpa

Samadhi or Sahaj Samadhi (sahaja means "spontaneous" in Sanskrit). Only the truly Enlightened (Satguru) can be and remain spontaneously free.

In Nirvikalpa Samadhi, all attachment to the material world and all karma is dissolved. All awareness is withdrawn step by step from the physical, astral and causal bodies until self-realization or oneness with the soul is achieved. During this process, breathing ceases and the heart stops beating.

Aware and fully conscious oneness with soul is then achieved in a most loving way, and all cells of the physical body are flooded with the Ocean of Divine Love and Divine Bliss for any period of duration-hours, days, weeks, until the individual shifts his awareness from the soul back to the physical body. Being fully functional in this world, his awareness stays in connection with the Divine. But some "strange" conditions accompany this state-better health (the body is sustained by Divine Grace), better feelings (even for other people who may contact the body which the enlightened soul has reidentified with) and various miraculous happenings may occur in connection with the Enlightened one.

Mahasamadhi (literally great samadhi) is the Hindi term for a realized yogi's conscious departure from the physical body at death. Which is also known as Ṅirvana (see above).

Mahasamadhi is the final conscious exit from the physical body. Every infinitesimal piece of attachment or karma is completely surrendered unto God and dissolved into the Divine Ocean of Love. The individual transcends to worlds beyond karma and returns to God, merging into transcendental Bliss.

Samadhi in Bhakti

The Vaishnava Bhakti Schools of Yoga define Samadhi as "complete absorption into the object of one's love (Krishna)." Rather than thinking of "nothing," true samadhi is said to be achieved only when one has pure, unmotivated love of God. Thus samadhi can be entered into through meditation on the personal form of God, even while performing daily activities a practitioner can strive for full samadhi.

"Anyone who is thinking of Krishna always within himself, he is first-class yogi." If you want perfection in yoga system, don't be satisfied only by practising a course of asana. You have to go further. Actually, the perfection of yoga system means when you are in samadhi, always thinking of the Vishnu form of the Lord within your heart, without being disturbed... Controlling all the senses and the mind. You have to control the mind, control the senses, and concentrate everything on the form of Vishnu. That is called perfection of yoga"-A. C. Bhaktivedanta Swami Prabhupada

"Meditation means to absorb your mind in the Supreme Personality of Godhead. That is meditation, real meditation. In all the standard scriptures and in yoga practice formula, the whole aim is to concentrate one's mind in the Supreme Personality of Godhead. That is called samadhi, samadhi, ecstasy. So that ecstasy is immediately brought by this chanting process. You begin chanting and hear for the few seconds or few minutes: you immediately become on the platform of ecstasy."-A. C. Bhaktivedanta Swami Prabhupada

Samadhi, a Description

In his book Autobiography of a Yogi, Paramahansa Yogananda, a reputed modern-day spiritual saint of India and teacher of Kriya Yoga, gives this stirring description of Samadhi consciousness:

My body became immovably rooted; breath was drawn out of my lungs as if by some huge magnet. Soul and mind instantly lost their physical bondage, and streamed out like a fluid piercing light from my every pore. The flesh was as though dead, yet in my intense awareness I knew that never before had I been fully alive. My sense of identity was no longer narrowly confined to a body, but embraced the circumambient atoms. People on distant streets seemed to be moving gently over my own remote periphery. The roots of plants and trees appeared through a dim transparency of the soil; I discerned the inward flow of their sap.

The whole vicinity lay bare before me. My ordinary frontal vision was now changed to a vast spherical sight, simultaneously all perceptive. Through the back of my head I saw men strolling far down Rai Ghat Road, and noticed also a white cow who was leisurely approaching. When she reached the space in front of the open ashram gate, I observed her with my two physical eyes. As she passed by, behind the brick wall, I saw her clearly still. All objects within my panoramic gaze trembled and vibrated like quick motion pictures. My body, Master's, the pillared courtyard, the furniture and floor, the trees and sunshine, occasionally became violently agitated, until all melted into a luminescent sea; even as sugar crystals, thrown into a glass of water, dissolve after being shaken. The unifying light alternated with materialisations of form, the metamorphoses revealing the law of cause and effect in creation.

An oceanic joy broke upon calm endless shores of my soul. The Spirit of God, I realized, is exhaustless Bliss; His body is countless tissues of light. A swelling glory within me began to envelop towns, continents, the earth, solar and stellar systems, tenuous nebulae, and floating universes. The entire cosmos, gently luminous, like a city seen afar at night, glimmered within the infinitude of my being. The sharply etched global outlines faded somewhat at the farthest edges; there I could see a mellow radiance, ever undiminished. It was indescribably subtle; the planetary pictures were formed of a grosser light.

The divine dispersion of rays poured from an Eternal Source, blazing into galaxies, transfigured with ineffable auras. Again and again I saw the creative beams condense into constellations, then resolve into sheets of transparent flame. By rhythmic reversion, sextillion worlds passed into diaphanous luster; fire became firmament.

I cognized the center of the empyrean as a point of intuitive perception in my heart. Irradiating splendour issued from my nucleus to every part of the universal structure. Blissful amrita, the nectar of immortality, pulsed through me with a quicksilver-like fluidity. The creative voice of God I heard resounding as Aum, the vibration of the Cosmic Motor.

Suddenly the breath returned to my lungs. With a disappointment almost unbearable, I realized that my infinite immensity was lost. Once more I was limited to the humiliating cage of a body, not easily accommodative to the Spirit. Like a prodigal child, I had run away from my macrocosmic home and imprisoned myself in a narrow microcosm.

Samadhi as Leaving the Body

Advanced yogis have been said to consciously leave (or disidentify with) their bodies as a vital step in the attainment of this final samadhi, or soul-liberation. It is at this time that the soul knows a complete and unbroken union with the Heavenly Godhead, and, being free from the limitations of the body, merges effortlessly into the transcendent amrita of Divine Bliss. It is said that sometimes the yogi leaves the body and returns. According to Meher Baba, Jesus entered into nirvikalpa samadhi at the time of his crucifixion.

Samadhi in Buddhism

Samadhi, or concentration of the mind (one-pointedness of mind, cittassa-ekaggata), is the third division of the Eightfold Path of the Buddha's teaching: panna (wisdom), sila (conduct), samadhi (concentration). It developed by samatha meditation. It has been taught by the Buddha using 40 different objects of meditation, according to the Visuddhimagga, an ancient commentarial text. These objects include the breath (anapanasati meditation), loving kindness (metta meditation), various colours, earth, fire, etc. (kasina meditation).

Upon development of samadhi, one's mind becomes temporary purified of defilements, calm, tranquil, and luminous. Once the meditator achieves a strong and powerful concentration, his mind is ready to penetrate and see into the ultimate nature of reality, eventually obtaining release from all suffering.

Important components of Buddhist meditation, frequently discussed (1, 2) by the Buddha, are the successively higher meditative states known as the four jhanas which in the language of the eight-fold path, is "right concentration". Right concentration has also been defined as concentration arising due to the previous 7 steps of the noble eightfold path in the Mahacattsarika sutta/MN.

Four developments of samadhi are mentioned in the Pali Canon:

1) Jhana
2) Increased alertness
3) Insight into the true nature of phenomena (knowledge and vision)
4) Final liberation

There are different types of samadhi mentioned as well:

1) access concentration (upacara samadhi)
2) fixed concentration (appana samadhi)
3) momentary samadhi (khanikha samadhi)
4) "concentraion without interruption" (anantharika samadhi)
5) immeasurable concentration (appamana samadhi)

Not all types of samadhi are recommended either. Those which focus and multiply the Five Hindrances are not suitable for development.

The Buddhist suttas also mention that samadhi practitioners may develop supernormal powers (abhijna, also see siddhis), and list several that the Buddha developed, but warn that these should not be allowed to distract the practitioner from the larger goal of complete freedom from suffering.

The bliss of Samadhi is not the goal of Buddhism; but it remains an important tool in reaching the goal of enlightenment. It has been said that Samatha/samadhi meditation and vipassana/insight meditation are the two wheels of the chariot of the noble eightfold path and the Buddha strongly recommended developing them both.

Analogous Concepts

According to the book "God Speaks" by Meher Baba, the Sufi words fana-fillah and baqa-billah are analogous to nirvikalpa samadhi and sahaj samadhi respectively. The Christian state of "receiving the Holy Spirit" could also be viewed as analogous to laja samadhi. This is also similar to the Don Juan concept of "stopping the world" as described in the Carlos Castaneda books.

States of consciousness with some of the features of Samadhi are experienced by individuals with no religious or spiritual preparation or disposition. Such episodes occur spontaneously and appear to be triggered by physically or emotionally charged peak experiences such as in runner's high or orgasmic ecstasy, however even mundane activities such as revelling in a sunset, dancing or a hard day's work have, in rare instances, induced the entire range of Samadhi from Laja to Nirvikalpa.

The only distinction in these spontaneous secular samadhi from Vedic and Buddhist descriptions is that in the state of non-duality equivalent to Nirvikalpa, there is no record of any supernormal physical effects as purported in the literature such as the breath and heart-beat stopping or any degree of conscious control during the event. Also absent are siddhis-like special powers as an aftermath although virtually all experiencers report they became imbued with a holistic and compassionate world view and no longer feared death.

As consciousness is in a state of duality in Laja and Savikalpa Samadhi there are some similarities to those described in NDEs near death experiences or Bardo in which interactions with archetypal events or entities may occur. In contrast-once swept into Nirvikalpa Samadhi-consciousness is transformed to a state of absolute non-duality whose only manifestations are light, bliss and love.

Chakra

Chakra is a Sanskrit term meaning wheel. There is a wide literature on chakra models, philosophy and lore that underpin many philosophical systems and spiritual energy practices, religious observance and personal discipline. Theories on chakras fit within systems that link the human body and mind into a single unit, sometimes called the bodymind. The philosophical theories and models of chakras as centers of energy were identified through the mystical practice of yoga in Ancient India where they were first codified.

Working Definitions

Judith (1996: p.5) provides a useful working definition for chakras:

A chakra is a center of activity that receives, assimilates, and expresses life force energy. The word chakra literally translates as wheel or disk and refers to a spinning sphere of bioenergetic activity emanating from the major nerve ganglia branching forward from the spinal column. There are seven of these wheels stacked in a column of energy that spans from the base of the spine to the top of the head. There are also minor chakras in the hands, feet, fingertips, and shoulders. Literally, any vortex of activity could be called a chakra. It is the seven major chakras that correlate with basic states of consciousness...

In other words, chakra are energy centers in the body located at major branchings of the human nervous system, beginning with the base of the spinal column and moving upward. Chakras are considered to be a touch point or nexus of metaphysical and/or biophysical energy of the human body.

Chakra are explained in different ways, depending on who is doing the explaining. In Chinese medicine, they are often explained in relation to acupuncture points. In some Eastern thought, chakras are considered to be gradations of consciousness and reflect states of the soul—these systems rely less on proof than on experience (under the assumption that 'proving' the existence of chakras is asking to 'prove' the existence of the thought process). A mystic may deal with chakra as a model for their internal and external experience, and when talking about 'energy centers', may be talking about subtle electromagnetic forces which connect to the physical, emotional, mental and spiritual aspects of a person.

Organisational Constructs

As Bucknell and Stuart-Fox (1986: p.vii) concisely state in implying a dichotomy between Indian Vajrayana and Himalayan Vajrayana:

In the Vajrayana tradition, now preserved mainly in Tibetan sects, it has long been recognized that certain important teachings are expressed in a form of secret symbolic language known as sàndhya-bhana, 'Twilight Language'. Mudras and mantras, mashalas and cakras, those mysterious devices and diagrams that were so much in vogue in the pseudo-Buddhist hippie culture of the 1960s, were all examples of Twilight Language....

History

Judith (1996: p.5) outlines that:

The chakra system originated in India more than four thousand years ago. Chakras were referred to in the ancient literature of the Vedas, the later Upanishads, the Yoga Sutras of Patanjali, and most thoroughly in the 16th century by an Indian yogi in a text called the Sat-Chakra-Nirupana. In the 1920s, chakras were brought to the West by Arthur Avalon with his book, The Serpent Power."

What is construed as the New Age movement, and to some degree the distinctly different New Thought movement, have adopted and developed the chakra meme.

Etymology

The English word chakra is derived from the Sanskrit cakram meaning "wheel" or "circle". More generally, the term refers to circular objects or formations, and Apte provides 23 different definitions for cakram used as a noun. Examples include "discus" (a type of divine weapon, particularly associated with the god Vishnu), a potter's wheel, a form of military array, etc.

Bhattacharyya's review of Tantric history says that the word chakra is used to mean several different things in the Sanskrit sources:

1. "Circle", used in a variety of senses, symbolizing endless rotation of shakti.
2. A circle of people. In rituals there are different cakra-sadhana in which adherents assemble and perform rites. According to the Niruttaratantra, chakras in the sense of assemblies are of 5 types.
3. The term chakra also is used to denote yantras or mystic diagrams, variously known as trikona-cakra, ashakona-cakra, etc.
4. Different "nerve plexi within the body".

In Buddhist literature the Sanskrit term cakra (Pali cakka) is used in a different sense of "circle", referring to a Buddhist conception of the 4 circles or states of existence in which gods or men may find themselves.

Chakra Models

Chakrology is a neologism sometimes employed by Alternative Medicine practitioners or esoteric philosophers for the study of chakras. There are many different chakrologies, some of them based on ancient Indian Hindu Tantric esoteric traditions, New Age interpretations, or Western occult analyses, as well as ancient Greek and Christian references.

There are numerous traditional and modern models of the chakra system of the human subtle energetic body. As the system is subtle, these differences may co-exist and be perceived as foregrounding and backgrounding different qualities or attributes for specific reasons or purposes rather than perceived as vying for ascendancy. That said, the bodymind is a system, refer systems theory and no chakra is supreme. Chakra work in dialogue and in relationship to each other and that is how Ayurvedic Medicine energetic interplay which is directly comparable to the human endocrine system and how different glands chemically signal and communicate to each other.

Hindu Model

In Hinduism, the concept of chakras is part of a complex of ideas related to esoteric anatomy. These ideas occur most often in the class of texts that are called Agamas or Tantras. This is a large body of scripture, most of which is rejected by orthodox Brahmins.

There are many variations on these concepts in the Sanskrit source texts. In earlier texts there are various systems of chakras and nadis, with varying connections between them. Various traditional sources list 5, 6, 7, or 8 chakras. Over time, one system of 6 or 7 chakras along the body's axis became the dominant model, adopted by most schools of yoga. This particular system may have originated in about the 11th century AD, and rapidly became widely popular. It is in this model where

Kundalini is said to "rise" upward, piercing the various centers until reaching the crown of the head, resulting in union with the Divine.

This is the conventional arrangement cited by Monier-Williams, where the chakras are defined as "6 in number, one above the other".

Atal Behari Ghosh presents the 6-chakra model but notes that "Opinion is divided as to the number of these cakras; some say that there are 16, and others that there are more."

The Hindu sadhana of Laya yoga works with the chakra system.

Tantric Model

The chakras are described in the tantric texts the Sat-Cakra-Nirupana, and the Padaka-Pancaka , in which they are described as emanations of consciousness from Brahman, an energy emanating from the spiritual which gradually turns concrete, creating these distinct levels of chakras, and which eventually finds its rest in the Muladhara chakra. They are therefore part of an emanationist theory, like that of the kabbalah in the west, lataif-e-sitta in Sufism or neoplatonism. The energy that was unleashed in creation, called the Kundalini, lies coiled and sleeping at the base of the spine. It is the purpose of the tantric or kundalini forms of yoga to arouse this energy, and cause it to rise back up through the increasingly subtler chakras, until union with God is achieved in the Sahasrara chakra at the crown of the head.

The Tantric sadhana of Laya yoga works with the chakra system.

The Tantric Chakras

Tantra (Shakta or Shaktism) describes eight primary inner chakras:

1. Muladhara (Sanskrit: Muladhara) tip of the tailbone, spiritual potential
2. Swadhisthana (Sanskrit: Svadhisthana) tailbone, unconscious emotion or desire

3. Manipura (Sanskrit: Manipura) navel, dynamism
4. Anahata (Sanskrit: Anahata) heart, love based decisions
5. Vishuddha (Sanskrit: Visuddha) neck, discrimination and wisdom
6. Ajna (Sanskrit: Ajna) eyebrow, mind
7. Bindu (Sanskrit: Bindu) a dot at the back of the head, prayer and Aum
8. Sahasrara (Sanskrit: Sahasrara) top of head, higher consciousness

Vajrayana and Tantric Buddhist Model

According to contemporary buddhist teacher Tarthang Tulku, the heart chakra is very important for the feeling of existential fullfilment.

A result of energetic imbalance between chakras is an almost continuous feeling of dissatisfaction. When the heart chakra is agitated, people lose touch with feelings and sensations, and that breeds the sense of dissatisfaction. That leads to looking outside for fullfilment.

When people live in their heads, feelings are secondary, they are interpretations of mental images that are fed back to the individual. When awareness is focused on memories of past experiences and mental verbalizations, the energy flow to the head chakra increases and the energy flow to the heart chakra lessens. Without nurturing feelings of the heart a subtle form of anxiety arises which results in the self reaching out for experience.

When the throat chakra settles and energy is distributed evenly between the head and the heart chakras, one is able to truly contact one's senses and touch real feelings.

Chogyal Namkai Norbu Rinpoche teaches a version of the Six Lokas sadhana which works with the chakra system.

Bon Model

Chakras, as pranic centers of the body, according to the Himalayan Bonpo tradition, influence the quality of experience, because movement of prana can not be separated from experience. Each of six major chakras are linked to experiential qualities of one of the six realms of existence.

A modern teacher, Tenzin Wangyal Rinpoche uses a computer analogy: main chakras are like hard drives. Each hard drive has many files. One of the files is always open in each of the chakras, no matter how "closed" that particular chakra may be. What is displayed by the file shapes experience.

The tsa lung practices such as those embodied in Trul Khor lineages open channels so lung (Lung is a Tibetan term cognate with prana or qi) may move without obstruction. Yoga opens chakras and evokes positive qualities associated with a particular chakra. In the hard drive analogy, the screen is cleared and a file is called up that contains positive, supportive qualities. A seed syllable (Sanskrit bija) is used both as a password that evokes the positive quality and the armour that sustains the quality.

Tantric practice eventually transforms all experience into bliss. The practice liberates from negative conditioning and leads to control over perception and cognition.

Tenzin Wangyal Rinpoche teaches a version of the Six Lokas sadhana which works with the chakra system.

Chinese Model

Traditional Chinese medicine also relies on a similar model of the human body as an energy system, except that it involves the circulation of qi energy , rather than a simple ascent as in kundalini yoga.

In the circuit of qi, called the Microcosmic orbit, energy also comes back down the front torso channel (equivalent to the nadis of Hatha yoga), and enters the tan tiens: when it returns to the heart (and cycles down and reascends to the head) further meditation/contemplation or union with deity develops In Macrocosmic orbit the qi is also guided through the main channels in the limbs.

With the front tan tiens (autonomic plexuses to organs/ glands) branching from cerebrospinal chakras) and two levels of a vitality triangle on/in the back (spleen and behind a 'belly chakra/tantien', and by the arm-nadi branch) on the back, there are 7 (or 8) chakra spots outside the cerebrospinal nadis.

Common Currency and Popular Models

The chakras are described as being aligned in an ascending column from the base of the spine to the top of the head. In New Age practices, each chakra is often associated with a certain colour.

In various traditions chakras are associated with multiple physiological functions, an aspect of consciousness, a classical element, and other distinguishing characteristics. They are visualized as lotuses/flowers with a different number of petals in every chakra.

The chakras are thought to vitalize the physical body and to be associated with interactions of a physical, emotional and mental nature. They are considered loci of life energy or prana, also called shakti, qi (Chinese; ki in Japanese), coach-ha-guf (Hebrew), bios (Greek) and aether (English), which is thought to flow among them along pathways called nadis. The function of the chakras is to spin and draw in this energy to keep the spiritual, mental, emotional and physical health of the body in balance.

The New Age movement has led to an increased interest in the West regarding chakras. Many in this movement point to a correspondence between the position and role of the chakras and those of the glands in the endocrine system. These ideas first appear in the writings of theosophical authors like C. W. Leadbeater, who wrote a book on the Chakras.

The seven principal chakras are said by some to reflect how the unified consciousness of humanity (the immortal human being or the soul), is divided to manage different aspects of earthly life (body/instinct/vital energy/deeper emotions/communication/having an overview of life/contact to God).

The chakras are placed at differing levels of spiritual subtlety, with Sahasrara at the top being concerned with pure consciousness, and Muladhara at the bottom being concerned with matter, which is seen simply as crudified consciousness.

Hesychastic Centres of Prayer

Hesychasm specifies four centres :

1. Cerebrofrontal centre: Positioned between the eyebrows (compare with Ajna).
2. Buccolaryngeal centre.
3. Pectoral centre: Positioned in the upper and median region of the chest.
4. Cardiac centre: Positioned near the upper part of the heart (compare with Anahata).

In the Hesychastic Tradition (and Christian Ascetical Theology as well) the ascetical methods and meditation which lead to an inner Knowledge of the Heart are often referred as Cardiognosis

Western Derivative Models and Interpretations

The first western reference on chakra commonly accepted by modern scholars is from a disceple of Jakob Bohme namely Johann Georg Gichtel. Gichtel, in his book Theosophia Practica (1696), directly refer to inner force centres which are strictly related with eastern chakra doctrines . Anyway it is the shakta theory of 7 main chakras that many people in the West adhere to, largely thanks to a translation of two Indian texts, the Sat-Cakra-Nirupana, and the Padaka-Pancaka, by Sir John Woodroffe, alias Arthur Avalon, in a book entitled The Serpent Power. This book is extremely detailed and complex, and later the ideas were developed into what is predominant western view of the Chakras by the Theosophists, and largely the controversial (in theosophical circles) C. W. Leadbeater in his book The Chakras, which are in large part his own meditations and insights on the matter.

Rudolf Steiner (one-time Theosophist, and founder of Anthroposophy) says much about the Chakras that is unusual, especially that the chakra system is dynamic and evolving and is very different for modern people than it was in ancient times, and will in turn be radically different in future times. In contrast to the traditional eastern teachings, Steiner describes a sequence of development from the top down rather than the bottom up.

This is the so called 'Christos Path' which has not always been available to humanity. He also seems to ignore the Thousand Petaled at the crown of the head and mentions cryptically an Eight Petaled chakra located between the Ten Petaled and the Six Petaled. In his book How to Know Higher Worlds Steiner gives clear instructions on how to develop the chakras safely into maturity. These are more like life disciplines than exercises and can take considerable time. He warns that while quicker methods exist, they can be dangerous to one's health, character, or sanity.

Many New Age writers, such as the Danish author and musician Peter Kjaerulff in his book, The Ringbearer's Diary or Anodea Judith in her book Wheels of Life, have written their opinions about the chakras in great detail, including the reasons for their appearance and functions.

Additionally, some chakra system models describe one or more Transpersonal chakras above the crown chakra, and an Earth star chakra below the feet. There are also held to be many minor chakras, for example between the major chakras.

Chakras and the Endocrine System

However, there are those who believe that chakras have a physical manifestation as well. Some authors allege that there is a relationship between the positions and functions of the chakras, and of the various organs of the endocrine system (Sivananda 1953).

It is noted by many that there is a marked similarity between the positions and roles described for chakras, and the positions and roles of the glands in the endocrine system, and also by the positions of the nerve ganglia (also known as "plexuses") along the spinal cord (branching to plexuses by endocrine glands or organs), opening the possibility that two vastly different systems of conceptualization have been brought to bear to systemize insights about the same phenomenon. By some, chakras are thought of as having their physical manifestation in the body as these glands, and their subjective manifestation as the associated emotional, mental and spiritual experiences. . However, as there are important organs located at virtually any point in the body, the correspondence of certain biological systems or organs with the traditional locations of chakras is unsurprising and may be considered inevitable.

A Popular Chakra Model

Sahasrara

Sahasrara or the crown chakra is generally considered to be the chakra of consciousness. Its role may be envisioned somewhat similar to that of the pituitary gland, which secretes hormones to communicate to the rest of the endocrine system and also connects to the central nervous system via the hypothalamus. The thalamus is thought to have a key role in the physical basis of consciousness. Symbolised by a lotus with nine hundred seventy-two petals, it is located above the head outside the body.

Ajna

Ajna (along with Bindu, either or both are considered to correspond to the third eye) is linked to the pineal gland which may inform a model of its envisioning. Ajna is held as the chakra of time, awareness and of light. The pineal gland is a light sensitive gland that produces the hormone melatonin which regulates sleep and awakening. Symbolised by a lotus with ninety-six petals.

Vishuddha

Vishuddha (also Vishuddhi) or the throat chakra may be envisioned as relating to communication and growth, growth being a form of expression. This chakra is paralleled to the thyroid, a gland that is also in the throat and which produces thyroid hormone, responsible for growth and maturation. Symbolised by a lotus with sixteen petals.

Anahata

Anahata or the heart chakra is related to complex emotion, compassion, love, equilibrium and wellbeing. It is related to the thymus, located in the chest. The thymus is an element of the immune system as well as being part of the endocrine system. It produces T cells responsible for fending off disease and may be adversely affected by stress. Symbolised by a lotus with twelve petals. See also heartmind.

Manipura/Nabhi

Manipura (also Nabhi) or the solar plexus chakra is related to the transition from simple or base to complex emotion, energy, assimilation and digestion, and is held to correspond to the roles played by the pancreas and the outer adrenal glands, the adrenal cortex. These play a valuable role in digestion, the conversion of food matter into energy for the body. Symbolised by a lotus with ten petals.

Swadhisthana

Swadhisthana or the sacral chakra is located in the groin and is related to base emotion, sexuality and creativity. This chakra is considered to correspond to the testicles or the ovaries that produce the various sex hormones involved in the reproductive cycle which may cause dramatic mood swings. Symbolised by a lotus with six petals.

Muladhara

Muladhara or the base or root chakra is related to instinct, security, survival and also to basic human potentiality. This centre is located in the region between the genitals and the anus. Although no endocrine organ is placed here, it is said to relate to the inner adrenal glands, the adrenal medulla, responsible for the fight and flight response when survival is under threat. In this region is located a muscle that controls ejaculation in the sexual act in the human male. A parallel is charted between the sperm cell and the ovum where the genetic code lies coiled and the kundalini. Symbolised by a lotus with for petals.

3

Modern Yoga

Yoga has been integral part of Indian life since the time immemorial. The world "Yoga" is derived from the Sanskrit root 'Yuj' meaning to bind and yoke.

It is true union of ourselves with our core level which is Aatm Brahm(self GOD).

The various paths, practices and disciplines of Yoga are intended to help us realize our eternal or Divine nature, which is pure awareness transcending all duality and desire. This is the ultimate goal of human existence for which all other labours are merely preparatory. Yet since the beginning of history we have always imagined a quick and easy way to God, a spiritual path without tears or struggle, a path free of pitfalls we can follow to the end quickly, without great effort or sacrifice.

But genuine attainment is not possible without preparation. An instructive image occurs in the Vedas: before we are able to drink the Divine Soma (the nectar of immortality) we must have a properly prepared vessel, one that can contain this hot and penetrating nectar without breaking. If the nectar is poured into an unbaked vessel, it will shatter and the soma will be lost. We are the vessels, and yoga is a methodology for preparing us to contain the Divine Soma or inner bliss. We are properly prepared when we have attained a certain degree of purity, maturity, and strength of body, mind, and heart. Without preparation, we are like unbaked soma vessels, running after the spiritual nectar without concerning ourselves with our ability to handle it.

There are many types of Yoga, namely Karm Yoga (Way of realizing God by detached actions), Bhakti Yoga (Way of realizing God by devotion), Sankhya Yoga (Way of realizing God by Meditation and Austerity).

To understand the first two type of Yoga you should read Bhagvadgita. Bhagvadgita is a portion of great historical epic Mahabharata. This is the largest epic in the world. It compiles the facts about Krishn, Pandav and Kaurav. Bhagvadgita covers the section where Krishn(Manisfestation of GOD) explains His friend and devotee Arjun the greatest secret and reverred truth of the universe. He explains to him the immortal nature of the soul and how it derives from Him. He also describes to Arjuna how this whole universe is created and how it is inhaled by Him. Here we are going to discuss Astanga Yoga (Eight Part Yoga). It falls under the category of Sankhya Yoga (Way of realizing God by Meditation).

Asthanga Yoga

Astanga Yoga falls under the category of Sankhya Yoga (Way of realizing God by Meditation). It consists of eight stages. The following are these eight stages.

1. Yama (Social Discipline)

Yama means restraint or abstension. It refers to five moral practices. They are :Ahinsa (nonviolence), Satya (truthfulness), Asteya (nonstealing), Brahamcharya (moderation in sex) and Aparigraha (nonacquisitiveness).

Ahinsa (nonviolence) means not to hurt any creature mentally or physically through mind, speech or action.

Satya (truthfulness) is the presentation of the matter as perceived with the help of sense organs.

Asteya (nonstealing) means not to covet and acquire physically, mentally or by speech other's possessions.

Brahamcharya (moderation in sex) does not mean lifelong celibacy, but moderation in sex between married couples.

Aparigraha (nonacquisitiveness) means abandoning wealth and means of sensual pleasurs.

2. Niyama (Individual Discipline)

It means rules of conduct towards oneself. It consists of certain disciplines which are both physical and mental.

These are five in number. Shaucha (cleanliness), Santosha (contentment), Tapas (austerity), Svadhyaya (self-study) and Ishvara Pranidhana (surrender to Braham).

Shaucha (cleanliness) means internal and external purification of the body and the mind.

Santosha (contentment) is a state of mind by which one lives happily and satisfied in congenial or uncongenial atmosphere.

Tapas (austerity or penance) is the conquest of all desire or sensual pleasures by practising purity in thought, speech and action.

Svadhyaya (self-study/discussion of Braham related knowledge) means exchange of thoughts in order to secure purity in thought and accomplish knowledge.

Ishvara Pranidhana (surrender to Braham) consists of pure devotion to GOD and surrender of all actions to Him.

3. Aasana (Postures)

It means holding the body in a particular posture to bring stability to the body and poise to the mind. The practice of Aasana brings purity in the tubular channels, firmness to the body and vitality to the body and the mind.

4. Pranayama (Breath Control)

The literal meaning of the Pranayama is Breath Control. The aim of practising Pranayama is to stimulate, regulate and harmonize vital energy of the body. Just as bath is required for purifying the body, so also Pranayama is required for purifying the mind.

5. Pratyahara (Discipline of Senses)

The extroversion of the sense organs due to their hankering after worldly objects has to be restrained and directed inwards towards the source of all existence (Braham). This process of drawing the senses inwards is Pratyahara

6. Dharna (Concentration)

It means focusing the pure mind on Brahm. The practice of Dharana helps the mind to concentrate on a particular object.

7. Dhyana (Meditation)

When one sustains and maintains the focus of attention through Dharana unbounded by space and time, it becomes Dhyana. Deep concentration destroys the Rajas Gunas and Tamas Gunas of the mind and develops Satvika Gunas. Please read Bhagvadgita to understand the Gunas (charasterstics) of the mind and body.

8. Samadhi (Self-realisation)

The eighh and final stage of Yoga is Samadhi. At this stage one's identity becomes both externally and internally immersed in Braham. This is like salt mixing in sea. The meditator, the act of meditation, and the object meditated upon all three shed their individual characterstics and merge with one single vision of the entire cosmos and become Braham only, which is the true nature of every object. Supreme happiness free from pleasure, pain or misery, is expeerienced. Samadhi is the climax of Dhyana.

The group of last three stages, namely, Dharana, Dhyana and Samadhi is called Samyam and is referred to as Internal Yoga in the Science of Yoga. These come by practice. And one who is able to realise oneself is eternal even in this body, one gets Mokcha. Please read Bhagvadgita to understand it more.

The first five stages-Yama, Niyama, Asana, Pranayama and Pratyahara constitute the External Yoga. If all these five stages are practised and followed in life, virtues like morality develop in human. Besides there is allround progress in human life, physically, intellectually and spiritually and human attains physical fitness and mental equanimity.

Padmasana

Padma means lotus. Padmasana acquires its name because when performed this resembles a lotus. This is also known as

Kamalasana. This is best suited for meditation and for reciting mantras. It is beneficial to both men and women.

Technique: Sit on the ground. Spread the legs forwards and place the right foot on the left thigh and left foot on the right thigh. Let the left hand rest on the left knee and the right hand on the right knee. Let the tips of the thumbs of both the hands touch the tips of the index fingers. Keep the head and spinal column erect. Keep your eyes close or open.

Those who can place only one leg on the thigh should practise this aasana daily with zeal. They will be able to perform this aasana easily after some practice.

Stay in the final position for one or two minutes in the initial stage. Later gradually increase the time.

Advantages:

1) This Aasana is useful for Japa, Pranayama, Dharana (Retention or Concentration) and Samadhi.
2) This Aasana stimulates the endocrine glands.
3) This Aasana is useful to cure diseases like asthma, insomnia and hysteria. It is greatly beneficial to the persons suffering from insomnia.
4) The Aasana relieves the body of its excessive fat and it increases the vitality.

Baddha Padmasana

This is a variation of Padmasana. This Aasana is not meant for meditation. It is chiefly meant for health-improvement and for making the body strong. This Aasana is difficult to perform. Those who are unable to practise this Aasana should not be disappointed. They should patiently try to accomplish the final position.

Technique: Sit in Padmasana with legs crossed. The heels should touch the lower part pf the abdomen. Swing the right armbehind the back of the shoulder and bring the hand near the left hip. Catch the left big toe. Similarly, swing the left arm and and hold the right big toe.

If you experience difficulty in holding the toes, bend slightly forward and make it convenient to hold the big toe.

After catching the toes, sit erect as before and breathe normally. Stay in this position for one or two minutes in the initial stage. Gradually increase the time till you can stay in the position for ten minutes.

Advantages:

1) In this Aasana the weight of the body is borne by the knees and the ankel-joints, so the joints of the leg become strong.
2) Both the heels of the legs get sufficient exercise.
3) The continuous practice of the Aasana helps the person to gradually overcome the weakness of the heart, the lungs, the stomach, the liver and the spine. Moreover it reduces the pain in the knees and the ankle-joints.
4) The Aasana helps to cure ailments like indigestion. fatulence, stomach-ache, etc.
5) By practising this Aasana one can get all the advantages of the Padmasana.

Parvatasana

Parvat means a mountain. This aasan is also known as Viyogasana, because it involves a special technique of Yoga. Only healthy persons should practise this aasana.

Technique: Sit in Padmasana with legs crossed. Join the palms of the hands. Stretch the arms vertically up over the head.

Advantages:

1) As both the arms are kept vertically up in this aasana, the Pran is sublimated.
2) If Suryabheda Pranayama is practised for fifteen minutes before performing this Parvatasana, the lungs, the abdomen and the spine become strong and healthy.
3) This aasana gives sufficient exercise to the muscles of the arms.

Utthita Padmasana (Lolasana)

This aasan is a variation of Padmasana. In this aasana the body is lifted up with both the hands on floor. This is the reason why it is named so. This aasana is more difficult than Padmasan because in this aasan the whole body is balanced on both the hands.

Technique: Sit in Padmasana with legs crossed. Rest the palms on the floor beside the hips. Slowly raise the trunk without a jerk. The body should not quiver.

Retain the breath in the lungs as long as the body is in raised position. Exhale when body is lowered down. While performing this aasan some beginners experience tremor in the hands because of some weakness. But this should not daunt them. They should practise the aasan with patience and perseverance.

Advantages:

1) This aasan strengthens the joints and muscles of the arms.
2) This aasan helps to cure intestinal weakness, constipation, indigestion, dysentery, drowsiness, impurities of tubular channels etc..
3) This aasan works as an appetiser which is a good characterstics of of health.

Kukkut Aasan

Kukkut is a Sanskrit word which means a cock. This aasan or posture resembles that of a cock and hence the name is Kukkut Aasan.

Technique: Sit in Padmasana with legs crossed. Insert the hands through the gap between the thighs and calves near the knees. Start with the fingers and gradually push the hands upto elbows. Inhale and raise the body off the floor.

Then continue normal breathing. Legs should be raised off the floor upto the level of elbows. Hands can easily be inserted in the gap if the Padmasan position is slightly raised. Pot-bellied persons will find it difficult to insert the hands in the gap between the calves and the thighs. In the beginning remain in this position for ten seconds and gradually increase the time to a minute depending on age and ability to aspirant.

Advantages:

1) All the benefits derived from Utthita Padmasan are derived from this aasan.
2) This aasan is beneficial to those who have worms in their intestines.
3) This aasan is very useful to woman as it cures uneasiness, pain in the hips and heaviness caused by menstruation.
4) This aasan gives sufficient exercise to the arms.
5) This aasan invigorates the body and delights the mind.

Garbh Aasan

When this aasan is performed, the pose achieved resembles that of a human foetus in the womb. So this aasan is called Grabh Aasan.

Technique: As in Kukkut Aasan, insert the hands between the thighs and the calves. Push the arms forward till the elbows can be easily bent. Then hold the lobe of the right ear with the right hand and of the left ear with the left hand. Stay in this position very cautiously to avoid tumbling.

The constant practice of this aasan will enable you to balance the body on the coccyx (the tail bone).

If aspirants experience difficulty in performing this aasan in Padmasan position, it should be practised without Padmasan. While performing this aasan, let the legs be stretched on the floor. This aasan should be formed 8 to 10 seconds in the beginning. Later the time of the rentention of the aasan can be increased to one minute depending on age and ability of the aspirants and benefits expected.

Advantages:

1) This aasan helps to cure diseases like colic pain, flatuence, enteritis, chronic fever, constipation et-cetera.
2) This aasan keeps the abdominal organs trim. It cures gas trouble and increases the digestive power.
3) The abdominal organs, the breast and the joints of the arms and the legs get sufficient exercise through this aasan and their ailments disaapear.

4) This aasan helps to preserve the semen and the mind begins to have communion with the Aatama(self).

Yoga—Bibliography

The word yoga comes from a Sanskrit verbal root meaning "to yoke, harness" and in general refers to one or another of the many psycho-physical techniques in Indian religions designed to obtain discipline and control over the body and mind. In its classical contexts, yoga could refer to any one of a whole variety of such self-disciplinary practices. In India, yoga transcended sectarian boundaries.

There are, for example, both Hindu and Buddhist forms of yoga and within each of these religious traditions many different kinds of spiritual methods and practices are designated by this term. None of these "yogic" methods is solely physical. All entail some form of mental discipline, which can be labelled meditation; in Indian religions yoga and meditation almost always went hand in hand. The physical practices of yoga were usually seen at best to be only preliminary to the more spiritual forms of yoga that utilize various kinds of meditation techniques.

It is possible that yoga goes back to the earliest period of Indian history. Figurines and seals found at sites of the Indus Valley civilization, dating back to the second millennium B.C., have sometimes been interpreted to indicate the practice of yoga there. In particular, one seal depicts what appears to be a deity sitting in a posture typical of later yoga.

In the earliest Sanskrit texts of the Vedic period (c. 1500-1200 BC.) there are references to ascetics and ecstatics called munis ("silent sages") who are depicted with long hair, are said to be "girdled by the wind" (meaning, possibly, naked), and are described as having some of the superhuman powers later associated with advanced yoga practice.

The Atharva Veda mentions a group called the vratyas who practice asceticism (they are said to be able to stand for a year) and assume other physical postures as part of their disciplinary regimen. They also seemed to have practised some kind of breath control and envisioned correlations between their bodies and the cosmos. Also already in the Vedic texts we encounter the theory and practice of tapas or "ascetic heat" which, when obtained by the practitioner through various methods of physical and mental asceticism, was said to impart similar powers and spiritual purity. Tapas was in later texts to come to the forefront of the essential disciplinary practices that were involved in yoga.

By the time of the later texts of the Vedic period, the Upanishads of the third or fourth centuries BC., the word and conceptualizations of yoga are encountered frequently. In these texts, yoga means primarily the control of the mind and the senses. The senses are likened to horses which must be "yoked" or "disciplined" by the yogin (yogi) whose "mind is constantly held firm" and whose "senses are under control like the good horses of a charioteer.... They consider yoga to be the firm restraint of the senses. Then one becomes undistracted" (Katha Upanishad 3.6; 6.11).

In these texts some of the physical practices of yoga are also described. The practitioner is advised to retreat to a pleasant place in the wilderness where he should assume a particular physical posture (or asana) and "breathe through his nostrils with diminished breath" (the practice of breath-control called in later yogic texts by the name of pranayama). Yoga is defined in one such Upanishad as "the unity [another possible translation of the word "yoga"] of the breath, mind, and senses, and the relinquishment of all conditions of existence" (Maitri Upanishad 6.25).

As the yogin progresses in his practice his body and mind are said to change: "Lightness, healthiness, freedom from desires, clearness of countenance and pleasantness of speech, sweetness of odour and scanty exertions-these, they say, are the first stage in the progress of yoga" (Shvetashvatara Upanishad 2.13). The final stage of the practice, the goal of yoga, is also depicted in the Upanishads-and will become standard in later yogic texts. It is nothing less that the state of deathlessness or eternal life, often imagined in a body of light that never degenerates or grows old.

Yoga was systematized in different ways in two foundational texts dating to around the turn of the Common Era. In the first of these classical treatises, the Bhagavad Gita or "Song of the Lord," yoga is used to describe three apparently distinct but practically interrelated "paths" or spiritual methods. The first of these is called jnana yoga or the "yoga of wisdom." This path consists of deep contemplation on the nature of reality and recognizing the difference between the phenomenal world of change and the unchanging self. Through such meditation, the yogin penetrates the illusory nature of appearances and realizes the ultimate unity of all things and beings. As the Gita is also a theistic (or pantheistic) text, jnana yoga also entails recognizing God or Krishna in all things.

The second kind of yoga in this syncretistic work is karma yoga, the yoga of action. This method is one of "doing one's duty" as it is laid out by the strictures of caste and stage of life (and not renouncing action in the world as seemed to be required by the earlier Upanishadic treatises). Such worldly activity must, however, be performed in a "yogic" and self-disciplined way. While one cannot avoid action, the yogin should act not out of desire for the fruits of action but rather in a desireless and self-sacrificial way. Renouncing the ends or goals, the practitioner of karma yoga was to perform desireless action dedicated to God. The third yoga outlined in the Bhagavad Gita was termed bhakti, "devotion," and was nothing other than the "yoking" or "union" of the self and God. It is depicted as the easiest of the three methods but also the most efficacious.

The other text of this period to synthesize yoga was the Yoga Sutra of Patanjali. Patanjali defines yoga as the "cessation of the turnings of thought," that is, the purification and becalming of the mind and the correlative attainment of higher states of consciousness. Yoga for Patanjali involves eight "limbs" or parts (ashtanga), each one leading to the next and culminating in release from suffering and rebirth.

The first two limbs provide the ethical foundation thought to be necessary for any further progress in yoga. The first consists of the five "moral restraints" (yamas): nonviolence, truthfulness, not stealing, chastity, and the avoidance of greed.

The second limb, the internal "observances" (niyama's), provides a second set of five virtues the practitioner should perfect. These are mental and physical purity, contentment, tapas or the practice of austerities and asceticism, the study of sacred texts, and devotion to the "Lord" (God or the guru).

The third part of Patanjali's eightfold path consists of the physical postures or asana's. When the yogin has disciplined his or her moral life, the next step is to discipline the physical body. The later traditions of yoga have greatly expanded this dimension of the yogic path.

The physical practices are sometimes referred to as hatha yoga (the "yoga of exertion") and are conceived of in terms of a rigorous program of physical exercise and digestive constraint thought to be preparatory to the more advanced and subtle forms of yoga. Some texts claim there are 840,000 yogic physical postures; a standard list gives 84 including, most famously, the "lotus position" (padma asana). Such postures are designed to make the practitioner's body supple and healthy and help in the general training of self-discipline. Patanjali, however, devotes a mere three verses to the purely physical dimension of yoga, saying only that one should take a position that is "steady and comfortable," for then one is ready to pursue the true goal of yoga, the state of mind wherein one is "unconstrained by opposing dualities."

More subtle than the physical body is the breath, and it is the "restraining of the breath" (pranayama) that forms the fourth limb of the practice. Here again, later yogic texts go into much greater detail about the various practices of breath awareness and control, including methods for retention of the breath over long periods of time.

The breath is regarded as the fundamental life force in yoga, and control and manipulation of it is essential for rejuvenating and immortalizing the body. Its power is such that some texts warn about the dangers entailed in the pranayama practices and, as always, insist that the yogin should only practice under the watchful guidance of a master. Patanjali has little to say about it, restricting his observations to the fact that it basically refers to the control of inhalation, exhalation, and retention of breath and that it has as its purpose the making of a "mind fit for concentration."

The next stage of Patanjali's system is named the "withdrawal of the senses" (pratyahara) by which is meant the kind of "yoking" of the sense organs that was likened to the reining in of horses. Another very common image for this portion of the yogic training is that of a tortoise who withdraws its limbs into its shell. So too should the yogin disengage the sense organs from the objects of senses and, by means of such detachment, gain mastery over them. The ability to turn away from the distractions of the object of senses and to increasingly turn attention to the mind itself in a concentrated fashion is, of course, crucial for the meditative pursuits that describe the highest and most subtle forms of yoga.

The sixth, seventh, and eighth limbs of Patanjali's yogic system are progressively higher states of meditative ability and attainment. The sixth is called "concentration" (dharana), defined as the ability to "bind thought in one place" for long periods of time; it is the essence of what is sometimes known as "one-pointedness" of mind. The mastery of concentration leads the yogin to the next the stage of the path, which is called "meditation" per se (dhyana), the unwavering attention of the concentrated mind on the meditative object. The culmination of yoga is the attainment of the eighth limb, pure contemplation accompanied by ecstasy or, otherwise described, the trance-like state of pure "enstasis," which is termed samadhi. The end of the yogic path is defined by Patanjali as "meditation that illumines the object alone, as if the subject were devoid of intrinsic form." The "yogin yoked in samadhi" is, according to a later text in this tradition, completed liberated-free from the "pairs of opposites" or all duality, not bound by the forces of karma, unconquerable, "without inhalation and exhalation," invulnerable to all weapons, and immortal (Hatha Yoga Pradipika 4.108ff.).

Indeed, much of the third chapter of Patanjali's classic text is given over to the extraordinary powers (the "accomplishments" or siddhi's) that are claimed to come along with advanced practice of yoga. These include the ability to know the past and future, the languages of animals, one's previous lives, the thoughts of others, and so on. It is, in fact, said that the perfected yogin becomes omniscient. He or she also attains the power to become invisible, gets the "strength of an elephant," and wins the capability to grow larger or smaller at will. In later texts, abilities such as these are summarized as the eight "great powers" (mahasiddhi's): miniaturization, magnification, levitation, extension, irresistible will, mastery, lordship over the universe, and fulfilment of all desires.

The yoga systematized in Patanjali's Yoga Sutras is sometimes referred to as "classical" or "royal" yoga (raja yoga), especially in contrast to the hatha yoga, which is envisioned as preparatory to the higher spiritual practices of Patanjali's later limbs. It also came to be the charter text of the school of Hindu philosophy (darshana) called "Yoga," which in turn was closely related to the dualistic philosophical school known as "Samkhya" (the main difference being the atheistic quality of the latter, although the "Lord" of the Yoga Sutras is more of a Divine Yogin than a creator god). In these philosophical traditions, the purpose of yoga was understood to be the "distinction" or "discrimination" between material nature and the eternal spirit. The spirit or pure consciousness (purusha) is to be "isolated" from both matter and from ordinary awareness and its afflicted mental experiences. When the purusha becomes thus disentangled, its pure nature can shine forth and the yogin becomes liberated.

The term yoga, as has already been shown, can be applied to a variety of practices and disciplines. Another important use of the term is in the phrase mantra yoga, the "yoga of sacred, efficacious sound." Here yoga refers to the concentration on and repetition of sacred sounds, utterances, syllables, or prayers composed from the Sanskrit language and thought to have inherent transformative power. Such mantras are transmitted from teacher to pupil in an initiatory setting, and it is indeed thought to be primarily the power of the guru that gives the mantra its efficacy. The most famous of such mantras is the sound "om" (sometimes written as "aum" to emphasize the three verbal parts of the utterance) which is regarded as the aural essence of the universe itself. While the texts do claim that mantra yoga will also lead to liberation, it is usually said to be suitable mainly for the practitioner of inferior intellectual capabilities.

Yoga also plays a major role in both Hindu and Buddhist "tantric" or esoteric traditions, which arose around the middle of the first millennium C.E. In Buddhism, tantric practice is divided into four classes, each one regarded higher than the other: action tantras, performance tantras, yoga tantras, and highest yoga tantras. In all forms of tantra, the goal is to transmute the physical body into a body of light, a "rainbow body," through the manipulation of the subtle energies, channels, and power centers (cakra's) of the mystical inner body. This is done through the practices known as guru yoga, the "yoking" of oneself to a tutelary deity or yidam, and the carrying out of a series of visualizations in which one assumes the being of that deity and meditates in that way. There is also a form of "Taoist yoga" in China that bears comparison to the Indian yogas.

Yoga has entered the West mostly as physical exercise and often not as the holistic worldview it was in its original contexts. Increasingly, however, Westerners are aware of the ethical and meditative dimensions to yoga and these elements are finding their way into the practice of yoga outside of India.

Yoga

Yoga is a way of life. It is predominantly concerned with maintaining a state of equanimity at all costs. All yoga schools of thought emphasize the importance of the mind remaining calm, because as the saying goes, only when the water is still can you see through it. Yoga Darshan or Yoga Philosophy also happens to be a valid discipline of Indian metaphysics (Brahma Vidya). It is the result of human wisdom and insight on physiology, psychology, ethics and spirituality collected together and practised over thousands of years for the well being of humanity.

The basic idea of yoga is to unite the atma or individual soul with the paramatma or the Universal Soul. According to

Yoga philosophy, by cleansing one's mind and controlling one's thought processes one can return to that primeval state, when the individual self was nothing but a part of the Divine Self. This is the sense encapsulated in the term samadhi. The aim of the yogi is to be able to perceive the world in its true light and to accept that truth in its entirety.

In Sanskrit, the term 'yoga' stands for 'union'. A yogi's ultimate aim is to be able to attain this 'union' with the Eternal Self with the help of certain mental and physical exercises. It is often said that Hiranyagarbha (The Cosmic Womb) Himself had originally advocated the traditional system of yoga, from which all other yoga schools have evolved. But for all extant knowledge of yoga and its practices, such as yogasanas and pranayama, the entire credit goes to Maharishi Patanjali.

Patanjali systematized the various yogic practices and traditions of his times by encapsulating them in the form of aphorisms in his Yoga Sutra. In this momentous work, he describes the aim of yoga as knowledge of the self and outlines the eight steps or methods of achieving it. These are:

— Yamas or eternal vows,
— Niyamas or observances,
— Yogasanas or yoga postures,
— Pranayama or breath control exercises,
— Pratyahara or withdrawal of the senses from distractions of the outside world,
— Dharana or concentration on an object, place or subject,
— Dhyana or the continuance of this concentration-meditation and
— Samadhi or the ultimate stage of yoga meditation.

The collation of these eight steps is known as Patanjali's Ashtanga Yoga.

Ashtanga Yoga

Yoga is more than just a physical discipline. It is a way of life-a rich philosophical path. And the yamas (restraints) and niyamas (observances) are ten good common-sense guidelines for leading a healthier, happier life for bringing spiritual awareness into a social context. They are for you to think about and ponder over with a rational mind, because yoga is not about mindlessly accepting externally imposed rules-it is about finding the truth for yourself-and 'connecting' with it.

Yamas: There are many interpretations of and opinions about the yamas and niyamas. While the ancient Indian text, the Bhagavata Purana assigns 12 yogic restraints the Parashar Smriti, another text, puts forward ten. But the yamas as described in Patanjali's Yoga Sutra are only five, which are also known as the great universal vows or the sarvabhauma maha vratas, because they are not limited by either class, creed, time or circumstances. They are the guidelines for how we interact with the outer world, the social disciplines to guide us in our relationships with others. These five are:

— Ahimsa (nonviolence),

— Satya (truthfulness),

— Asteya (non-stealing),

— Brahmacharya (celibacy) and

— Aparigraha (non-covetousness)

According to the Yajnavalkya Samhita, ahimsa or nonviolence is the awareness and practice of nonviolence in thought, speech and action. It advocates the practices of compassion, love, understanding, patience, self-love, and worthiness.

Patanjali describes truthfulness as: "To be in harmony with mind, word and action, to conduct speech and mind according to truth, to express through speech and to retain it in the intellect what has been seen, understood or heard." A perfectly truthful person is he who expresses in his speech exactly what he thinks in his mind and in the end acts according to it.

Non-stealing or asteya is the third constituent of the yamas of Ashtanga Yoga. It upholds forgoing the unauthorized possession of thought, speech and action. Asteya stands against covetousness and envy. It advocates the cultivation of a sense of completeness and self-sufficiency in order to progress beyond base cravings.

The Vedas, Smritis and Puranas all glorify the fourth constituent of celibacy. It is believed to be a behaviour, which brings man nearer to the Divine. This yama believes in avoiding all sensual pleasures, whether mental, vocal or physical.

The literal meaning of apigraha, the fifth yama, is the non-accumulation of worldly objects, caused by covetousness and attachment. The commentator Vyasa says that this last state of yama is attained when one remains totally detached from sensual pleasures of all kinds and so effectively refrains from committing himsa or violence of any sort.

Niyamas: The niyamas are the second constituents of Ashtanga Yoga. How we interact with ourselves, our internal world. The niyamas are about self-regulation-helping us maintain a positive environment in which to grow. Their practice harnesses the energy generated from the cultivation of the earlier yamas. According to sage Yajnavalkya, there are ten niyamas and the Bhagavad Gita lists 11 constituents. But Patanjali names only five:

— Shaucha or purity,
— Santosha or contentment,
— Tapa or austerity,
— Swadhyaya or self-education and
— Ishwar-Pranidhan or meditation on the Divine

Shaucha implies both external as well as internal purity. In the words of sage Manu, water purifies the body; truthfulness the mind; true knowledge the intellect and the soul is purified by knowledge and austerity. It advocates the practices of intellectual purity, purity of speech and of the body.

The second niyama is that of contentment, which is described as not desiring more than what one has earned by his honest labour. This state of mind is about maintaining equanimity through all that life offers. Santosha involves the practice of gratitude and joyfulness-maintaining calm at all costs. This state of mind does not depend on any external causes.

Austerity, the third niyama, is described in Yoga philosophy as power to stand thirst and hunger, cold and heat, discomforts of place and postures, silent meditation and ritual fasts. It also maintains that the perfect man is he who practices both mental as well as physical austerity.

According to the commentator Vyas, self-education or swadhyaya consists of scriptural studies. The scripture being, the Vedas and Upanishads together with the recitation of the Gayatri Mantra and the Om mantra.

Commentators describe Ishwar-Pranidhan, the last of the niyamas, as the dedication of all our actions, performed either by intellect, speech or body, to the Divine. The results of all such actions are by definition, therefore, dependent upon Divine decision. The mortal mind can simply aspire to realize the Divine through dedication, purification, tranquilization and concentration of the mind. This Divine contemplation spills over to all aspects of the yogi's life.

The Benefits of Practising Yamas and Niyamas: The yamas and niyamas help in managing our energy in an integrative manner, complementing our outer life to our inner development. They help us view ourselves with compassion and awareness. They help in respecting the values of this life, in balancing our inner growth with outer restraint. In short they help us to lead a conscious life.

Yamas and niyamas are not about right and wrong. They are about being honest with the true Self. Living according to these principles are about living our lives in a better way, about moving towards an understanding, about making it possible to 'connect' with the Divine.

A yogasana is a posture in harmony with one's inner consciousness. It aims at the attainment of a sustained and comfortable sitting posture to facilitate meditation. Asanas also help in balancing and harmonizing the basic structure of the human body, which is why they have a range of therapeutic uses too.

Functions of Yogasanas

Asanas basically perform five functions:

— Conative,

— Cognitive,
— Mental,
— Intellectual and
— Spiritual.

Conative action is the voluntary exercise of the organs of action. The asanas being the main yogic instrument of balancing the body, they consist of various physical postures, which are designed to release tension, improve flexibility and maximize the flow of vital energy. The purpose of the asanas is to create a flow of positive energy so that our concentration is directed within ourselves and the mind is able to perceive (parokshya jnana) the effects of our purposive action. That is cognitive action.

When the earlier two actions are fused, our mind's discriminative faculty guides these organs to perform the asanas more correctly. The resultant rhythmic energy flow and awareness leads to a mental state of pure joy (ananda). Physical postures, therefore, end up affecting the various interrelated channels (nadis) of the mind-body complex. And ultimately the performance of a perfect yogasana leads to the absolute intellectual absorption of the mind on a single task (dharana), which in turn leads to the fusion of the individual spirit with the Divine Self (dhyana).

Benefits of Yogasanas

The regular practice of yogasanas has an immense amount of therapeutic value. Besides various physiological benefits, they positively affect our minds, our life force energies as well as our creative intelligence.

Regular practice helps to keep our body fit, controls cholesterol level, reduces weight, normalizes blood pressure and improves heart performance. Physical fitness thus achieved leads to reduction of physical stress and greater vitality. Asanas harmonize our pranic ability and mental energy flow by clearing any blockages in the subtle body leading to mental equilibrium and calmness. They make the mind strong thus enabling our human body to suffer pain and unhappiness stoically and with fortitude.

Various Categories of Yogasanas

Consummate mastery over the entire gamut of asanas is no doubt time-consuming, but what is of vital importance is the will to remain in the present moment and to let both the mind and body relax completely.

The various categories of asanas are:

— Standing Asanas,

— Forward Bending Asanas,

— Supine Asanas,

— Inverted Asanas,

— Abdominal and Lumbar Asanas,

— Twisting Asanas,

— Back Bending Asanas and

— Balancing Asanas.

Standing Asanas: Beginners should start with these as they bring elasticity in joints and muscles and build up stamina and physical stability. This constitutes the most basic training in the early stages of yoga practice. Some basic standing poses are, Tadasana, Utthita Trikonasana, Virabhadrasana, Ardha Chandrasana and Utthita Parsvakonasana.

Forward Bending Asanas: In these postures the posterior half of the body is stretched. These prepare you to proceed further in yoga and bring consistency in the development of physical and mental pliability. Examples of such asanas are, Upavisthakonasana and Paschimotanasana.

Sitting and Supine Asanas: Sitting upright and supine extending positions help a sadhaka prepare physically and mentally for pranayama. Some of them are, Baddhakonasana, Supta Baddhakonasana, Supta Padangusthanasana, Padmasana, Vajrasana, Simhasana, Virasana and so on.

Inverted Asanas: These help recover from everyday stress. They give vitality, mental balance and emotional stability. These are Adho Mukha Svanasa and Urdhva Mukha Svanasa.

Abdominal and Lumbar Asanas: These tone and massage the abdominal organs and strengthen the pelvic and lumbar areas. Bharadvajasana and Marichyasana are some examples of such asanas.

Twisting Asanas: It consists of lateral stretching and twisting of the spine, toning the internal organs and reaching new horizons while tranquilizing the mind. These are, Ardha Matsyendrasana and Jathara Parivartanasana.

Back Bending Asanas: These bring physical and mental sharpness and alertness. The postures are the opposite of forward bends as are the effects. In forward bends the posterior spine is extended, bringing consistency and mental peace, whereas in back bends the anterior spine is extended and stretched. The effect is invigorating and enlivening. Such asanas are, Ustrasana, Bhujangasana and Matsyasana.

Balancing Asanas: These strengthen the arms and wrists and exercise the abdominal organs. They also make the body feel light and help attain a good bearing. Salamba Sirsasana, Niralamba Sarvangasana and Salamba Sarvangasana are some of the balancing asanas.

'Pranayama' is a compound term ('prana' and 'yama') meaning the maintenance of prana in a healthy throughout one's life. More than a breath-control exercise, pranayama is all about controlling the life force or prana. Ancient yogis, who understood the essence of prana, studied it and devised methods and practices to master it. These practices are better known as pranayama. Since breath or prana is basic to life, the practice of pranayama helps in harnessing the prana in and around us, and by deepening and extending it, pranayama leads to a state of inner peace.

According to Hatha Yoga, pranayamas can be classified under:

— Sahita Kumbhaka,

— Surya Bhedi,

— Ujjayi,

— Sitali,

— Bhastrika,

— Bhramari,

— Murchha and

— Kewali.

The first is a breath retention technique, which gives agility, strength and flexibility to the body. They also quieten the mind and the sense organs besides enabling the meditator to control his hunger and thirst.

The Surya Bhedi pranayama consists of inhaling through the right nostril and exhaling through the left. This practice promotes good digestion and through perspiration, it purges the body of all its impurities.

Ujjayi pranayama involves the travel of breath between the nose and the heart only. It acts like an expectorant and increases digestion together with removing all impurities of nerves as well as thoughts. Bhramari pranayama involves a very concentrated and fixed breathing exercise. It helps in strengthening one's breath besides quietening the mind and increasing the powers of concentration. This breathing technique is very helpful in the last meditative stage of samadhi.

Murchha pranayama is an extreme form of breath retention, which only experienced yogis can achieve. This practice quietens the mind and helps it to reach the near-unconscious state.

The last technique of Kewali pranayama, is a breath retention technique in which, the yogi stops both inhalation as well as exhalation. This form balances inhalation and exhalation besides helping the mind to concentrate better.

Benefits of Pranayama

The practices of pranayama-the correct breathing technique helps to manipulate our energies. Most of us breathe incorrectly, using only half of our lung capacity. Pranayama is a technique, which re-educates our breathing process, helps us to release tensions and develop a relaxed state of mind. It also balances our nervous system and encourages creative thinking. In addition, by increasing the amount of oxygen to our brain it improves mental clarity, alertness and physical well being.

When practised along with yogasanas the benefits of pranayama are more pronounced. According to Patanjali's Yoga

Sutra, pranayama enables the mind to acquire the capacity to concentrate on any given object of attention.

It also says that scientific breathing helps in unveiling true knowledge from the darkness of ignorance. But it is eminently advisable to be aware of all the do's and don'ts of pranayama before practising them.

Various Stages of Pranayama

The following are the stages of pranayama:

— Inhalation or puraka,

— Exhalation or rechaka,

— Stambhavritti pranayama and

— Bahyabhyantarakshepi pranayama.

Puraka or inhalation techniques are about regular and controlled inhalation. It also teaches regulating the entire breathing process and reducing the number of inhalations per minute. Rechaka or exhalation exercises teach slow and ordered breathing besides reducing the number of inhalations and exhalations per minute.

The third stage consists of retaining the breath after stopping natural inhalation and exhalation. The last stage of pranayama is about converting both exhalation and inhalation into retention and storing the retained breathe in various internal organs for various lengths of time.

Pratyahara

Pratyahara involves rightly managing the senses and going beyond them instead of simply closing and suppressing them. It involves reining in the senses for increased attention rather than distraction. Pratyahara may be practised with mantra meditation and visualization techniques.

Benefits of Pratyahara

It is essential to practice pratyahara for achieving the three meditative stages of dharana, dhyana and samadhi. Perfecting this technique of yoga is also essential in order to break out from the eternal cycle of rebirths.

Dharana

The last three limbs of Ashtanga Yoga are the three essential stages of meditation. Dharana involves developing and extending our powers of concentration. This consists of various ways of directing and controlling our attention and mind-fixing skills, such as concentrating on the chakras or turning inwards.

Dhyana

Dhyana is the state of meditation, when the mind attains the ability to sustain its attention without getting distracted. Strictly speaking, unlike the other six limbs of yoga, this is not a technique but rather a state of mind, a delicate state of awareness. This state rightfully precedes the final state of samadhi.

Samadhi

Samadhi, or total absorption, is the ability to become one with the True Self and merge into the object of concentration. In this state of mind, the perceiver and the object of perception unite through the very act of perception-a true unity of all thought and action. This is the acme of all yogic endeavors-the ultimate 'yoga' or connection between the individual and the universal Soul!

Patanjali's Yoga Sutra categorizes and grades the levels of samadhi in the first chapter or Samadhi Pada:

— Samprajnata Samadhi or distinguished contemplation and

— Asamprajnata Samadhi or non-distinguished contemplation,

— Savitarka Samadhi or deliberated absorption and

— Nirvitarka Samadhi or non-deliberated absorption,

— Savichara Samadhi or reflective meditation and

— Nirvichara Samadhi or non-reflective meditation,

— Sabija Samadhi, where the mind continues to carry seeds of earthly impressions and

— Nirbija Samadhi, where each seed of earthly impressions have been erased.

Yoga Schools

The different yoga schools simply adhere to different applications of inner discipline, all of which ultimately lead to the liberation of the soul and to a unique understanding of the Divine Unity.

The schools are merely named according to the yogi's objective of self-transformation and the instrument chosen for such anticipated change.

The yoga schools are:

Ashtanga Yoga and it's different variations, for the most part, aim at the fullest development of any one human faculty-the mind, emotions, life-force or the physical body. Such partial perfection is then allowed to spill over to one's entire being.

But Sri Aurobindo's Purna Yoga or Integral Yoga focuses on the whole being in order to bring about total transformation. The approach, objective and means of Purna Yoga are all integral in essence.

The main stages of Purna Yoga are:

— Aspiration for the Divine.

— Surrender of the individual soul to the Universal Soul.

— Rejection of all obstructions to the path of total transformation.

Realizing the Divine within oneself is the first step of Integral Yoga. The means of achieving this state of Divine awareness is through a regular practice of either concentration, meditation or prayer.

The next step involves the realization of the Divine in entities beyond the subjective self. A realization of all constituent consciousnesses of the universe-an acceptance of a common origin of all beings.

The third stage consists of a true identification with the "Transcendental Divine", which is neither limited within the being of a single individual nor within any other constituents of existence. According to Sri Aurobindo, unless this crucial Truth is realized, it is impossible for the sadhak or seeker to attain liberation.

In his philosophy, Rishi Aurobindo termed this rarefied region of higher consciousness as the "Supramental Consciousness", the attainment of which is necessary for the liberation of the soul. The Master believed this stage of spiritual awareness to be potentially the ultimate rung on the human evolutionary ladder. And the realization of this "Supramental Consciousness" is the principal aspiration of Sri Aurobindo's Purna Yoga or Integral Yoga.

Jnana Yoga

Jnana refers to knowledge but the emphasis is not on acquiring information but on developing the analytical powers of the mind. The manner in which the power of analysis is applied depends on the metaphysical system within which it is practised. In the Samkhya system of Indian philosophy, the focus is on understanding one's own inner self. In Advaita Vedanta (non-dualist Vedanta philosophy), the idea is to understand the difference between reality and illusion.

Bhakti Yoga

Bhakti Yoga is all about getting in touch with the Divine Being by following the outpourings of one's heart. The term 'bhakti' can be roughly translated to mean 'devotion', and this emotion coupled with the Christian concept of faith leads to a state of mind which can be described as being immersed in bhakti. This strand of yoga principally advocates love and devotion as the path to moksha or liberation.

Karma Yoga

Originally, it was believed that the practice of Karma Yoga, accompanied by the observance of certain rituals, would lead to liberation from the cycle of birth and death. In the Bhagavad Gita, lord Krishna further extended the semantics of the term karma to mean detached action, that is, subjugation of the individual will to Divine purpose.

According to the Bhagavad Gita, these three different paths of yoga (jnana, bhakti and karma) help to define three different categories of men-reflective, emotional and active, respectively-distinguished on account of the distribution of emphasis on the theoretical, emotional and practical aspects of human personalities.

Raja Yoga

Raja Yoga or Ashtanga Yoga, which was formulated by Patanjali into a definite system from classical yoga, forms one of the Shad-Darshanas or classical systems of Indian philosophy. The school of Raja Yoga prescribes to a particular meditative system, which focuses on the analysis and control of the field of human consciousness. Often known as the 'royal road' or the 'royal path' ('raja' in Sanskrit denotes 'king' or 'royal'), it offers a comprehensive method for controlling waves of thought by channeling mental and physical energies into spiritual energy.

Hatha Yoga

The school of Hatha Yoga attaches a lot of importance to the perfect physical form, believing it to be a way of attaining spiritual perfection. And to this end it takes the help of pranayama (breath-control exercises) and mudras (hand gestures) to attain self-realization. Often seen as part of Raja Yoga, the origins of Hatha Yoga can be traced to Gorakhnath, the 12th-century founder of the Kanphata Yogis. The word 'hatha' is derived from the two root terms, 'ha' meaning 'the sun' and 'tha' meaning 'the moon'. Taken together, the term stands for 'union of force'. Hence, central to Hatha Yoga disciplines is the harmonizing of its positive (sun) and negative (moon) currents.

Kundalini Yoga

Kundalini is the potential form of prana or life force, lying dormant in our bodies. It is conceptualized as a coiled up serpent (literally, 'kundalini' in Sanskrit is 'coiled up') lying at the base of our spine, which can spring awake when activated by spiritual disciplines. The practitioners of Kundalini Yoga concentrate on psychic centers or chakras in the body in order to generate a spiritual power, which is known as kundalini energy. The practice comprises of awakening and then forcing this energy, flowing through nadis or channels, up the psychic channel of the sushumna, which runs from the base of the spine to the brain.

The three main channels running alongside the spinal cord are ida, pingala and the sushumna. When this kundalini energy, pictured as the serpent residing in the first chakra at the root of the spine (muladhar chakra), is raised up through the rest of the chakras until it reaches the seventh and the highest chakra (sahasrara) located at the crown of the head-self-realization occurs. This induces the blissful state of samadhi. The school of Sahaja Yoga is very similar to the Kundalini school.

Mantra Yoga

Mantra Yoga refers to the repetition of mantras (words or sounds) during various yoga meditation techniques. This ritualistic chanting helps bind the mind to a single thought until it attains the state of samadhi.

Tantra Yoga

The roots of Tantra Yoga go back to ancient fertility cults of India. The history of this strain of yoga, like the Kundalini school, is linked with the worship of Shakti, the primordial female energy. The objective of Tantra Yoga is to merge with the Ultimate by the arousal and channeling of sexual energy.

The Tantra school equates spiritual awakening with the awakening and rising of the kundalini power. According to Tantra, the kundalini is present in everything, even in the smallest of particles, in the form of cosmic energy. Only a fraction of it is operative, while an unmeasured residuum is left 'coiled up' and untapped at the 'base root'.

4

Sadhana the Relation of the Individual to the Universe

The civilisation of ancient Greece was nurtured within city walls. In fact, all the modern civilisations have their cradles of brick and mortar.

These walls leave their mark deep in the minds of men. They set up a principle of "divide and rule" in our mental outlook, which begets in us a habit of securing all our conquests by fortifying them and separating them from one another. We divide nation and nation, knowledge and knowledge, man and nature. It breeds in us a strong suspicion of whatever is beyond the barriers we have built, and everything has to fight hard for its entrance into our recognition.

When the first Aryan invaders appeared in India it was a vast land of forests, and the new-comers rapidly took advantage of them. These forests afforded them shelter from the fierce heat of the sun and the ravages of tropical storms, pastures for cattle, fuel for sacrificial fire, and materials for building cottages. And the different Aryan clans with their patriarchal heads settled in the different forest tracts which had some special advantage of natural protection, and food and water in plenty.

Thus in India it was in the forests that our civilisation had its birth, and it took a distinct character from this origin and environment. It was surrounded by the vast life of nature, was fed and clothed by her, and had the closest and most constant intercourse with her varying aspects.

Such a life, it may be thought, tends to have the effect of dulling human intelligence and dwarfing the incentives to progress by lowering the standards of existence. But in ancient India we find that the circumstances of forest life did not overcome man's mind, and did not enfeeble the current of his energies, but only gave to it a particular direction. Having been in constant contact with the living growth of nature, his mind was free from the desire to extend his dominion by erecting boundary walls around his acquisitions. His aim was not to acquire but to realise, to enlarge his consciousness by growing with and growing into his surroundings. He felt that truth is all-comprehensive, that there is no such thing as absolute isolation in existence, and the only way of attaining truth is through the interpenetration of our being into all objects. To realise this great harmony between man's spirit and the spirit of the world was the endeavour of the forest-dwelling sages of ancient India.

In later days there came a time when these primeval forests gave way to cultivated fields, and wealthy cities sprang up on all sides. Mighty kingdoms were established, which had communications with all the great powers of the world. But even in the heyday of its material prosperity the heart of India ever looked back with adoration upon the early ideal of strenuous self-realisation, and the dignity of the simple life of the forest hermitage, and drew its best inspiration from the wisdom stored there.

The west seems to take a pride in thinking that it is subduing nature; as if we are living in a hostile world where we have to wrest everything we want from an unwilling and alien arrangement of things. This sentiment is the product of the city-wall habit and training of mind. For in the city life man naturally directs the concentrated light of his mental vision upon his own life and works, and this creates an artificial dissociation between himself and the Universal Nature within whose bosom he lies.

But in India the point of view was different; it included the world with the man as one great truth. India put all her emphasis on the harmony that exists between the individual and the universal. She felt we could have no communication whatever with our surroundings if they were absolutely foreign to us. Man's complaint against nature is that he has to acquire most of his necessaries by his own efforts. Yes, but his efforts are not in vain; he is reaping success every day, and that shows there is a rational connection between him and nature, for we never can make anything our own except that which is truly related to us.

We can look upon a road from two different points of view. One regards it as dividing us from the object of our desire; in that case we count every step of our journey over it as something attained by force in the face of obstruction. The other sees it as the road which leads us to our destination; and as such it is part of our goal. It is already the beginning of our attainment, and by journeying over it we can only gain that which in itself it offers to us. This last point of view is that of India with regard to nature. For her, the great fact is that we are in harmony with nature; that man can think because his thoughts are in harmony with things; that he can use the forces of nature for his own purpose only because his power is in harmony with the power which is universal, and that in the long run his purpose never can knock against the purpose which works through nature.

In the west the prevalent feeling is that nature belongs exclusively to inanimate things and to beasts, that there is a sudden unaccountable break where human-nature begins. According to it, everything that is low in the scale of beings is merely nature, and whatever has the stamp of perfection on it, intellectual or moral, is human-nature. It is like dividing the bud and the blossom into two separate categories, and putting their grace to the credit of two different and antithetical principles. But the Indian mind never has any hesitation in acknowledging its kinship with nature, its unbroken relation with all.

The fundamental unity of creation was not simply a philosophical speculation for India; it was her life-object to realise this great harmony in feeling and in action. With mediation and service, with a regulation of life, she cultivated her consciousness in such a way that everything had a spiritual meaning to her. The earth, water and light, fruits and flowers, to her were not merely physical phenomena to be turned to use and then left aside. They were necessary to her in the attainment of her ideal of perfection, as every note is necessary to the completeness of the symphony. India intuitively felt that the essential fact of this world has a vital meaning for us; we have to be fully alive to it and establish a conscious relation with it, not merely impelled by scientific curiosity or greed of material advantage, but realising it in the spirit of sympathy, with a large feeling of joy and peace.

The man of science knows, in one aspect, that the world is not merely what it appears to be to our senses; he knows that earth and water are really the play of forces that manifest themselves to us as earth and water—how, we can but partially apprehend. Likewise the man who has his spiritual eyes open knows that the ultimate truth about earth and water lies in our apprehension of the eternal will which works in time and takes shape in the forces we realise under those aspects. This is not mere knowledge, as science is, but it is a preception of the soul by the soul.

This does not lead us to power, as knowledge does, but it gives us joy, which is the product of the union of kindred things. The man whose acquaintance with the world does not lead him deeper than science leads him, will never understand what it is that the man with the spiritual vision finds in these natural phenomena. The water does not merely cleanse his limbs, but it purifies his heart; for it touches his soul. The earth does not merely hold his body, but it gladdens his mind; for its contact is more than a physical contact—it is a living presence. When a man does not realise his kinship with the world, he lives in a prison-house whose walls are alien to him.

When he meets the eternal spirit in all objects, then is he emancipated, for then he discovers the fullest significance of the world into which he is born; then he finds himself in perfect truth, and his harmony with the all is established. In India men are enjoined to be fully awake to the fact that they are in the closest relation to things around them, body and soul, and that they are to hail the morning sun, the flowing water, the fruitful earth, as the manifestation of the same living truth which holds them in its embrace.

Thus the text of our everyday meditation is the Gayathri, a verse which is considered to be the epitome of all the Vedas. By its help we try to realise the essential unity of the world with the conscious soul of man; we learn to perceive the unity held together by the one Eternal Spirit, whose power creates the earth, the sky, and the stars, and at the same time irradiates our minds with the light of a consciousness that moves and exists in unbroken continuity with the outer world.

It is not true that India has tried to ignore differences of value in different things, for she knows that would make life impossible. The sense of the superiority of man in the scale of creation has not been absent from her mind. But she has had her own idea as to that in which his superiority really consists. It is not in the power of possession but in the power of union. Therefore India chose her places of pilgrimage wherever there was in nature some special grandeur or beauty, so that her mind could come out of its world of narrow necessities and realise its place in the infinite. This was the reason why in India a whole people who once were meat-eaters gave up taking animal food to cultivate the sentiment of universal sympathy for life, an event unique in the history of mankind.

India knew that when by physical and mental barriers we violently detach ourselves from the inexhaustible life of nature; when we become merely man, but not man-in-the-universe, we create bewildering problems, and having shut off the source of their solution, we try all kinds of artificial methods each of which brings its own crop of interminable difficulties.

When man leaves his resting-place in universal nature, when he walks on the single rope of humanity, it means either a dance or a fall for him, he has ceaselessly to strain every nerve and muscle to keep his balance at each step, and then, in the intervals of his weariness, he fulminates against Providence and feels a secret pride and satisfaction in thinking that he has been unfairly dealt with by the whole scheme of things.

But this cannot go on for ever. Man must realise the wholeness of his existence, his place in the infinite; he must know that hard as he may strive he can never create his honey within the cells of his hive; for the perennial supply of his life food is outside their walls. He must know that when man shuts himself out from the vitalising and purifying touch of the infinite, and falls back upon himself for his sustenance and his healing, then he goads himself into madness, tears himself into shreds, and eats his own substance. Deprived of the background of the whole, his poverty loses its one great quality, which is simplicity, and becomes squalid and shamefaced.

His wealth is no longer magnanimous; it grows merely extravagant. His appetites do not minister to his life, keeping to the limits of their purpose; they become an end in themselves and set fire to his life and play the fiddle in the lurid light of the conflagration. Then it is that in our self-expression we try to startle and not to attract; in art we strive for originality and lose sight of truth which is old and yet ever new; in literature we miss the complete view of man which is simple and yet great, but he appears as a psychological problem or the embodiment of a passion that is intense because abnormal and because exhibited in the glare of a fiercely emphatic light which is artificial.

When man's consciousness is restricted only to the immediate vicinity of his human self, the deeper roots of his nature do not find their permanent soil, his spirit is ever on the brink of starvation, and in the place of healthful strength he substitutes rounds of stimulation. Then it is that man misses his inner perspective and measures his greatness by its bulk and not by its vital link with the infinite, judges his activity by its movement and not by the repose of perfection—the repose which is in the starry heavens, in the ever-flowing rhythmic dance of creation.

The first invasion of India has its exact parallel in the invasion of America by the European settlers. They also were confronted with primeval forests and a fierce struggle with aboriginal races. But this struggle between man and man, and man and nature lasted till the very end; they never came to any terms. In India the forests which were the habitation of the barbarians became the sanctuary of sages, but in America these great living cathedrals of nature had no deeper significance to man. The brought wealth and power to him, and perhaps at times they ministered to his enjoyment of beauty, and inspired a solitary poet. They never acquired a sacred association in the hearts of men as the site of some great spiritual reconcilement where man's soul has its meeting-place with the soul of the world.

I do not for a moment wish to suggest that these things should have been otherwise. It would be an utter waste of opportunities if history were to repeat itself exactly in the same manner in every place. It is best for the commerce of the spirit that people differently situated should bring their different products into the market of humanity, each of which is complementary and necessary to the others. All that I wish to say is that India at the outset of her career met with a special combination of circumstances which was not lost upon her. She had, according to her opportunities, thought and pondered, striven and suffered, dived into the depths of existence, and achieved something which surely cannot be without its value to people whose evolution in history took a different way altogether. Man for his perfect growth requires all the living elements that constitute his complex life; that is why his food has to be cultivated in different fields and brought from different sources.

Civilisation is a kind of mould that each nation is busy making for itself to shape its men and women according to its best ideal. All its institutions, its legislature, its standard of approbation and condemnation, its conscious and unconscious teachings tend toward that object. The modern civilisation of the west, by all its organised efforts, is trying to turn out men perfect in physical, intellectual, and moral efficiency. There the vast energies of the nations are employed in extending man's power over his surroundings, and people are combining and straining every faculty to possess and to turn to account all that they can lay their hands upon, to overcome every obstacle on their path of conquest. They are ever disciplining themselves to fight nature and other races; their armaments are getting more and more stupendous every day; their machines, their appliances, their organisations go on multiplying at an amazing rate. This is a splendid achievement, no doubt, and a wonderful manifestation of man's masterfulness which knows no obstacle, and which has for its object the supremacy of himself over everything else.

The ancient civilisation of India had its own ideal of perfection towards which its efforts were directed. Its aim was not attaining power, and it neglected to cultivate to the utmost its capacities, and to organise men for defensive and offensive purposes, for cooperation in the acquisition of wealth and for military and political ascendancy.

The ideal that India tried to realise led her best men to the isolation of a contemplative life, and the treasures that she gained for mankind by penetrating into the mysteries of reality cost her dear in the sphere of worldly success. Yet, this also was a sublime achievement,—it was a supreme manifestation of that human aspiration which knows no limit, and which has for its object nothing less than the realisation of the Infinite.

There were the virtuous, the wise, the courageous; there were the statesmen, kings and emperors of India; but whom amongst all these classes did she look up to and choose to be the representative of men?

They were the rishis. What were the rishis? They who having attained the supreme soul in knowledge were filled with wisdom, and having found him in union with the soul were in perfect harmony with the inner self; they having realised him in the heart were free from all selfish desires, and having experienced him in all the activities of the world, had attained calmness. The rishis were they who having reached the supreme God from all sides had found abiding peace, had become united with all, had entered into the life of the Universe.

Thus the state of realising our relationship with all, of entering into everything through union with God, was considered in India to be the ultimate end and fulfilment of humanity.

Man can destroy and plunder, earn and accumulate, invent and discover, but he is great because his soul comprehends all. It is dire destruction for him when he envelopes his soul in a dead shell of callous habits, and when a blind fury of works whirls round him like an eddying dust storm, shutting out the horizon.

That indeed kills the very spirit of his being, which is the spirit of comprehension. Essentially man is not a slave either of himself or of the world; but he is a lover. His freedom and fulfilment is in love, which is another name for perfect comprehension. By this power of comprehension, this permeation of his being, he is united with the all-pervading Spirit, who is also the breath of his soul. Where a man tries to raise himself to eminence by pushing and jostling all others, to achieve a distinction by which he prides himself to be more than everybody else, there he is alienated from that Spirit. This is why the Upanishads describe those who have attained the goal of human life as "peaceful" 2 and as "at-one-with-God," 3 meaning that they are in perfect harmony with man and nature, and therefore in undisturbed union with God.

We have a glimpse of the same truth in the teachings of Jesus when he says, "It is easier for a camel to pass through the eye of a needle than for a rich man to enter the kingdom of Heaven"—which implies that whatever we treasure for ourselves separates us from others; our possessions are our limitations. He who is bent upon accumulating riches is unable, with his ego continually bulging, to pass through the gates of comprehension of the spiritual world, which is the world of perfect harmony; he is shut up within the narrow walls of his limited acquisitions.

Hence the spirit of the teachings of Upanishad is: In order to find him you must embrace all. In the pursuit of wealth you really give up everything to gain a few things, and that is not the way to attain him who is completeness.

Some modern philosophers of Europe, who are directly or indirectly indebted to the Upanishads, far from realising their debt, maintain that the Brahma of India is a mere abstraction, a negation of all that is in the world. In a word, that the Infinite

Being is to be found nowhere except in metaphysics. It may be, that such a doctrine has been and still is prevalent with a section of our countrymen. But this is certainly not in accord with the pervading spirit of the Indian mind. Instead, it is the practice of realising and affirming the presence of the infinite in all things which has been its constant inspiration.

We are enjoined to see whatever. there is in the world as being enveloped by God.

I bow to God over and over again who is in fire and in water, who permeates the whole world, who is in the annual crops as well as in the perennial trees.

Can this be God abstracted from the world? Instead, it signifies not merely seeing him in all things, but saluting him in all the objects of the world. The attitude of the God-conscious man of the Upanishad towards the universe is one of a deep feeling of adoration. His object of worship is present everywhere. It is the one living truth that makes all realities true. This truth is not only of knowledge but of devotion. 'Namonamah,'— we bow to him everywhere, and over and over again. It is recognised in the outburst of the Rishi, who addresses the whole world in a sudden ecstasy of joy: Listen to me, ye sons of the immortal spirit, ye who live in the heavenly abode, I have known the Supreme Person whose light shines forth from beyond the darkness. Do we not find the overwhelming delight of a direct and positive experience where there is not the least trace of vagueness or passivity?

Buddha who developed the practical side of the teaching of Upanishads, preached the same message when he said, With everything, whether it is above or below, remote or near, visible or invisible, thou shalt preserve a relation of unlimited love without any animosity or without a desire to kill. To live in such a consciousness while standing or walking, sitting or lying down till you are asleep, is Brahma vihara, or, in other words, is living and moving and having your joy in the spirit of Brahma.

What is that spirit? The Upanishad says, The being who is in his essence the light and life of all, who is world-conscious, is Brahma. To feel all, to be conscious of everything, is his spirit. We are immersed in his consciousness body and soul. It is through his consciousness that the sun attracts the earth; it is through his consciousness that the light-waves are being transmitted from planet to planet.

Not only in space, but this light and life, this all-feeling being is in our souls. He is all-conscious in space, or the world of extension; and he is all-conscious in soul, or the world of intension.

Thus to attain our world-consciousness, we have to unite our feeling with this all-pervasive infinite feeling. In fact, the only true human progress is coincident with this widening of the range of feeling. All our poetry, philosophy, science, art and religion are serving to extend the scope of our consciousness towards higher and larger spheres. Man does not acquire rights through occupation of larger space, nor through external conduct, but his rights extend only so far as he is real, and his reality is measured by the scope of his consciousness.

We have, however, to pay a price for this attainment of the freedom of consciousness. What is the price? It is to give one's self away. Our soul can realise itself truly only by denying itself. The Upanishad says, Thou shalt gain by giving away 9, Thou shalt not covet.

In Gita we are advised to work disinterestedly, abandoning all lust for the result. Many outsiders conclude from this teaching that the conception of the world as something unreal lies at the root of the so-called disinterestedness preached in India. But the reverse is true.

The man who aims at his own aggrandisement underrates everything else. Compared to his ego the rest of the world is unreal. Thus in order to be fully conscious of the reality of all, one has to be free himself from the bonds of personal desires. This discipline we have to go through to prepare ourselves for our social duties—for sharing the burdens of our fellow-beings. Every endeavour to attain a larger life requires of man "to gain by giving away, and not to be greedy." And thus to expand gradually the consciousness of one's unity with all is the striving of humanity.

The Infinite in India was not a thin nonentity, void of all content. The Rishis of India asserted emphatically, "To know him in this life is to be true; not to know him in this life is the desolation of death." 11 How to know him then? "By realising him in each and all." 12 Not only in nature but in the family, in society, and in the state, the more we realise the World-conscious in all, the better for us. Failing to realise it, we turn our faces to destruction.

It fills me with great joy and a high hope for the future of humanity when I realise that there was a time in the remote past when our poet-prophets stood under the lavish sunshine of an Indian sky and greeted the world with the glad recognition of kindred. It was not an anthropomorphic hallucination. It was not seeing man reflected everywhere in grotesquely exaggerated images, and witnessing the human drama acted on a gigantic scale in nature's arena of flitting lights and shadows. On the contrary, it meant crossing the limiting barriers of the individual, to become more than man, to become one with the All.

It was not a mere play of the imagination, but it was the liberation of consciousness from all the mystifications and exaggerations of the self. These ancient seers felt in the serene depth of their mind that the same energy which vibrates and passes into the endless forms of the world manifests itself in our inner being as consciousness; and there is no break in unity. For these seers there was no gap in their luminous vision of perfection. They never acknowledged even death itself as creating a chasm in the field of reality. They said, His reflection is death as well as immortality. They did not recognise any essential opposition between life and death, and they said with absolute assurance, "It is life that is death." 14 They saluted with the same serenity of gladness "life in its aspect of appearing and in its aspect of departure"—That which is past is hidden in life, and that which is to come. They knew that mere appearance and disappearance are on the surface like waves on the sea, but life which is permanent knows no decay or diminution.

Everything has sprung from immortal life and is vibrating with life, for life is immense.

This is the noble heritage from our forefathers waiting to be claimed by us as our own, this ideal of the supreme freedom of consciousness. It is not merely intellectual or emotional, it has an ethical basis, and it must be translated into action. In the Upanishad it is said, The supreme being is all-pervading, therefore he is the innate good in all. To be truly united in knowledge, love, and service with all beings, and thus to realise one's self in the all-pervading God is the essence of goodness, and this is the keynote of the teachings of the Upanishads: Life is immense!

Soul Consciousness

We have seen that it was the aspiration of ancient India to live and move and have its joy in Brahma, the all-conscious and all-pervading Spirit, by extending its field of consciousness over all the world. But that, it may be urged, is an impossible task for man to achieve. If this extension of consciousness be an outward process, then it is endless; it is like attempting to cross the ocean after ladling out its water. By beginning to try to realise all, one has to end by realising nothing.

But, in reality, it is not so absurd as it sounds. Man has every day to solve this problem of enlarging his region and adjusting his burdens. His burdens are many, too numerous for him to carry, but he knows that by adopting a system he can lighten the weight of his load. Whenever they feel too complicated and unwieldy, he knows it is because he has not been able to hit upon the system which would have set everything in place and distributed the weight evenly. This search for system is really a search for unity, for synthesis; it is our attempt to harmonise the heterogeneous complexity of outward materials by an inner adjustment.

In the search we gradually become aware that to find out the One is to possess the All; that there, indeed, is our last and highest privilege. It is based on the law of that unity which is, if we only know it, our abiding strength. Its living principle is the power that is in truth; the truth of that unity which comprehends multiplicity. Facts are many, but the truth is one. The animal intelligence knows facts, the human mind has power to apprehend truth. The apple falls from the tree, the rain descends upon the earth—you can go on burdening your memory with such facts and never come to an end. But once you get hold of the law of gravitation you can dispense with the necessity of collecting facts ad infinitum.

You have got at one truth which governs numberless facts. This discovery of truth is pure joy to man—it is a liberation of his mind. For, a mere fact is like a blind lane, it leads only to itself—it has no beyond. But a truth opens up a whole horizon, it leads us to the infinite. That is the reason why, when a man like Darwin discovers some simple general truth about Biology, it does not stop there, but like a lamp shedding its light far beyond the object for which it was lighted, it illumines the whole region of human life and thought, transcending its original purpose. Thus we find that truth, while investing all facts, is not a mere aggregate of facts—it surpasses them on all sides and points to the infinite reality.

As in the region of knowledge so in that of consciousness, man must clearly realise some central truth which will give him an outlook over the widest possible field. And that is the object which the Upanishad has in view when it says, Know thine own Soul. Or, in other words, realise the one great principal of unity that there is in every man.

All our egoistic impulses, our selfish desires, obscure our true vision of the soul. For they only indicate our own narrow self. When we are conscious of our soul, we perceive the inner being that transcends our ego and has its deeper affinity with the All.

Children, when they begin to learn each separate letter of the alphabet, find no pleasure in it, because they miss the real purpose of the lesson; in fact, while letters claim our attention only in themselves and as isolated things, they fatigue us. They become a source of joy to us only when they combine into words and sentences and convey an idea.

Likewise, our soul when detached and imprisoned within the narrow limits of a self loses its significance. For its very essence is unity. It can only find out its truth by unifying itself with others, and only then it has its joy. Man was troubled and he lived in a state of fear so long as he had not discovered the uniformity of law in nature; till then the world was alien to him. The law that he discovered is nothing but the perception of harmony that prevails between reason which is of the soul of man and the workings of the world.

This is the bond of union through which man is related to the world in which he lives, and he feels an exceeding joy when he finds this out, for then he realises himself in his surroundings. To understand anything is to find in it something which is our own, and it is the discovery of ourselves outside us which makes us glad. This relation of understanding is partial, but the relation of love is complete. In love the sense of difference is obliterated and the human soul fulfils its purpose in perfection, transcending the limits of itself and reaching across the threshold of the infinite. Therefore love is the highest bliss that man can attain to, for through it alone he truly knows that he is more than himself, and that he is at one with the All.

This principal of unity which man has in his soul is ever active, establishing relations far and wide through literature, art, and science, society, statecraft, and religion. Our great Revealers are they who make manifest the true meaning of the soul by giving up self for the love of mankind. They face calumny and persecution, deprivation and death in their service of love. They live the life of the soul, not of the self, and thus they prove to us the ultimate truth of humanity. We call them Mahatmas, "the men of the great soul."

It is said in one of the Upanishads: It is not that thou lovest thy son because thou desirest him, but thou lovest thy son because thou desirest thine own soul. The meaning of this is, that whomsoever we love, in him we find our own soul in the highest sense. The final truth of our existence lies in this. Paramatma, the supreme soul, is in me, as well as in my son, and my joy in my son is the realisation of this truth. It has become quite a commonplace fact, yet it is wonderful to think upon, that the joys and sorrows of our loved ones are joys and sorrows to us—nay they are more. Why so? Because in them we have grown larger, in them we have touched that great truth which comprehends the whole universe. It very often happens that our love for our children, our friends, or other loved ones, debars us from the further realisation of our soul.

It enlarges our scope of consciousness, no doubt, yet it sets a limit to its freest expansion. Nevertheless, it is the first step, and all the wonder lies in this first step itself. It shows to us the true nature of our soul. From it we know, for certain, that our highest joy is in the losing of our egoistic self and in the uniting with others.

This love gives us a new power and insight and beauty of mind to the extent of the limits we set around it, but ceases to do so if those limits lose their elasticity, and militate against the spirit of love altogether; then our friendships become exclusive, our families selfish and inhospitable, our nations insular and aggressively inimical to other races. It is like putting a burning light within a sealed enclosure, which shines brightly till the poisonous gases accumulate and smother the flame. Nevertheless it has proved its truth before it dies, and made known the joy of freedom from the grip of darkness, blind and empty and cold.

According to the Upanishads, the key to cosmic consciousness, to God-consciousness, is in the consciousness of the soul. To know our soul apart from the self is the first step towards the realisation of the supreme deliverance. We must know with absolute certainty that essentially we are spirit. This we can do by winning mastery over self, by rising above all pride and greed and fear, by knowing that worldly losses and physical death can take nothing away from the truth and the greatness of our soul.

The chick knows when it breaks through the self-centered isolation of its egg that the hard shell which covered it so long was not really a part of its life. That shell is a dead thing, it has no growth, it affords no glimpse whatever of the vast beyond that lies outside it. However pleasantly perfect and rounded it may be, it must be given a blow to, it must be burst through and thereby the freedom of light and air be won, and the complete purpose of bird life be achieved. In Sanskrit, the bird has been called the twice-born. So too the man who has gone through the ceremony of the discipline of self-restraint and high thinking for a period of at least twelve years; who has come out simple in wants, pure in heart, and ready to take up all the responsibilities of life in a disinterested largeness of spirit. He is considered to have had his rebirth from the blind envelopment of self to the freedom of soul life; to have come into living relation with his surroundings; to have become at one with the All.

I have already warned my hearers, and must once more warn them against the idea that the teachers of India preached a renunciation of the world and of self which leads only to the blank emptiness of negation. Their aim was the realisation of the soul, or, in other words, gaining the world in perfect truth. When Jesus said, "Blessed are the meek, for they shall inherit the earth," he meant this. He proclaimed the truth that when man gets rid of his pride of self then he comes into his true inheritance. No more has he to fight his way into his position in the world; it is secure for him everywhere by the immortal right of his soul. Pride of self interferes with the proper function of the soul which is to realise itself by perfecting its union with the world and the world's God.

In his sermon to Sadhu Simha Buddha says, It is true, Simha, that I denounce activities, but only the activities that lead to the evil in words, thoughts, or deeds. It is true, Simha, that I preach extinction, but only the extinction of pride, lust, evil thought, and ignorance, not that of forgiveness, love, charity, and truth.

The doctrine of deliverance that Buddha preached was the freedom from the thraldom of Avidya. Avidya is the ignorance that darkens our consciousness, and tends to limit it within the boundaries of our personal self. It is this Avidya, this ignorance, this limiting of consciousness that creates the hard separateness of the ego, and thus becomes the source of all pride and greed and cruelty incidental to self-seeking. When a man sleeps he is shut up within the narrow activities of his physical life. He lives, but he knows not the varied relations of his life to his surroundings,—therefore he knows not himself. So when a man lives the life of Avidya he is confined within his self. It is a spiritual sleep; his consciousness is not fully awake to the highest reality that surrounds him, therefore he knows not the reality of his own soul. When he attains Bodhi, i.e. the awakenment from the sleep of self to the perfection of consciousness, he becomes Buddha.

Once I met two ascetics of a certain religious sect in a village of Bengal. "Can you tell me," I asked them, "wherein lies the special features of your religion?" One of them hesitated for a moment and answered, "It is difficult to define that." The other said, "No, it is quite simple. We hold that we have first of all to know our own soul under the guidance of our spiritual teacher, and when we have done that we can find him, who is the Supreme Soul, within us." "Why don't you preach your doctrine to all the people of the world?" I asked. "Whoever feels thirsty will of himself come to the river," was his reply. "But then, do you find it so? Are they coming?" The man gave a gentle smile, and with an assurance which had not the least tinge of impatience or anxiety, he said, "They must come, one and all."

Yes, he is right, this simple ascetic of rural Bengal. Man is indeed abroad to satisfy needs which are more to him than food and clothing. He is out to find himself. Man's history is the history of his journey to the unknown in quest of the realisation of his immortal self—his soul.

Through the rise and fall of empires; through the building up gigantic piles of wealth and the ruthless scattering of them upon the dust; through the creation of vast bodies of symbols that give shape to his dreams and aspirations, and the casting of them away like the playthings of an outworn infancy; through his forging of magic keys with which to unlock the mysteries of creation, and through his throwing away of this labour of ages to go back to his workshop and work up afresh some new form; yes, through it all man is marching from epoch to epoch towards the fullest realisation of his soul,—the soul which is greater than the things man accumulates, the deeds he accomplishes, the theories he builds; the soul whose onward course is never checked by death or dissolution. Man's mistakes and failures have by no means been trifling or small, they have strewn his path with colossal ruins; his sufferings have been immense, like birth-pangs for a giant child; they are the prelude of a fulfilment whose scope is infinite. Man has gone through and is still undergoing martyrdoms in various ways, and his institutions are the altars he has built whereto he brings his daily sacrifices, marvellous in kind and stupendous in quantity.

All this would be absolutely unmeaning and unbearable if all along he did not feel that deepest joy of the soul within him, which tries its divine strength by suffering and proves its exhaustless riches by renunciation. Yes, they are coming, the pilgrims, one and all—coming to their true inheritance of the world; they are ever broadening their consciousness, ever seeking a higher and higher unity, ever approaching nearer to the one central Truth which is all-comprehensive.

Man's poverty is abysmal, his wants are endless till he becomes truly conscious of his soul. Till then, the world to him is in a state of continual flux—a phantasm that is and is not. For a man who has realised his soul there is a determinate centre of the universe around which all else can find its proper place, and from thence only can he draw and enjoy the blessedness of a harmonious life.

There was a time when the earth was only a nebulous mass whose particles were scattered far apart through the expanding force of heat; when she had not yet attained her definiteness of form and had neither beauty nor purpose, but only heat and motion. Gradually, when her vapours were condensed into a unified rounded whole through a force that strove to bring all straggling matters under the control of a centre, she occupied her proper place among the planets of the solar system, like an emerald pendant in a necklace of diamonds. So with our soul. When the heat and motion of blind impulses and passions distract it on all sides, we can neither give nor receive anything truly. But when we find our centre in our soul by the power of self-restraint, by the force that harmonises all warring elements and unifies those that are apart, then all our isolated impressions reduce themselves to wisdom, and all our momentary impulses of heart find their completion in love;

then all the petty details of our life reveal an infinite purpose, and all our thoughts and deeds unite themselves inseparably in an internal harmony.

The Upanishads say with great emphasis, Know thou the One, the Soul. It is the bridge leading to the immortal being.

This is the ultimate end of man, to find the One which is in him; which is his truth, which is his soul; the key with which he opens the gate of the spiritual life, the heavenly kingdom. His desires are many, and madly they run after the varied objects of the world, for therein they have their life and fulfilment. But that which is one in him is ever seeking for unity—unity in knowledge, unity in love, unity in purposes of will; its highest joy is when it reaches the infinite one within its eternal unity. Hence the saying of the Upanishad, Only those of tranquil minds, and none else, can attain abiding joy, by realising within their souls the Being who manifests one essence in a multiplicity of forms.

[Transcriber's note: The above footnote contains the * mark in the original printed version. This has been retained as is.]

Through all the diversities of the world the one in us is threading its course towards the one in all; this is its nature and this is its joy. But by that devious path it could never reach its goal if it had not a light of its own by which it could catch the sight of what it was seeking in a flash. The vision of the Supreme One in our own soul is a direct and immediate intuition, not based on any ratiocination or demonstration at all. Our eyes naturally see an object as a whole, not by breaking it up into parts, but by bringing all the parts together into a unity with ourselves. So with the intuition of our Soul-consciousness, which naturally and totally realises its unity in the Supreme One.

Says the Upanishad: This deity who is manifesting himself in the activities of the universe always dwells in the heart of man as the supreme soul. Those who realise him through the immediate perception of the heart attain immortality.

He is Vishvakarma; that is, in a multiplicity of forms and forces lies his outward manifestation in nature; but his inner manifestation in our soul is that which exists in unity. Our pursuit of truth in the domain of nature therefore is through analysis and the gradual methods of science, but our apprehension of truth in our soul is immediate and through direct intuition. We cannot attain the supreme soul by successive additions of knowledge acquired bit by bit even through all eternity, because he is one, he is not made up of parts; we can only know him as heart of our hearts and soul of our soul; we can only know him in the love and joy we feel when we give up our self and stand before him face to face.

The deepest and the most earnest prayer that has ever risen from the human heart has been uttered in our ancient tongue: — thou self-revealing one, reveal thyself in me. We are in misery because we are creatures of self—the self that is unyielding and narrow, that reflects no light, that is blind to the infinite. Our self is loud with its own discordant clamour—it is not the tuned harp whose chords vibrate with the music of the eternal. Sighs of discontent and weariness of failure, idle regrets for the past and anxieties for the future are troubling our shallow hearts because we have not found our souls, and the self-revealing spirit has not been manifest within us.

Hence our cry, — thou awful one, save me with thy smile of grace ever and evermore. It is a stifling shroud of death, this self-gratification, this insatiable greed, this pride of possession, this insolent alienation of heart. Rudra, — thou awful one, rend this dark cover in twain and let the saving beam of thy smile of grace strike through this night of gloom and waken my soul.

From unreality lead me to the real, from darkness to the light, from death to immortality. But how can one hope to have this prayer granted? For infinite is the distance that lies between truth and untruth, between death and deathlessness. Yet this measureless gulf is bridged in a moment when the self revealing one reveals himself in the soul. There the miracle happens, for there is the meeting-ground of the finite and infinite. Father, completely sweep away all my sins! 28 For in sin man takes part with the finite against the infinite that is in him. It is the defeat of his soul by his self. It is a perilously losing game, in which man stakes his all to gain a part. Sin is the blurring of truth which clouds the purity of our consciousness. In sin we lust after pleasures, not because they are truly desirable, but because the red light of our passions makes them appear desirable; we long for things not because they are great in themselves, but because our greed exaggerates them and makes them appear great.

These exaggerations, these falsifications of the perspective of things, break the harmony of our life at every step; we lose the true standard of values and are distracted by the false claims of the varied interests of life contending with one another. It is this failure to bring all the elements of his nature under the unity and control of the Supreme One that makes man feel the pang of his separation from God and gives rise to the earnest prayer, — God, — Father, completely sweep away all our sins. Give unto us that which is good 30, the good which is the daily bread of our souls.

In our pleasures we are confined to ourselves, in the good we are freed and we belong to all. As the child in its mother's womb gets its sustenance through the union of its life with the larger life of its mother, so our soul is nourished only through the good which is the recognition of its inner kinship, the channel of its communication with the infinite by which it is surrounded and fed. Hence it is said, "Blessed are they which do hunger and thirst after righteousness: for they shall be filled." For righteousness is the divine food of the soul; nothing but this can fill him, can make him live the life of the infinite, can help him in his growth towards the eternal. We bow to thee from whom come the enjoyments of our life. We bow also to thee from whom comes the good of our soul. We bow to thee who art good, the highest good 33, in whom we are united with everything, that is, in peace and harmony, in goodness and love.

Man's cry is to reach his fullest expression. It is this desire for self-expression that leads him to seek wealth and power. But he has to discover that accumulation is not realisation. It is the inner light that reveals him, not outer things. When this light is lighted, then in a moment he knows that Man's highest revelation is God's own revelation in him. And his cry is for this—the manifestation of his soul, which is the manifestation of God in his soul. Man becomes perfect man, he attains his fullest expression, when his soul realises itself in the Infinite being who is Avih whose very essence is expression.

The real misery of man is in the fact that he has not fully come out, that he is self-obscured, lost in the midst of his own desires. He cannot feel himself beyond his personal surroundings, his greater self is blotted out, his truth is unrealised. The prayer that rises up from his whole being is therefore, Thou, who art the spirit of manifestation, manifest thyself in me. This longing for the perfect expression of his self is more deeply inherent in man than his hunger and thirst for bodily sustenance, his lust for wealth and distinction. This prayer is not merely one born individually of him; it is in depth of all things, it is the ceaseless urging in him of the Avih, of the spirit of eternal manifestation. The revealment of the infinite in the finite, which is the motive of all creation, is not seen in its perfection in the starry heavens, in the beauty of flowers. It is in the soul of man. For there will seeks its manifestation in will, and freedom turns to win its final prize in the freedom of surrender.

Therefore, it is the self of man which the great King of the universe has not shadowed with his throne—he has left it free. In his physical and mental organism, where man is related with nature, he has to acknowledge the rule of his King, but in his self he is free to disown him. There our God must win his entrance. There he comes as a guest, not as a king, and therefore he has to wait till he is invited. It is the man's self from which God has withdrawn his commands, for there he comes to court our love. His armed force, the laws of nature, stand outside its gate, and only beauty, the messenger of his love, finds admission within its precincts.

It is only in this region of will that anarchy is permitted; only in man's self that the discord of untruth and unrighteousness hold its reign; and things can come to such a pass that we may cry out in our anguish, "Such utter lawlessness could never prevail if there were a God!" Indeed, God has stood aside from our self, where his watchful patience knows no bounds, and where he never forces open the doors if shut against him. For this self of ours has to attain its ultimate meaning, which is the soul, not through the compulsion of God's power but through love, and thus become united with God in freedom.

He whose spirit has been made one with God stands before man as the supreme flower of humanity. There man finds in truth what he is; for there the Avih is revealed to him in the soul of man as the most perfect revelation for him of God; for there we see the union of the supreme will with our will, our love with the love everlasting.

Therefore, in our country he who truly loves God receives such homage from men as would be considered almost sacrilegious in the west. We see in him God's wish fulfilled, the most difficult of all obstacles to his revealment removed, and God's own perfect joy fully blossoming in humanity. Through him we find the whole world of man overspread with a divine homeliness. His life, burning with God's love, makes all our earthly love resplendent. All the intimate associations of our life, all its experience of pleasure and pain, group themselves around this display of the divine love, and from the drama that we witness in him. The touch of an infinite mystery passes over the trivial and the familiar, making it break out into ineffable music. The trees and the stars and the blue hills appear to us as symbols aching with a meaning which can never be uttered in words. We seem to watch the Master in the very act of creation of a new world when a man's soul draws her heavy curtain of self aside, when her veil is lifted and she is face to face with her eternal lover.

But what is this state? It is like a morning of spring, varied in its life and beauty, yet one and entire. When a man's life rescued from distractions finds its unity in the soul, then the consciousness of the infinite becomes at once direct and natural to it as the light is to the flame. All the conflicts and contradictions of life are reconciled; knowledge, love and action harmonized; pleasure and pain become one in beauty, enjoyment and renunciation equal in goodness; the breach between the finite and the infinite fills with love and overflows; every moment carries its message of the eternal; the formless appears to us in the form of the flower, of the fruit; the boundless takes us up in his arms as a father and walks by our side as a friend. It is only the soul, the One in man which by its very nature can overcome all limits, and finds its affinity with the Supreme One. While yet we have not attained the internal harmony, and the wholeness of our being, our life remains a life of habits. The world still appears to us as a machine, to be mastered where it is useful, to be guarded against where it is dangerous, and never to be known in its full fellowship with us, alike in its physical nature and in its spiritual life and beauty.

The Problem of Evil

The question why there is evil in existence is the same as why there is imperfection, or, in other words, why there is creation at all. We must take it for granted that it could not be otherwise; that creation must be imperfect, must be gradual, and that it is futile to ask the question, Why we are?

But this is the real question we ought to ask: Is this imperfection the final truth, is evil absolute and ultimate? The river has its boundaries, its banks, but is a river all banks? or are the banks the final facts about the river? Do not these obstructions themselves give its water an onward motion? The towing rope binds a boat, but is the bondage its meaning? Does it not at the same time draw the boat forward?

The current of the world has its boundaries, otherwise it could have no existence, but its purpose is not shown in the boundaries which restrain it, but in its movement, which is towards perfection. The wonder is not that there should be obstacles and sufferings in this world, but that there should be law and order, beauty and joy, goodness and love. The idea of God that man has in his being is the wonder of all wonders. He has felt in the depths of his life that what appears as imperfect is the manifestation of the perfect; just as a man who has an ear for music realises the perfection of a song, while in fact he is only listening to a succession of notes. Man has found out the great paradox that what is limited is not imprisoned within its limits; it is ever moving, and therewith shedding its fainted every moment. In fact, imperfection is not a negation of perfectness; fainted is not contradictory to infinity: they are but completeness manifested in parts, infinity revealed within bounds.

Pain, which is the feeling of our finiteness, is not a fixture in our life. It is not an end in itself, as joy is. To meet with it is to know that it has no part in the true permanence of creation. It is what error is in our intellectual life. To go through the history of the development of science is to go through the maze of mistakes it made current at different times. Yet no one really believes that science is the one perfect mode of disseminating mistakes. The progressive ascertainment of truth is the important thing to remember in the history of science, not its innumerable mistakes. Error, by its nature, cannot be stationary; it cannot remain with truth; like a tramp, it must quit its lodging as soon as it fails to pay its score to the full.

As in intellectual error, so in evil of any other form, its essence is impermanence, for it cannot accord with the whole. Every moment it is being corrected by the totality of things and keeps changing its aspect. We exaggerate its importance by imagining it as a standstill. Could we collect the statistics of the immense amount of death and putrefaction happening every moment in this earth, they would appal us. But evil is ever moving; with all its incalculable immensity it does not effectually clog the current of our life; and we find that the earth, water, and air remain sweet and pure for living beings. All statistics consist of our attempts to represent statistically what is in motion; and in the process things assume a weight in our mind which they have not in reality.

For this reason a man, who by his profession is concerned with any particular aspect of life, is apt to magnify its proportions; in laying undue stress upon facts he loses his hold upon truth. A detective may have the opportunity of studying crimes in detail, but he loses his sense of their relative places in the whole social economy. When science collects facts to illustrate the struggle for existence that is going on in the kingdom of life, it raises a picture in our minds of "nature red in tooth and claw." But in these mental pictures we give a fixity to colours and forms which are really evanescent. It is like calculating the weight of the air on each square inch of our body to prove that it must be crushingly heavy for us. With every weight, however, there is an adjustment, and we lightly bear our burden. With the struggle for existence in nature there is reciprocity. There is the love for children and for comrades; there is the sacrifice of self, which springs from love; and this love is the positive element in life.

If we kept the search-light of our observation turned upon the fact of death, the world would appear to us like a huge charnel-house; but in the world of life the thought of death has, we find, the least possible hold upon our minds. Not because it is the least apparent, but because it is the negative aspect of life; just as, in spite of the fact that we shut our eyelids every second, it is the openings of the eye that count. Life as a whole never takes death seriously. It laughs, dances and plays, it builds, hoards and loves in death's face. Only when we detach one individual fact of death do we see its blankness and become dismayed. We lose sight of the wholeness of a life of which death is part. It is like looking at a piece of cloth through a microscope. It appears like a net; we gaze at the big holes and shiver in imagination. But the truth is, death is not the ultimate reality. It looks black, as the sky looks blue; but it does not blacken existence, just as the sky does not leave its stain upon the wings of the bird.

When we watch a child trying to walk, we see its countless failures; its successes are but few. If we had to limit our observation within a narrow space of time, the sight would be cruel. But we find that in spite of its repeated failures there is an impetus of joy in the child which sustains it in its seemingly impossible task. We see it does not think of its falls so much as of its power to keep its balance though for only a moment.

Like these accidents in a child's attempts to walk, we meet with sufferings in various forms in our life every day, showing the imperfections in our knowledge and our available power, and in the application of our will. But if these revealed our weakness to us only, we should die of utter depression. When we select for observation a limited area of our activities, our individual failures and miseries loom large in our minds; but our life leads us instinctively to take a wider view. It gives us an ideal of perfection which ever carries us beyond our present limitations. Within us we have a hope which always walks in front of our present narrow experience; it is the undying faith in the infinite in us; it will never accept any of our disabilities as a permanent fact; it sets no limit to its own scope; it dares to assert that man has oneness with God; and its wild dreams become true every day.

We see the truth when we set our mind towards the infinite. The ideal of truth is not in the narrow present, not in our immediate sensations, but in the consciousness of the whole which give us a taste of what we should have in what we do have. Consciously or unconsciously we have in our life this feeling of Truth which is ever larger than its appearance; for our life is facing the infinite, and it is in movement. Its aspiration is therefore infinitely more than its achievement, and as it goes on it finds that no realisation of truth ever leaves it stranded on the desert of finality, but carries it to a region beyond. Evil cannot altogether arrest the course of life on the highway and rob it of its possessions.

For the evil has to pass on, it has to grow into good; it cannot stand and give battle to the All. If the least evil could stop anywhere indefinitely, it would sink deep and cut into the very roots of existence. As it is, man does not really believe in evil, just as he cannot believe that violin strings have been purposely made to create the exquisite torture of discordant notes, though by the aid of statistics it can be mathematically proved that the probability of discord is far greater than that of harmony, and for one who can play the violin there are thousands who cannot.

The potentiality of perfection outweighs actual contradictions. No doubt there have been people who asserted existence to be an absolute evil, but man can never take them seriously. Their pessimism is a mere pose, either intellectual or sentimental; but life itself is optimistic: it wants to go on. Pessimism is a form of mental dipsomania, it disdains healthy nourishment, indulges in the strong drink of denunciation, and creates an artificial dejection which thirsts for a stronger draught. If existence were an evil, it would wait for no philosopher to prove it. It is like convicting a man of suicide, while all the time he stands before you in the flesh. Existence itself is here to prove that it cannot be an evil.

An imperfection which is not all imperfection, but which has perfection for its ideal, must go through a perpetual realisation. Thus, it is the function of our intellect to realise the truth through untruths, and knowledge is nothing but the continually burning up of error to set free the light of truth. Our will, our character, has to attain perfection by continually overcoming evils, either inside or outside us, or both; our physical life is consuming bodily materials every moment to maintain the life fire; and our moral life too has its fuel to burn.

This life process is going on—we know it, we have felt it; and we have a faith which no individual instances to the contrary can shake, that the direction of humanity is from evil to good. For we feel that good is the positive element in man's nature, and in every age and every clime what man values most is his ideals of goodness. We have known the good, we have loved it, and we have paid our highest reverence to men who have shown in their lives what goodness is.

The question will be asked, What is goodness; what does our moral nature mean? My answer is, that when a man begins to have an extended vision of his self, when he realises that he is much more than at present he seems to be, he begins to get conscious of his moral nature. Then he grows aware of that which he is yet to be, and the state not yet experienced by him becomes more real than that under his direct experience. Necessarily, his perspective of life changes, and his will takes the place of his wishes.

For will is the supreme wish of the larger life, the life whose greater portion is out of our present reach, most of whose objects are not before our sight. Then comes the conflict of our lesser man with our greater man, of our wishes with our will, of the desire for things affecting our senses with the purpose that is within our heart. Then we begin to distinguish between what we immediately desire and what is good. For good is that which is desirable for our greater self. Thus the sense of goodness comes out of a truer view of our life, which is the connected view of the wholeness of the field of life, and which takes into account not only what is present before us but what is not, and perhaps never humanly can be.

Man, who is provident, feels for that life of his which is not yet existent, feels much more that than for the life that is with him; therefore he is ready to sacrifice his present inclination for the unrealised future. In this he becomes great, for he realises truth. Even to be efficiently selfish one has to recognise this truth, and has to curb his immediate impulses—in other words, has to be moral. For our moral faculty is the faculty by which we know that life is not made up of fragments, purposeless and discontinuous.

This moral sense of man not only gives him the power to see that the self has a continuity in time, but it also enables him to see that he is not true when he is only restricted to his own self. He is more in truth than he is in fact. He truly belongs to individuals who are not included in his own individuality, and whom he is never even likely to know. As he has a feeling for his future self which is outside his present consciousness, so he has a feeling for his greater self which is outside the limits of his personality. There is no man who has not this feeling to some extent, who has never sacrificed his selfish desire for the sake of some other person, who has never felt a pleasure in undergoing some loss or trouble because it pleased somebody else.

It is a truth that man is not a detached being, that he has a universal aspect; and when he recognises this he becomes great. Even the most evilly-disposed selfishness has to recognise this when it seeks the power to do evil; for it cannot ignore truth and yet be strong. So in order to claim the aid of truth, selfishness has to be unselfish to some extent. A band of robbers must be moral in order to hold together as a band; they may rob the whole world but not each other. To make an immoral intention successful, some of its weapons must be moral. In fact, very often it is our very moral strength which gives us most effectively the power to do evil, to exploit other individuals for our own benefit, to rob other people of their rights. The life of an animal is unmoral, for it is aware only of an immediate present; the life of a man can be immoral, but that only means that it must have a moral basis.

What is immoral is imperfectly moral, just as what is false is true to a small extent, or it cannot even be false. Not to see is to be blind, but to see wrongly is to see only in an imperfect manner. Man's selfishness is a beginning to see some connection, some purpose in life; and to act in accordance with its dictates requires self-restraint and regulation of conduct. A selfish man willingly undergoes troubles for the sake of the self, he suffers hardship and privation without a murmur, simply because he knows that what is pain and trouble, looked at from the point of view of a short space of time, are just the opposite when seen in a larger perspective. Thus what is a loss to the smaller man is a gain to the greater, and vice versa.

To the man who lives for an idea, for his country, for the good of humanity, life has an extensive meaning, and to that extent pain becomes less important to him. To live the life of goodness is to live the life of all. Pleasure is for one's own self, but goodness is concerned with the happiness of all humanity and for all time. From the point of view of the good, pleasure and pain appear in a different meaning; so much so, that pleasure may be shunned, and pain be courted in its place, and death itself be made welcome as giving a higher value to life. From these higher standpoints of a man's life, the standpoints of the good, pleasure and pain lose their absolute value. Martyrs prove it in history, and we prove it every day in our life in our little martyrdoms.

When we take a pitcherful of water from the sea it has its weight, but when we take a dip into the sea itself a thousand pitchersful of water flow above our head, and we do not feel their weight. We have to carry the pitcher of self with our strength; and so, while on the plane of selfishness pleasure and pain have their full weight, on the moral plane they are so much lightened that the man who has reached it appears to us almost superhuman in his patience under crushing trails, and his forbearance in the face of malignant persecution. To live in perfect goodness is to realise one's life in the infinitive. This is the most comprehensive view of life which we can have by our inherent power of the moral vision of the wholeness of life.

And the teaching of Buddha is to cultivate this moral power to the highest extent, to know that our field of activities is not bound to the plane of our narrow self. This is the vision of the heavenly kingdom of Christ. When we attain to that universal life, which is the moral life, we become freed from the bonds of pleasure and pain, and the place vacated by our self becomes filled with an unspeakable joy which springs from measureless love. In this state the soul's activity is all the more heightened, only its motive power is not from desires, but in its own joy. This is the Karma-yoga of the Gita, the way to become one with the infinite activity by the exercise of the activity of disinterested goodness.

When Buddha mentioned upon the way of realising mankind from the grip of misery he came to this truth: that when man attains his highest end by merging the individual in the universal, he becomes free from the thraldom of pain. Let us consider this point more fully.

A student of mine once related to me his adventure in a storm, and complained that all the time he was troubled with the feeling that this great commotion in nature behaved to him as if he were no more than a mere handful of dust. That he was a distinct personality with a will of his own had not the least influence upon what was happening.

I said, "If consideration for our individuality could sway nature from her path, then it would be the individuals who would suffer most."

But he persisted in his doubt, saying that there was this fact which could not be ignored—the feeling that I am. The "I" in us seeks for a relation which is individual to it.

I replied that the relation of the "I" is with something which is "not-I." So we must have a medium which is common to both, and we must be absolutely certain that it is the same to the

"I" as it is to the "not-I." This is what needs repeating here. We have to keep in mind that our individuality by its nature is impelled to seek for the universal. Our body can only die if it tries to eat its own substance, and our eye loses the meaning of its function if it can only see itself.

Just as we find that the stronger the imagination the less is it merely imaginary and the more is it in harmony with truth, so we see the more vigorous our individuality the more does it widen towards the universal. For the greatness of a personality is not in itself but in its content, which is universal, just as the depth of a lake is judged not by the size of its cavity but by the depth of its water.

So, if it is a truth that the yearning of our nature is for reality, and that our personality cannot be happy with a fantastic universe of its own creation, then it is clearly best for it that our will can only deal with things by following their law, and cannot do with them just as it pleases. This unyielding sureness of reality sometimes crosses our will, and very often leads us to disaster, just as the firmness of the earth invariably hurts the falling child who is learning to walk. Nevertheless it is the same firmness that hurts him which makes his walking possible. Once, while passing under a bridge, the mast of my boat got stuck in one of its girders. If only for a moment the mast would have bent an inch or two, or the bridge raised its back like a yawning cat, or the river given in, it would have been all right with me.

But they took no notice of my helplessness. That is the very reason why I could make use of the river, and sail upon it with the help of the mast, and that is why, when its current was inconvenient, I could rely upon the bridge. Things are what they are, and we have to know them if we would deal with them, and knowledge of them is possible because our wish is not their law. This knowledge is a joy to us, for the knowledge is one of the channels of our relation with the things outside us; it is making them our own, and thus widening the limit of our self.

At every step we have to take into account others than ourselves. For only in death are we alone. A poet is a true poet when he can make his personal idea joyful to all men, which he could not do if he had not a medium common to all his audience. This common language has its own law which the poet must discover and follow, by doing which he becomes true and attains poetical immortality.

We see then that man's individuality is not his highest truth; there is that in him which is universal. If he were made to live in a world where his own self was the only factor to consider, then that would be the worst prison imaginable to him, for man's deepest joy is in growing greater and greater by more and more union with the all. This, as we have seen, would be an impossibility if there were no law common to all. Only by discovering the law and following it, do we become great, do we realise the universal; while, so long as our individual desires are at conflict with the universal law, we suffer pain and are futile.

There was a time when we prayed for special concessions, we expected that the laws of nature should be held in abeyance for our own convenience. But now we know better. We know that law cannot be set aside, and in this knowledge we have become strong. For this law is not something apart from us; it is our own. The universal power which is manifested in the universal law is one with our own power.

It will thwart us where we are small, where we are against the current of things; but it will help us where we are great, where we are in unison with the all. Thus, through the help of science, as we come to know more of the laws of nature, we gain in power; we tend to attain a universal body. Our organ of sight, our organ of locomotion, our physical strength becomes world-wide; steam and electricity become our nerve and muscle.

Thus we find that, just as throughout our bodily organisation there is a principle of relation by virtue of which we can call the entire body our own, and can use it as such, so all through the universe there is that principle of uninterrupted relation by virtue of which we can call the whole world our extended body and use it accordingly. And in this age of science it is our endeavour fully to establish our claim to our world-self. We know all our poverty and sufferings are owing to our inability to realise this legitimate claim of ours. Really, there is no limit to our powers, for we are not outside the universal power which is the expression of universal law. We are on our way to overcome disease and death, to conquer pain and poverty; for through scientific knowledge we are ever on our way to realise the universal in its physical aspect. And as we make progress we find that pain, disease, and poverty of power are not absolute, but that is only the want of adjustment of our individual self to our universal self which gives rise to them.

It is the same with our spiritual life. When the individual man in us chafes against the lawful rule of the universal man we become morally small, and we must suffer. In such a condition our successes are our greatest failures, and the very fulfilment of our desires leaves us poorer. We hanker after special gains for ourselves, we want to enjoy privileges which none else can share with us. But everything that is absolutely special must keep up a perpetual warfare with what is general. In such a state of civil war man always lives behind barricades, and in any civilisation which is selfish our homes are not real homes, but artificial barriers around us.

Yet we complain that we are not happy, as if there were something inherent in the nature of things to make us miserable. The universal spirit is waiting to crown us with happiness, but our individual spirit would not accept it. It is our life of the self that causes conflicts and complications everywhere, upsets the normal balance of society and gives rise to miseries of all kinds. It brings things to such a pass that to maintain order we have to create artificial coercions and organised forms of tyranny, and tolerate infernal institutions in our midst, whereby at every moment humanity is humiliated.

We have seen that in order to be powerful we have to submit to the laws of the universal forces, and to realise in practice that they are our own. So, in order to be happy, we have to submit our individual will to the sovereignty of the universal will, and to feel in truth that it is our own will. When we reach that state wherein the adjustment of the finite in us to the infinite is made perfect, then pain itself becomes a valuable asset. It becomes a measuring rod with which to gauge the true value of our joy. The most important lesson that man can learn from his life is not that there is pain in this world, but that it depends upon him to turn it into good account, that it is possible for him to transmute it into joy.

The lesson has not been lost altogether to us, and there is no man living who would willingly be deprived of his right to suffer pain, for that is his right to be a man. One day the wife of a poor labourer complained bitterly to me that her eldest boy was going to be sent away to a rich relative's house for part of the year. It was the implied kind intention of trying to relieve her of her trouble that gave her the shock, for a mother's trouble is a mother's own by her inalienable right of love, and she was not going to surrender it to any dictates of expediency. Man's freedom is never in being saved troubles, but it is the freedom to take trouble for his own good, to make the trouble an element in his joy.

It can be made so only when we realise that our individual self is not the highest meaning of our being, that in us we have the world-man who is immortal, who is not afraid of death or sufferings, and who looks upon pain as only the other side of joy. He who has realised this knows that it is pain which is our true wealth as imperfect beings, and has made us great and worthy to take our seat with the perfect. He knows that we are not beggars; that it is the hard coin which must be paid for everything valuable in this life, for our power, our wisdom, our love; that in pain is symbolised the infinite possibility of perfection, the eternal unfolding of joy; and the man who loses all pleasure in accepting pain sinks down and down to the lowest depth of penury and degradation.

It is only when we invoke the aid of pain for our self-gratification that she becomes evil and takes her vengeance for the insult done to her by hurling us into misery. For she is the vestal virgin consecrated to the service of the immortal perfection, and when she takes her true place before the altar of the infinite she casts off her dark veil and bares her face to the beholder as a revelation of supreme joy.

The Problem of Self

At one pole of my being I am one with stocks and stones. There I have to acknowledge the rule of universal law. That is where the foundation of my existence lies, deep down below. Its strength lies in its being held firm in the clasp of comprehensive world, and in the fullness of its community with all things.

But at the other pole of my being I am separate from all. There I have broken through the cordon of equality and stand alone as an individual. I am absolutely unique, I am I, I am incomparable. The whole weight of the universe cannot crush out this individuality of mine. I maintain it in spite of the tremendous gravitation of all things. It is small in appearance but great in reality. For it holds its own against the forces that would rob it of its distinction and make it one with the dust.

This is the superstructure of the self which rises from the indeterminate depth and darkness of its foundation into the open, proud of its isolation, proud of having given shape to a single individual idea of the architect's which has no duplicate in the whole universe. If this individuality be demolished, then though no material be lost, not an atom destroyed, the creative joy which was crystallised therein is gone. We are absolutely bankrupt if we are deprived of this specialty, this individuality, which is the only thing we can call our own; and which, if lost, is also a loss to the whole world. It is most valuable because it is not universal. And therefore only through it can we gain the universe more truly than if we were lying within its breast unconscious of our distinctiveness. The universal is ever seeking its consummation in the unique. And the desire we have to keep our uniqueness intact is really the desire of the universe acting in us. It is our joy of the infinite in us that gives us our joy in ourselves.

That this separateness of self is considered by man as his most precious possession is proved by the sufferings he undergoes and the sins he commits for its sake. But the consciousness of separation has come from the eating of the fruit of knowledge. It has led man to shame and crime and death; yet it is dearer to him than any paradise where the self lies, securely slumbering in perfect innocence in the womb of mother nature.

It is a constant striving and suffering for us to maintain the separateness of this self of ours. And in fact it is this suffering which measures its value. One side of the value is sacrifice, which represents how much the cost has been. The other side of it is the attainment, which represents how much has been gained. If the self meant nothing to us but pain and sacrifice, it could have no value for us, and on no account would we willingly undergo such sacrifice. In such case there could be no doubt at all that the highest object of humanity would be the annihilation of self.

But if there is a corresponding gain, if it does not end in a void but in a fullness, then it is clear that its negative qualities, its very sufferings and sacrifices, make it all the more precious. That it is so has been proved by those who have realised the positive significance of self, and have accepted its responsibilities with eagerness and undergone sacrifices without flinching.

With the foregoing introduction it will be easy for me to answer the question once asked by one of my audience as to whether the annihilation of self has not been held by India as the supreme goal of humanity?

In the first place we must keep in mind the fact that man is never literal in the expression of his ideas, except in matters most trivial. Very often man's words are not a language at all, but merely a vocal gesture of the dumb. They may indicate, but do not express his thoughts. The more vital his thoughts the more have his words to be explained by the context of his life. Those who seek to know his meaning by the aid of the dictionary only technically reach the house, for they are stopped by the outside wall and find no entrance to the hall. This is the reason why the teachings of our greatest prophets give rise to endless disputations when we try to understand them by following their words and not be realising them in our own lives. The men who are cursed with the gift of the literal mind are the unfortunate ones who are always busy with their nets and neglect the fishing.

It is not only in Buddhism and the Indian religions, but in Christianity too, that the ideal of selflessness is preached with all fervour. In the last the symbol of death has been used for expressing the idea of man's deliverance from the life which is not true. This is the same as Nirvnana, the symbol of the extinction of the lamp.

In the typical thought of India it is held that the true deliverance of man is the deliverance from avidya, from ignorance. It is not in destroying anything that is positive and real, for that cannot be possible, but that which is negative, which obstructs our vision of truth. When this obstruction, which is ignorance, is removed, then only is the eyelid drawn up which is no loss to the eye.

It is our ignorance which makes us think that our self, as self, is real, that it has its complete meaning in itself. When we take that wrong view of self then we try to live in such a manner as to make self the ultimate object of our life. Then we are doomed to disappointment like the man who tries to reach his destination by firmly clutching the dust of the road. Our self has no means of holding us, for its own nature is to pass on; and by clinging to this thread of self which is passing through the loom of life we cannot make it serve the purpose of the cloth into which it is being woven. When a man, with elaborate care, arranges for an enjoyment of the self, he lights a fire but has no dough to make his bread with; the fire flares up and consumes itself to extinction, like an unnatural beast that eats its own progeny and dies.

In an unknown language the words are tyrannically prominent. They stop us but say nothing. To be rescued from this fetter of words we must rid ourselves of the avidya, our ignorance, and then our mind will find its freedom in the inner idea. But it would be foolish to say that our ignorance of the language can be dispelled only by the destruction of the words. No, when the perfect knowledge comes, every word remains in its place, only they do not bind us to themselves, but let us pass through them and lead us to the idea which is emancipation. Thus it is only avidya which makes the self our fetter by making us think that it is an end in itself, and by preventing our seeing that it contains the idea that transcends its limits. That is why the wise man comes and says, "Set yourselves free from the avidya; know your true soul and be saved from the grasp of the self which imprisons you."

We gain our freedom when we attain our truest nature. The man who is an artist finds his artistic freedom when he finds his ideal of art. Then is he freed from laborious attempts at imitation, from the goadings of popular approbation. It is the function of religion not to destroy our nature but to fulfil it.

The Sanskrit word dharma which is usually translated into English as religion has a deeper meaning in our language. Dharma is the innermost nature, the essence, the implicit truth, of all things. Dharma is the ultimate purpose that is working in our self. When any wrong is done we say that dharma is violated, meaning that the lie has been given to our true nature.

But this dharma, which is the truth in us, is not apparent, because it is inherent. So much so, that it has been held that sinfulness is the nature of man, and only by the special grace of God can a particular person be saved. This is like saying that the nature of the seed is to remain enfolded within its shell, and it is only by some special miracle that it can be grown into a tree. But do we not know that the appearance of the seed contradicts its true nature? When you submit it to chemical analysis you may find in it carbon and proteid and a good many other things, but not the idea of a branching tree. Only when the tree begins to take shape do you come to see its dharma, and then you can affirm without doubt that the seed which has been wasted and allowed to rot in the ground has been thwarted in its dharma, in the fulfilment of its true nature.

In the history of humanity we have known the living seed in us to sprout. We have seen the great purpose in us taking shape in the lives of our greatest men, and have felt certain that though there are numerous individual lives that seem ineffectual, still it is not their dharma to remain barren; but it is for them to burst their cover and transform themselves into a vigorous spiritual shoot, growing up into the air and light, and branching out in all directions.

The freedom of the seed is in the attainment of its dharma, its nature and destiny of becoming a tree; it is the non-accomplishment which is its prison. The sacrifice by which a thing attains its fulfilment is not a sacrifice which ends in death; it is the casting-off of bonds which wins freedom.

When we know the highest ideal of freedom which a man has, we know his dharma, the essence of his nature, the real meaning of his self. At first sight it seems that man counts that as freedom by which he gets unbounded opportunities of self gratification and self-aggrandisement. But surely this is not borne out by history. Our revelatory men have always been those who have lived the life of self-sacrifice. The higher nature in man always seeks for something which transcends itself and yet is its deepest truth; which claims all its sacrifice, yet makes this sacrifice its own recompense. This is man's dharma, man's religion, and man's self is the vessel which is to carry this sacrifice to the altar.

We can look at our self in its two different aspects. The self which displays itself, and the self which transcends itself and thereby reveals its own meaning. To display itself it tries to be big, to stand upon the pedestal of its accumulations, and to retain everything to itself. To reveal itself it gives up everything it has; thus becoming perfect like a flower that has blossomed out from the bud, pouring from its chalice of beauty all its sweetness.

The lamp contains its oil, which it holds securely in its close grasp and guards from the least loss. Thus is it separate from all other objects around it and is miserly. But when lighted it finds its meaning at once; its relation with all things far and near is established, and it freely sacrifices its fund of oil to feed the flame.

Such a lamp is our self. So long as it hoards its possessions it keeps itself dark, its conduct contradicts its true purpose.

When it finds illumination it forgets itself in a moment, holds the light high, and serves it with everything it has; for therein is its revelation. This revelation is the freedom which Buddha preached. He asked the lamp to give up its oil. But purposeless giving up is a still darker poverty which he never could have meant. The lamp must give up its oil to the light and thus set free the purpose it has in its hoarding. This is emancipation. The path Buddha pointed out was not merely the practice of self-abnegation, but the widening of love. And therein lies the true meaning of Buddha's preaching.

When we find that the state of Nirvana preached by Buddha is through love, then we know for certain that Nirvana is the highest culmination of love. For love is an end unto itself. Everything else raises the question "Why?" in our mind, and we require a reason for it. But when we say, "I love," then there is no room for the "why"; it is the final answer in itself.

Doubtless, even selfishness impels one to give away. But the selfish man does it on compulsion. That is like plucking fruit when it is unripe; you have to tear it from the tree and bruise the branch. But when a man loves, giving becomes a matter of joy to him, like the tree's surrender of the ripe fruit. All our belongings assume a weight by the ceaseless gravitation of our selfish desires; we cannot easily cast them away from us. They seem to belong to our very nature, to stick to us as a second skin, and we bleed as we detach them. But when we are possessed by love, its force acts in the opposite direction. The things that closely adhered to us lose their adhesion and weight, and we find that they are not of us. Far from being a loss to give them away, we find in that the fulfilment of our being.

Thus we find in perfect love the freedom of our self. That only which is done for love is done freely, however much pain it may cause. Therefore working for love is freedom in action. This is the meaning of the teaching of disinterested work in the Gita.

The Gita says action we must have, for only in action do we manifest our nature. But this manifestation is not perfect so long as our action is not free. In fact, our nature is obscured by work done by the compulsion of want or fear. The mother reveals herself in the service of her children, so our true freedom is not the freedom from action but freedom in action, which can only be attained in the work of love.

God's manifestation is in his work of creation and it is said in the Upanishad, Knowledge, power, and action are of his nature 35 ; they are not imposed upon him from outside. Therefore his work is his freedom, and in his creation he realises himself. The same thing is said elsewhere in other words: From joy does spring all this creation, by joy is it maintained, towards joy does it progress, and into joy does it enter. It means that God's creation has not its source in any necessity; it comes from his fullness of joy; it is his love that creates, therefore in creation is his own revealment.

The artist who has a joy in the fullness of his artistic idea objectifies it and thus gains it more fully by holding it afar. It is joy which detaches ourselves from us, and then gives it form in creations of love in order to make it more perfectly our own. Hence there must be this separation, not a separation of repulsion but a separation of love. Repulsion has only the one element, the element of severance. But love has two, the element of severance, which is only an appearance, and the element of union which is the ultimate truth. Just as when the father tosses his child up from his arms it has the appearance of rejection but its truth is quite the reverse.

So we must know that the meaning of our self is not to be found in its separateness from God and others, but in the ceaseless realisation of yoga, of union; not on the side of the canvas where it is blank, but on the side where the picture is being painted.

This is the reason why the separateness of our self has been described by our philosophers as maya, as an illusion, because it has no intrinsic reality of its own. It looks perilous; it raises its isolation to a giddy height and casts a black shadow upon the fair face of existence; from the outside it has an aspect of a sudden disruption, rebellious and destructive; it is proud, domineering and wayward; it is ready to rob the world of all its wealth to gratify its craving of a moment; to pluck with a reckless, cruel hand all the plumes from the divine bird of beauty to deck its ugliness for a day; indeed man's legend has it that it bears the black mark of disobedience stamped on its forehead for ever; but still all this maya, envelopment of avidya; it is the mist, it is not the sun; it is the black smoke that presages the fire of love.

Imagine some savage who, in his ignorance, thinks that it is the paper of the banknote that has the magic, by virtue of which the possessor of it gets all he wants. He piles up the papers, hides them, handles them in all sorts of absurd ways, and then at last, wearied by his efforts, comes to the sad conclusion that they are absolutely worthless, only fit to be thrown into the fire. But the wise man knows that the paper of the banknote is all maya, and until it is given up to the bank it is futile.

It is only avidya, our ignorance, that makes us believe that the separateness of our self like the paper of the banknote is precious in itself, and by acting on this belief our self is rendered valueless. It is only when the avidya is removed that this very self comes to us with a wealth which is priceless. For He manifests Himself in forms which His joy assumes. These forms are separate from Him, and the value that these forms have is only what his joy has imparted to them. When we transfer back these forms into that original joy, which is love, then we cash them in the bank and we find their truth.

When pure necessity drives man to his work it takes an accidental and contingent character, it becomes a mere makeshift arrangement; it is deserted and left in ruins when necessity changes its course. But when his work is the outcome of joy, the forms that it takes have the elements of immortality. The immortal in man imparts to it its own quality of permanence.

Our self, as a form of God's joy, is deathless. For his joy is amritham, eternal. This it is in us which makes us sceptical of death, even when the fact of death cannot be doubted. In reconcilement of this contradiction in us we come to the truth that in the dualism of death and life there is a harmony. We know that the life of a soul, which is finite in its expression and infinite in its principle, must go through the portals of death in its journey to realise the infinite. It is death which is monistic, it has no life in it. But life is dualistic; it has an appearance as well as truth; and death is that appearance, that maya, which is an inseparable companion to life. Our self to live must go through a continual change and growth of form, which may be termed a continual death and a continual life going on at the same time. It is really courting death when we refuse to accept death; when we wish to give the form of the self some fixed changelessness; when the self feels no impulse which urges it to grow out of itself; when it treats its limits as final and acts accordingly. Then comes our teacher's call to die to this death; not a call to annihilation but to eternal life. It is the extinction of the lamp in the morning light; not the abolition of the sun. It is really asking us consciously to give effect to the innermost wish that we have in the depths of our nature.

We have a dual set of desires in our being, which it should be our endeavour to bring into a harmony. In the region of our physical nature we have one set of which we are conscious always. We wish to enjoy our food and drink, we hanker after bodily pleasure and comfort. These desires are self-centered; they are solely concerned with their respective impulses. The wishes of our palate often run counter to what our stomach can allow.

But we have another set, which is the desire of our physical system as a whole, of which we are usually unconscious. It is the wish for health. This is always doing its work, mending and repairing, making new adjustments in cases of accident, and skilfully restoring the balance wherever disturbed. It has no concern with the fulfilment of our immediate bodily desires, but it goes beyond the present time. It is the principle of our physical wholeness, it links our life with its past and its future and maintains the unity of its parts. He who is wise knows it, and makes his other physical wishes harmonise with it.

We have a greater body which is the social body. Society is an organism, of which we as parts have our individual wishes. We want our own pleasure and license. We want to pay less and gain more than anybody else. This causes scramblings and fights. But there is that other wish in us which does its work in the depths of the social being. It is the wish for the welfare of the society. It transcends the limits of the present and the personal. It is on the side of the infinite.

He who is wise tries to harmonise the wishes that seek for self-gratification with the wish for the social good, and only thus can he realise his higher self.

In its finite aspect the self is conscious of its separateness, and there it is ruthless in its attempt to have more distinction than all others. But in its infinite aspect its wish is to gain that harmony which leads to its perfection and not its mere aggrandisement.

The emancipation of our physical nature is in attaining health, of our social being in attaining goodness, and of our self in attaining love. This last is what Buddha describes as extinction—the extinction of selfishness—which is the function of love, and which does not lead to darkness but to illumination. This is the attainment of bodhi, or the true awakening; it is the revealing in us of the infinite joy by the light of love.

The passage of our self is through its selfhood, which is independent, to its attainment of soul, which is harmonious. This harmony can never be reached through compulsion. So our will, in the history of its growth, must come through independence and rebellion to the ultimate completion. We must have the possibility of the negative form of freedom, which is licence, before we can attain the positive freedom, which is love.

This negative freedom, the freedom of self-will, can turn its back upon its highest realisation, but it cannot cut itself away from it altogether, for then it will lose its own meaning. Our self-will has freedom up to a certain extent; it can know what it is to break away from the path, but it cannot continue in that direction indefinitely. For we are finite on our negative side. We must come to an end in our evil doing, in our career of discord. For evil is not infinite, and discord cannot be an end in itself. Our will has freedom in order that it may find out that its true course is towards goodness and love. For goodness and love are infinite, and only in the infinite is the perfect realisation of freedom possible. So our will can be free not towards the limitations of our self, not where it is maya and negation, but towards the unlimited, where is truth and love. Our freedom cannot go against its own principle of freedom and yet be free; it cannot commit suicide and yet live. We cannot say that we should have infinite freedom to fetter ourselves, for the fettering ends the freedom.

So in the freedom of our will, we have the same dualism of appearance and truth—our self-will is only the appearance of freedom and love is the truth. When we try to make this appearance independent of truth, then our attempt brings misery and proves its own futility in the end. Everything has this dualism of maya and satyam, appearance and truth. Words are maya where they are merely sounds and finite, they are satyam where they are ideas and infinite. Our self is maya where it is merely individual and finite, where it considers its separateness as absolute; it is satyam where it recognises its essence in the universal and infinite, in the supreme self, in paramatman. This is what Christ means when he says, "Before Abraham was I am." This is the eternal I am that speaks through the I am that is in me. The individual I am attains its perfect end when it realises its freedom of harmony in the infinite I am. Then is it mukti, its deliverance from the thraldom of maya, of appearance, which springs from avidya, from ignorance; its emancipation in shantam shivam advaitam, in the perfect repose in truth, in the perfect activity in goodness, and in the perfect union in love.

Not only in our self but also in nature is there this separateness from God, which has been described as maya by our philosophers, because the separateness does not exist by itself, it does not limit God's infinity from outside. It is his own will that has imposed limits to itself, just as the chess-player restricts his will with regard to the moving of the chessmen. The player willingly enters into definite relations with each particular piece and realises the joy of his power by these very restrictions. It is not that he cannot move the chessmen just as he pleases, but if he does so then there can be no play. If

God assumes his rôle of omnipotence, then his creation is at an end and his power loses all its meaning. For power to be a power must act within limits. God's water must be water, his earth can never be other than earth. The law that has made them water and earth is his own law by which he has separated the play from the player, for therein the joy of the player consists.

As by the limits of law nature is separated from God, so it is the limits of its egoism which separates the self from him. He has willingly set limits to his will, and has given us mastery over the little world of our own. It is like a father's settling upon his son some allowance within the limit of which he is free to do what he likes. Though it remains a portion of the father's own property, yet he frees it from the operation of his own will. The reason of it is that the will, which is love's will and therefore free, can have its joy only in a union with another free will. The tyrant who must have slaves looks upon them as instruments of his purpose.

It is the consciousness of his own necessity which makes him crush the will out of them, to make his self-interest absolutely secure. This self-interest cannot brook the least freedom in others, because it is not itself free. The tyrant is really dependent on his slaves, and therefore he tries to make them completely useful by making them subservient to his own will. But a lover must have two wills for the realisation of his love, because the consummation of love is in harmony, the harmony between freedom and freedom.

So God's love from which our self has taken form has made it separate from God; and it is God's love which again establishes a reconciliation and unites God with our self through the separation. That is why our self has to go through endless renewals. For in its career of separateness it cannot go on for ever. Separateness is the fainted where it finds its barriers to come back again and again to its infinite source. Our self has ceaselessly to cast off its age, repeatedly shed its limits in oblivion and death, in order to realise its immortal youth. Its personality must merge in the universal time after time, in fact pass through it every moment, ever to refresh its individual life. It must follow the eternal rhythm and touch the fundamental unity at every step, and thus maintain its separation balanced in beauty and strength.

The play of life and death we see everywhere—this transmutation of the old into the new. The day comes to us every morning, naked and white, fresh as a flower. But we know it is old. It is age itself. It is that very ancient day which took up the newborn earth in its arms, covered it with its white mantle of light, and sent it forth on its pilgrimage among the stars.

Yet its feet are untired and its eyes undimmed. It carries the golden amulet of ageless eternity, at whose touch all wrinkles vanish from the forehead of creation. In the very core of the world's heart stands immortal youth. Death and decay cast over its face momentary shadows and pass on; they leave no marks of their steps—and truth remains fresh and young.

This old, old day of our earth is born again and again every morning. It comes back to the original refrain of its music. If its march were the march of an infinite straight line, if it had not the awful pause of its plunge in the abysmal darkness and its repeated rebirth in the life of the endless beginning, then it would gradually soil and bury truth with its dust and spread ceaseless aching over the earth under its heavy tread. Then every moment would leave its load of weariness behind, and decrepitude would reign supreme on its throne of eternal dirt.

But every morning the day is reborn among the newly-blossomed flowers with the same message retold and the same assurance renewed that death eternally dies, that the waves of turmoil are on the surface, and that the sea of tranquillity is fathomless. The curtain of night is drawn aside and truth emerges without a speck of dust on its garment, without a furrow of age on its lineaments.

We see that he who is before everything else is the same today. Every note of the song of creation comes fresh from his voice. The universe is not a mere echo, reverberating from sky to sky, like a homeless wanderer—the echo of an old song sung once for all in the dim beginning of things and then left orphaned.

Every moment it comes from the heart of the master, it is breathed in his breath.

And that is the reason why it overspreads the sky like a thought taking shape in a poem, and never has to break into pieces with the burden of its own accumulating weight. Hence the surprise of endless variations, the advent of the unaccountable, the ceaseless procession of individuals, each of whom is without a parallel in creation. As at the first so to the last, the beginning never ends—the world is ever old and ever new.

It is for our self to know that it must be born anew every moment of its life. It must break through all illusions that encase it in their crust to make it appear old, burdening it with death. For life is immortal youthfulness, and it hates age that tries to clog its movements—age that belongs not to life in truth, but follows it as the shadow follows the lamp.

Our life, like a river, strikes its banks not to find itself closed in by them, but to realise anew every moment that it has its unending opening towards the sea. It is a poem that strikes its metre at every step not to be silenced by its rigid regulations, but to give expression every moment to the inner freedom of its harmony.

The boundary walls of our individuality thrust us back within our limits, on the one hand, and thus lead us, on the other, to the unlimited. Only when we try to make these limits infinite are we launched into an impossible contradiction and court miserable failure.

This is the cause which leads to the great revolutions in human history. Whenever the part, spurning the whole, tries to run a separate course of its own, the great pull of the all gives it a violent wrench, stops it suddenly, and brings it to the dust. Whenever the individual tries to dam the ever-flowing current of the world-force and imprison it within the area of his particular use, it brings on disaster. However powerful a king may be, he cannot raise his standard or rebellion against the infinite source of strength, which is unity, and yet remain powerful.

It has been said, By unrighteousness men prosper, gain what they desire, and triumph over their enemies, but at the end they are cut off at the root and suffer extinction. Our roots must go deep down into the universal if we would attain the greatness of personality.

It is the end of our self to seek that union. It must bend its head low in love and meekness and take its stand where great and small all meet. It has to gain by its loss and rise by its surrender. His games would be a horror to the child if he could not come back to his mother, and our pride of personality will be a curse to us if we cannot give it up in love. We must know that it is only the revelation of the Infinite which is endlessly new and eternally beautiful in us, and which gives the only meaning to our self.

Realisation in Love

We come now to the eternal problem of co-existence of the infinite and the finite, of the supreme being and our soul. There is a sublime paradox that lies at the root of existence. We never can go round it, because we never can stand outside the problem and weigh it against any other possible alternative. But the problem exists in logic only; in reality it does not offer us any difficulty at all. Logically speaking, the distance between two points, however near, may be said to be infinite because it is infinitely divisible. But we do cross the infinite at every step, and meet the eternal in every second. Therefore some of our philosophers say there is no such thing as fainted; it is but a maya, an illusion. The real is the infinite, and it is only maya, the unreality, which causes the appearance of the finite. But the word maya is a mere name, it is no explanation. It is merely saying that with truth there is this appearance which is the opposite of truth; but how they come to exist at one and the same time is incomprehensible.

We have what we call in Sanskrit dvandva, a series of opposites in creation; such as, the positive pole and the negative, the centripetal force and the centrifugal, attraction and repulsion. These are also mere names, they are no explanations. They are only different ways of asserting that the world in its essence is a reconciliation of pairs of opposing forces. These forces, like the left and the right hands of the creator, are acting in absolute harmony, yet acting from opposite directions.

There is a bond of harmony between our two eyes, which makes them act in unison. Likewise there is an unbreakable continuity of relation in the physical world between heat and cold, light and darkness, motion and rest, as between the bass and treble notes of a piano. That is why these opposites do not bring confusion in the universe, but harmony. If creation were but a chaos, we should have to imagine the two opposing principles as trying to get the better of each other. But the universe is not under martial law, arbitrary and provisional. Here we find no force which can run amok, or go on indefinitely in its wild road, like an exiled outlaw, breaking all harmony with its surroundings; each force, on the contrary, has to come back in a curved line to its equilibrium. Waves rise, each to its individual height in a seeming attitude of unrelenting competition, but only up to a certain point; and thus we know of the great repose of the sea to which they are all related, and to which they must all return in a rhythm which is marvellously beautiful.

In fact, these undulations and vibrations, these risings and fallings, are not due to the erratic contortions of disparate bodies, they are a rhythmic dance. Rhythm never can be born of the haphazard struggle of combat. Its underlying principle must be unity, not opposition.

This principle of unity is the mystery of all mysteries. The existence of a duality at once raises a question in our minds, and we seek its solution in the One. When at last we find a relation between these two, and thereby see them as one in essence, we feel that we have come to the truth. And then we give utterance to this most startling of all paradoxes, that the One appears as many, that the appearance is the opposite of truth and yet is inseparably related to it.

Curiously enough, there are men who lose that feeling of mystery, which is at the root of all our delights, when they discover the uniformity of law among the diversity of nature.

As if gravitation is not more of a mystery than the fall of an apple, as if the evolution from one scale of being to the other is not something which is even more shy of explanation than a succession of creations. The trouble is that we very often stop at such a law as if it were the final end of our search, and then we find that it does not even begin to emancipate our spirit. It only gives satisfaction to our intellect, and as it does not appeal to our whole being it only deadens in us the sense of the infinite.

A great poem, when analysed, is a set of detached sounds. The reader who finds out the meaning, which is the inner medium that connects these outer sounds, discovers a perfect law all through, which is never violated in the least; the law of the evolution of ideas, the law of the music and the form.

But law in itself is a limit. It only shows that whatever is can never be otherwise. When a man is exclusively occupied with the search for the links of causality, his mind succumbs to the tyranny of law in escaping from the tyranny of facts. In learning a language, when from mere words we reach the laws of words we have gained a great deal. But if we stop at that point, and only concern ourselves with the marvels of the formation of a language, seeking the hidden reason of all its apparent caprices, we do not reach the end—for grammar is not literature, prosody is not a poem.

When we come to literature we find that though it conforms to rules of grammar it is yet a thing of joy, it is freedom itself. The beauty of a poem is bound by strict laws, yet it transcends them. The laws are its wings, they do not keep it weighed down, they carry it to freedom. Its form is in law but its spirit is in beauty. Law is the first step towards freedom, and beauty is the complete liberation which stands on the pedestal of law. Beauty harmonises in itself the limit and the beyond, the law and the liberty.

In the world-poem, the discovery of the law of its rhythms, the measurement of its expansion and contraction, movement and pause, the pursuit of its evolution of forms and characters, are true achievements of the mind; but we cannot stop there. It is like a railway station; but the station platform is not our home. Only he has attained the final truth who knows that the whole world is a creation of joy.

This leads me to think how mysterious the relation of the human heart with nature must be. In the outer world of activity nature has one aspect, but in our hearts, in the inner world, it presents an altogether different picture.

Take an instance—the flower of a plant. However fine and dainty it may look, it is pressed to do a great service, and its colours and forms are all suited to its work. It must bring forth the fruit, or the continuity of plant life will be broken and the earth will be turned into a desert ere long. The colour and the smell of the flower are all for some purpose therefore; no sooner is it fertilised by the bee, and the time of its fruition arrives, than it sheds its exquisite petals and a cruel economy compels it to give up its sweet perfume.

It has no time to flaunt its finery, for it is busy beyond measure. Viewed from without, necessity seems to be the only factor in nature for which everything works and moves. There the bud develops into the flower, the flower into the fruit, the fruit into the seed, the seed into a new plant again, and so forth, the chain of activity running on unbroken. Should there crop up any disturbance or impediment, no excuse would be accepted, and the unfortunate thing thus choked in its movement would at once be labelled as rejected, and be bound to die and disappear post-haste. In the great office of nature there are innumerable departments with endless work going on, and the fine flower that you behold there, gaudily attired and scented like a dandy, is by no means what it appears to be, but rather, is like a labourer toiling in sun and shower, who has to submit a clear account of his work and has no breathing space to enjoy himself in playful frolic.

But when this same flower enters the heart of men its aspect of busy practicality is gone, and it becomes the very emblem of leisure and repose. The same object that is the embodiment of endless activity without is the perfect expression of beauty and peace within.

Science here warns us that we are mistaken, that the purpose of a flower is nothing but what is outwardly manifested, and that the relation of beauty and sweetness which we think it bears to us is all our own making, gratuitous and imaginary.

But our heart replies that we are not in the least mistaken. In the sphere of nature the flower carries with it a certificate which recommends it as having immense capacity for doing useful work, but it brings an altogether different letter of introduction when it knocks at the door of our hearts. Beauty becomes its only qualification. At one place it comes as a slave, and at another as a free thing. How, then, should we give credit to its first recommendation and disbelieve the second one? That the flower has got its being in the unbroken chain of causation is true beyond doubt; but that is an outer truth. The inner truth is: Verily from the everlasting joy do all objects have their birth.

A flower, therefore, has not its only function in nature, but has another great function to exercise in the mind of man. And what is that function? In nature its work is that of a servant who has to make his appearance at appointed times, but in the heart of man it comes like a messenger from the King. In the Ramayana, when Sita, forcibly separated from her husband, was bewailing her evil fate in Ravana's golden palace, she was met by a messenger who brought with him a ring of her beloved Ramachandra himself. The very sight of it convinced Sita of the truth of tidings he bore. She was at once reassured that he came indeed from her beloved one, who had not forgotten her and was at hand to rescue her.

Such a messenger is a flower from our great lover. Surrounded with the pomp and pageantry of worldliness, which may be linked to Ravana's golden city, we still live in exile, while the insolent spirit of worldly prosperity tempts us with allurements and claims us as its bride. In the meantime the flower comes across with a message from the other shore, and whispers in our ears, "I am come. He has sent me. I am a messenger of the beautiful, the one whose soul is the bliss of love. This island of isolation has been bridged over by him, and he has not forgotten thee, and will rescue thee even now. He will draw thee unto him and make thee his own. This illusion will not hold thee in thraldom for ever."

If we happen to be awake then, we question him: "How are we to know that thou art come from him indeed?" The messenger says, "Look! I have this ring from him. How lovely are its hues and charms!"

Ah, doubtless it is his—indeed, it is our wedding ring. Now all else passes into oblivion, only this sweet symbol of the touch of the eternal love fills us with a deep longing. We realise that the palace of gold where we are has nothing to do with us—our deliverance is outside it—and there our love has its fruition and our life its fulfilment.

What to the bee in nature is merely colour and scent, and the marks or spots which show the right track to the honey, is to the human heart beauty and joy untrammelled by necessity. They bring a love letter to the heart written in many-coloured inks.

I was telling you, therefore, that however busy our active nature outwardly may be, she has a secret chamber within the heart where she comes and goes freely, without any design whatsoever. There the fire of her workshop is transformed into lamps of a festival, the noise of her factory is heard like music. The iron chain of cause and effect sounds heavily outside in nature, but in the human heart its unalloyed delight seems to sound, as it were, like the golden strings of a harp.

It indeed seems to be wonderful that nature has these two aspects at one and the same time, and so antithetical—one being of thraldom and the other of freedom. In the same form, sound, colour, and taste two contrary notes are heard, one of necessity and the other of joy. Outwardly nature is busy and restless, inwardly she is all silence and peace. She has toil on one side and leisure on the other. You see her bondage only when you see her from without, but within her heart is a limitless beauty.

Our seer says, "From joy are born all creatures, by joy they are sustained, towards joy they progress, and into joy they enter."

Not that he ignores law, or that his contemplation of this infinite joy is born of the intoxication produced by an indulgence in abstract thought. He fully recognises the inexorable laws of nature, and says, "Fire burns for fear of him (i.e. by his law); the sun shines by fear of him; and for fear of him the wind, the clouds, and death perform their offices." It is a reign of iron rule, ready to punish the least transgression. Yet the poet chants the glad song, "From joy are born all creatures, by joy they are sustained, towards joy they progress, and into joy they enter."

The immortal being manifests himself in joy-form. His manifestation in creation is out of his fullness of joy. It is the nature of this abounding joy to realise itself in form which is law. The joy, which is without form, must create, must translate itself into forms. The joy of the singer is expressed in the form of a song, that of the poet in the form of a poem. Man in his rôle of a creator is ever creating forms, and they come out of his abounding joy.

This joy, whose other name is love, must by its very nature have duality for its realisation. When the singer has his inspiration he makes himself into two; he has within him his other self as the hearer, and the outside audience is merely an extension of this other self of his. The lover seeks his own other self in his beloved. It is the joy that creates this separation, in order to realise through obstacles of union.

The amritam, the immortal bliss, has made himself into two. Our soul is the loved one, it is his other self. We are separate; but if this separation were absolute, then there would have been absolute misery and unmitigated evil in this world. Then from untruth we never could reach truth, and from sin we never could hope to attain purity of heart; then all opposites would ever remain opposites, and we could never find a medium through which our differences could ever tend to meet. Then we could have no language, no understanding, no blending of hearts, no cooperation in life. But on the contrary, we find that the separateness of objects is in a fluid state. Their individualities are even changing, they are meeting and merging into each other, till science itself is turning into metaphysics, matter losing its boundaries, and the definition of life becoming more and more indefinite.

Yes, our individual soul has been separated from the supreme soul, but this has not been from alienation but from the fullness of love. It is for that reason that untruths, sufferings, and evils are not at a standstill; the human soul can defy them, can overcome them, nay, can altogether transform them into new power and beauty.

The singer is translating his song into singing, his joy into forms, and the hearer has to translate back the singing into the original joy; then the communion between the singer and the hearer is complete. The infinite joy is manifesting itself in manifold forms, taking upon itself the bondage of law, and we fulfil our destiny when we go back from forms to joy, from law to the love, when we untie the knot of the finite and hark back to the infinite.

The human soul is on its journey from the law to love, from discipline to liberation, from the moral plane to the spiritual. Buddha preached the discipline of self-restraint and moral life; it is a complete acceptance of law. But this bondage of law cannot be an end by itself; by mastering it thoroughly we acquire the means of getting beyond it. It is going back to Brahma, to the infinite love, which is manifesting itself through the finite forms of law. Buddha names it Brahma-vihara, the joy of living in Brahma. He who wants to reach this stage, according to Buddha, "shall deceive none, entertain no hatred for anybody, and never wish to injure through anger. He shall have measureless love for all creatures, even as a mother has for her only child, whom she protects with her own life. Up above, below, and all around him he shall extend his love, which is without bounds and obstacles, and which is free from all cruelty and antagonism. While standing, sitting, walking, lying down, till he fall asleep, he shall keep his mind active in this exercise of universal goodwill."

Want of love is a degree of callousness; for love is the perfection of consciousness. We do not love because we do not comprehend, or rather we do not comprehend because we do not love. For love is the ultimate meaning of everything around us. It is not a mere sentiment; it is truth; it is the joy that is at the root of all creation. It is the white light of pure consciousness that emanates from Brahma. So, to be one with this sarvanubhuh, this all-feeling being who is in the external sky, as well as in our inner soul, we must attain to that summit of consciousness, which is love: Who could have breathed or moved if the sky were not filled with joy, with love? 41 It is through the heightening of our consciousness into love, and extending it all over the world, that we can attain Brahma-vihara, communion with this infinite joy.

Love spontaneously gives itself in endless gifts. But these gifts lose their fullest significance if through them we do not reach that love, which is the giver. To do that, we must have love in our own heart. He who has no love in him values the gifts of his lover only according to their usefulness. But utility is temporary and partial. It can never occupy our whole being; what is useful only touches us at the point where we have some want. When the want is satisfied, utility becomes a burden if it still persists. On the other hand, a mere token is of permanent worth to us when we have love in our heart. For it is not for any special use. It is an end in itself; it is for our whole being and therefore can never tire us.

The question is, In what manner do we accept this world, which is a perfect gift of joy? Have we been able to receive it in our heart where we keep enshrined things that are of deathless value to us? We are frantically busy making use of the forces of the universe to gain more and more power; we feed and we clothe ourselves from its stores, we scramble for its riches, and it becomes for us a field of fierce competition. But were we born for this, to extend our proprietary rights over this world and make of it a marketable commodity? When our whole mind is bent only upon making use of this world it loses for us its true value. We make it cheap by our sordid desires; and thus to the end of our days we only try to feed upon it and miss its truth, just like the greedy child who tears leaves from a precious book and tries to swallow them.

In the lands where cannibalism is prevalent man looks upon man as his food. In such a country civilisation can never thrive, for there man loses his higher value and is made common indeed. But there are other kinds of cannibalism, perhaps not so gross, but not less heinous, for which one need not travel far. In countries higher in the scale of civilisation we find sometimes man looked upon as a mere body, and he is bought and sold in the market by the price of his flesh only. And sometimes he gets his sole value from being useful; he is made into a machine, and is traded upon by the man of money to acquire for him more money. Thus our lust, our greed, our love of comfort result in cheapening man to his lowest value. It is self deception on a large scale. Our desires blind us to the truth that there is in man, and this is the greatest wrong done by ourselves to our own soul. It deadens our consciousness, and is but a gradual method of spiritual suicide. It produces ugly sores in the body of civilisation, gives rise to its hovels and brothels, its vindictive penal codes, its cruel prison systems, its organised method of exploiting foreign races to the extent of permanently injuring them by depriving them of the discipline of self-government and means of self-defence.

Of course man is useful to man, because his body is a marvellous machine and his mind an organ of wonderful efficiency. But he is a spirit as well, and this spirit is truly known only by love. When we define a man by the market value of the service we can expect of him, we know him imperfectly. With this limited knowledge of him it becomes easy for us to be unjust to him and to entertain feelings of triumphant self-congratulation when, on account of some cruel advantage on our side, we can get out of him much more than we have paid for. But when we know him as a spirit we know him as our own. We at once feel that cruelty to him is cruelty to ourselves, to make him small is stealing from our own humanity, and in seeking to make use of him solely for personal profit we merely gain in money or comfort what we pay in truth.

One day I was out in a boat on the Ganges. It was a beautiful evening in autumn. The sun had just set; the silence of the sky was full to the brim with ineffable peace and beauty. The vast expanse of water was without a ripple, mirroring all the changing shades of the sunset glow. Miles and miles of a desolate sandbank lay like a huge amphibious reptile of some antediluvian age, with its scales glistening in shining colours.

As our boat was silently gliding by the precipitous river-bank, riddled with the nest-holes of a colony of birds, suddenly a big fish leapt up to the surface of the water and then disappeared, displaying on its vanishing figure all the colours of the evening sky. It drew aside for a moment the many-coloured screen behind which there was a silent world full of the joy of life.

It came up from the depths of its mysterious dwelling with a beautiful dancing motion and added its own music to the silent symphony of the dying day. I felt as if I had a friendly greeting from an alien world in its own language, and it touched my heart with a flash of gladness. Then suddenly the man at the helm exclaimed with a distinct note of regret, "Ah, what a big fish!" It at once brought before his vision the picture of the fish caught and made ready for his supper. He could only look at the fish through his desire, and thus missed the whole truth of its existence.

But man is not entirely an animal. He aspires to a spiritual vision, which is the vision of the whole truth. This gives him the highest delight, because it reveals to him the deepest harmony that exists between him and his surroundings. It is our desires that limit the scope of our self-realisation, hinder our extension of consciousness, and give rise to sin, which is the innermost barrier that keeps us apart from our God, setting up disunion and the arrogance of exclusiveness. For sin is not one mere action, but it is an attitude of life which takes for granted that our goal is finite, that our self is the ultimate truth, and that we are not all essentially one but exist each for his own separate individual existence.

So I repeat we never can have a true view of man unless we have a love for him. Civilisation must be judged and prized, not by the amount of power it has developed, but by how much it has evolved and given expression to, by its laws and institutions, the love of humanity. The first question and the last which it has to answer is, Whether and how far it recognises man more as a spirit than a machine? Whenever some ancient civilisation fell into decay and died, it was owing to causes which produced callousness of heart and led to the cheapening of man's worth; when either the state or some powerful group of men began to look upon the people as a mere instrument of their power; when, by compelling weaker races to slavery and trying to keep them down by every means, man struck at the foundation of his greatness, his own love of freedom and fair-play. Civilisation can never sustain itself upon cannibalism of any form. For that by which alone man is true can only be nourished by love and justice.

As with man, so with this universe. When we look at the world through the veil of our desires we make it small and narrow, and fail to perceive its full truth. Of course it is obvious that the world serves us and fulfils our needs, but our relation to it does not end there. We are bound to it with a deeper and truer bond than that of necessity. Our soul is drawn to it; our love of life is really our wish to continue our relation with this great world. This relation is one of love. We are glad that we are in it; we are attached to it with numberless threads, which extend from this earth to the stars. Man foolishly tries to prove his superiority by imagining his radical separateness from what he calls his physical world, which, in his blind fanaticism, he sometimes goes to the extent of ignoring altogether, holding it at his direst enemy.

Yet the more his knowledge progresses, the more it becomes difficult for man to establish this separateness, and all the imaginary boundaries he had set up around himself vanish one after another. Every time we lose some of our badges of absolute distinction by which we conferred upon our humanity the right to hold itself apart from its surroundings, it gives us a shock of humiliation. But we have to submit to this. If we set up our pride on the path of our self-realisation to create divisions and disunion, then it must sooner or later come under the wheels of truth and be ground to dust. No, we are not burdened with some monstrous superiority, unmeaning in its singular abruptness. It would be utterly degrading for us to live in a world immeasurably less than ourselves in the quality of soul, just as it would be repulsive and degrading to be surrounded and served by a host of slaves, day and night, from birth to the moment of death. On the contrary, this world is our compeer, nay, we are one with it.

Through our progress in science the wholeness of the world and our oneness with it is becoming clearer to our mind. When this perception of the perfection of unity is not merely intellectual, when it opens out our whole being into a luminous consciousness of the all, then it becomes a radiant joy, an overspreading love. Our spirit finds its larger self in the whole world, and is filled with an absolute certainty that it is immortal. It dies a hundred times in its enclosures of self; for separateness is doomed to die, it cannot be made eternal.

But it never can die where it is one with the all, for there is its truth, its joy. When a man feels the rhythmic throb of the soul-life of the whole world in his own soul, then is he free. Then he enters into the secret courting that goes on between this beautiful world-bride, veiled with the veil of the many-coloured finiteness, and the paramatmam, the bridegroom, in his spotless white. Then he knows that he is the partaker of this gorgeous love festival, and he is the honoured guest at the feast of immortality. Then he understands the meaning of the seer-poet who sings, "From love the world is born, by love it is sustained, towards love it moves, and into love it enters."

In love all the contradictions of existence merge themselves and are lost. Only in love are unity and duality not at variance. Love must be one and two at the same time.

Only love is motion and rest in one. Our heart ever changes its place till it finds love, and then it has its rest. But this rest itself is an intense form of activity where utter quiescence and unceasing energy meet at the same point in love.

In love, loss and gain are harmonised. In its balance-sheet, credit and debit accounts are in the same column, and gifts are added to gains. In this wonderful festival of creation, this great ceremony of self-sacrifice of God, the lover constantly gives himself up to gain himself in love. Indeed, love is what brings together and inseparably connects both the act of abandoning and that of receiving.

In love, at one of its poles you find the personal, and at the other the impersonal. At one you have the positive assertion—Here I am; at the other the equally strong denial—I am not.

Without this ego what is love? And again, with only this ego how can love be possible?

Bondage and liberation are not antagonistic in love. For love is most free and at the same time most bound. If God were absolutely free there would be no creation. The infinite being has assumed unto himself the mystery of fainted. And in him who is love the finite and the infinite are made one.

Similarly, when we talk about the relative values of freedom and non-freedom, it becomes a mere play of words. It is not that we desire freedom alone, we want thraldom as well. It is the high function of love to welcome all limitations and to transcend them. For nothing is more independent than love, and where else, again, shall we find so much of dependence? In love, thraldom is as glorious as freedom.

The Vaishnava religion has boldly declared that God has bound himself to man, and in that consists the greatest glory of human existence. In the spell of the wonderful rhythm of the finite he fetters himself at every step, and thus gives his love out in music in his most perfect lyrics of beauty. Beauty is his wooing of our heart; it can have no other purpose. It tells us everywhere that the display of power is not the ultimate meaning of creation; wherever there is a bit of colour, a note of song, a grace of form, there comes the call for our love. Hunger compels us to obey its behests, but hunger is not the last word for a man.

There have been men who have deliberately defied its commands to show that the human soul is not to be led by the pressure of wants and threat of pain. In fact, to live the life of man we have to resist its demands every day, the least of us as well as the greatest. But, on the other hand, there is a beauty in the world which never insults our freedom, never raises even its little finger to make us acknowledge its sovereignty. We can absolutely ignore it and suffer no penalty in consequence. It is a call to us, but not a command. It seeks for love in us, and love can never be had by compulsion. Compulsion is not indeed the final appeal to man, but joy is. Any joy is everywhere; it is in the earth's green covering of grass; in the blue serenity of the sky; in the reckless exuberance of spring; in the severe abstinence of grey winter; in the living flesh that animates our bodily frame; in the perfect poise of the human figure, noble and upright; in living; in the exercise of all our powers; in the acquisition of knowledge; in fighting evils; in dying for gains we never can share. Joy is there everywhere; it is superfluous, unnecessary; nay, it very often contradicts the most peremptory behests of necessity. It exists to show that the bonds of law can only be explained by love; they are like body and soul. Joy is the realisation of the truth of oneness, the oneness of our soul with the world and of the world-soul with the supreme lover.

Realisation in Action

It is only those who have known that joy expresses itself through law who have learnt to transcend the law. Not that the bonds of law have ceased to exist for them—but that the bonds have become to them as the form of freedom incarnate. The freed soul delights in accepting bonds, and does not seek to evade any of them, for in each does it feel the manifestation of an infinite energy whose joy is in creation.

As a matter of fact, where there are no bonds, where there is the madness of license, the soul ceases to be free. There is its hurt; there is its separation from the infinite, its agony of sin. Whenever at the call of temptation the soul falls away from the bondage of law, then, like a child deprived of the support of its mother's arms, it cries out, Smite me not! 42 "Bind me," it prays, "oh, bind me in the bonds of thy law; bind me within and without; hold me tight; let me in the clasp of thy law be bound up together with thy joy; protect me by thy firm hold from the deadly laxity of sin."

As some, under the idea that law is the opposite of joy, mistake intoxication for joy, so there are many in our country who imagine action to be opposed to freedom. They think that activity being in the material plane is a restriction of the free spirit of the soul. But we must remember that as joy expresses itself in law, so the soul finds its freedom in action. It is because joy cannot find expression in itself alone that it desires the law which is outside. Likewise it is because the soul cannot find freedom within itself that it wants external action. The soul of man is ever freeing itself from its own folds by its activity; had it been otherwise it could not have done any voluntary work.

The more man acts and makes actual what was latent in him, the nearer does he bring the distant Yet-to-be. In that actualisation man is ever making himself more and yet more distinct, and seeing himself clearly under newer and newer aspects in the midst of his varied activities, in the state, in society. This vision makes for freedom.

Freedom is not in darkness, nor in vagueness. There is no bondage so fearful as that of obscurity. It is to escape from this obscurity that the seed struggles to sprout, the bud to blossom. It is to rid itself of this envelope of vagueness that the ideas in our mind are constantly seeking opportunities to take on outward form. In the same way our soul, in order to release itself from the mist of indistinctness and come out into the open, is continually creating for itself fresh fields of action, and is busy contriving new forms of activity, even such as are not needful for the purposes of its earthly life. And why? Because it wants freedom. It wants to see itself, to realise itself.

When man cuts down the pestilential jungle and makes unto himself a garden, the beauty that he thus sets free from within its enclosure of ugliness is the beauty of his own soul: without giving it this freedom outside, he cannot make it free within. When he implants law and order in the midst of the waywardness of society, the good which he sets free from the obstruction of the bad is the goodness of his own soul: without being thus made free outside it cannot find freedom within. Thus is man continually engaged in setting free in action his powers, his beauty, his goodness, his very soul. And the more he succeeds in so doing, the greater does he see himself to be, the broader becomes the field of his knowledge of self.

The Upanishad says: In the midst of activity alone wilt thou desire to live a hundred years. It is the saying of those who had amply tasted of the joy of the soul. Those who have fully realised the soul have never talked in mournful accents of the sorrowfulness of life or of the bondage of action. They are not like the weakling flower whose stem-hold is so light that it drops away before attaining fruition. They hold on to life with all their might and say, "never will we let go till the fruit is ripe." They desire in their joy to express themselves strenuously in their life and in their work. Pain and sorrow dismay them not, they are not bowed down to the dust by the weight of their own heart.

With the erect head of the victorious hero they march through life seeing themselves and showing themselves in increasing resplendence of soul through both joys and sorrows. The joy of their life keeps step with the joy of that energy which is playing at building and breaking throughout the universe. The joy of the sunlight, the joy of the free air, mingling with the joy of their lives, makes one sweet harmony reign within and without. It is they who say, In the midst of activity alone wilt thou desire to live a hundred years.

This joy of life, this joy of work, in man is absolutely true. It is no use saying that it is a delusion of ours; that unless we cast it away we cannot enter upon the path of self-realisation. It will never do the least good to attempt the realisation of the infinite apart from the world of action.

It is not the truth that man is active on compulsion. If there is compulsion on one side, on the other there is pleasure; on the one hand action is spurred on by want, on the other it hies to its natural fulfilment. That is why, as man's civilisation advances, he increases his obligations and the work that he willingly creates for himself. One should have thought that nature had given him quite enough to do to keep him busy, in fact that it was working him to death with the lash of hunger and thirst,—but no. Man does not think that sufficient; he cannot rest content with only doing the work that nature prescribes for him in common with the birds and beasts. He needs must surpass all, even in activity.

No creature has to work so hard as man; he has been impelled to contrive for himself a vast field of action in society; and in this field he is for every building up and pulling down, making and unmaking laws, piling up heaps of material, and incessantly thinking, seeking and suffering. In this field he has fought his mightiest battles, gained continual new life, made death glorious, and, far from evading troubles, has willingly and continually taken up the burden of fresh trouble. He has discovered the truth that he is not complete in the cage of his immediate surroundings, that he is greater than his present, and that while to stand still in one place may be comforting, the arrest of life destroys his true function and the real purpose of his existence.

This mahati vinashtih—this great destruction he cannot bear, and accordingly he toils and suffers in order that he may gain in stature by transcending his present, in order to become that which he yet is not. In this travail is man's glory, and it is because he knows it, that he has not sought to circumscribe his field of action, but is constantly occupied in extending the bounds.

Sometimes he wanders so far that his work tends to lose its meaning, and his rushings to and fro create fearful eddies round different centres—eddies of self-interest, of pride of power. Still, so long as the strength of the current is not lost, there is no fear; the obstructions and the dead accumulations of his activity are dissipated and carried away; the impetus corrects its own mistakes. Only when the soul sleeps in stagnation do its enemies gain overmastering strength, and these obstructions become too clogging to be fought through. Hence have we been warned by our teachers that to work we must live, to live we must work; that life and activity are inseparably connected.

It is very characteristic of life that it is not complete within itself; it must come out. Its truth is in the commerce of the inside and the outside. In order to live, the body must maintain its various relations with the outside light and air—not only to gain life-force, but also to manifest it. Consider how fully employed the body is with its own inside activities; its heart-beat must not stop for a second, its stomach, its brain, must be ceaselessly working.

Yet this is not enough; the body is outwardly restless all the while. Its life leads it to an endless dance of work and play outside; it cannot be satisfied with the circulations of its internal economy, and only finds the fulfilment of joy in its outward excursions.

The same with the soul. It cannot live on its own internal feelings and imaginings. It is ever in need of external objects; not only to feed its inner consciousness but to apply itself in action, not only to receive but also to give.

The real truth is, we cannot live if we divide him who is truth itself into two parts. We must abide in him within as well as without. In whichever aspect we deny him we deceive ourselves and incur a loss. Brahma has not left me, let me not leave Brahma. If we say that we would realise him in introspection alone and leave him out of our external activity, that we would enjoy him by the love in our heart, but not worship him by outward ministrations; or if we say the opposite, and overweight ourselves on one side in the journey of our life's quest, we shall alike totter to our downfall.

In the great western continent we see that the soul of man is mainly concerned with extending itself outwards; the open field of the exercise of power is its field. Its partiality is entirely for the world of extension, and it would leave aside—nay, hardly believe in—that field of inner consciousness which is the field of fulfilment. It has gone so far in this that the perfection of fulfilment seems to exist for it nowhere. Its science has always talked of the never-ending evolution of the world. Its metaphysic has now begun to talk of the evolution of God himself. They will not admit that he is; they would have it that he also is becoming.

They fail to realise that while the infinite is always greater than any assignable limit, it is also complete; that on the one hand Brahma is evolving, on the other he is perfection; that in the one aspect he is essence, in the other manifestation—both together at the same time, as is the song and the act of singing. This is like ignoring the consciousness of the singer and saying that only the singing is in progress, that there is no song. Doubtless we are directly aware only of the singing, and never at any one time of the song as a whole; but do we not all the time know that the complete song is in the soul of the singer? It is because of this insistence on the doing and the becoming that we perceive in the west the intoxication of power. These men seem to have determined to despoil and grasp everything by force. They would always obstinately be doing and never be done—they would not allow to death its natural place in the scheme of things—they know not the beauty of completion.

In our country the danger comes from the opposite side. Our partiality is for the internal world. We would cast aside with contumely the field of power and of extension. We would realise Brahma in mediation only in his aspect of completeness, we have determined not to see him in the commerce of the universe in his aspect of evolution. That is why in our seekers we so often find the intoxication of the spirit and its consequent degradation.

Their faith would acknowledge no bondage of law, their imagination soars unrestricted, their conduct disdains to offer any explanation to reason. Their intellect, in its vain attempts to see Brahma inseparable from his creation, works itself stone-dry, and their heart, seeking to confine him within its own outpourings, swoons in a drunken ecstasy of emotion. They have not even kept within reach any standard whereby they can measure the loss of strength and character which manhood sustains by thus ignoring the bonds of law and the claims of action in the external universe.

But true spirituality, as taught in our sacred lore, is calmly balanced in strength, in the correlation of the within and the without. The truth has its law, it has its joy. On one side of it is being chanted the Bhayadasyagnistapati, on the other the Anandadhyeva khalvimani bhutani jayante. Freedom is impossible of attainment without submission to law, for Brahma is in one aspect bound by his truth, in the other free in his joy.

As for ourselves, it is only when we wholly submit to the bonds of truth that we fully gain the joy of freedom. And how? As does the string that is bound to the harp. When the harp is truly strung, when there is not the slightest laxity in the strength of the bond, then only does music result; and the string transcending itself in its melody finds at every chord its true freedom. It is because it is bound by such hard and fast rules on the one side that it can find this range of freedom in music on the other. While the string was not true, it was indeed merely bound; but a loosening of its bondage would not have been the way to freedom, which it can only fully achieve by being bound tighter and tighter till it has attained the true pitch.

The bass and treble strings of our duty are only bonds so long as we cannot maintain them steadfastly attuned according to the law of truth; and we cannot call by the name of freedom the loosening of them into the nothingness of inaction. That is why I would say that the true striving in the quest of truth, of dharma, consists not in the neglect of action but in the effort to attune it closer and closer to the eternal harmony. The text of this striving should be, Whatever works thou doest, consecrate them to Brahma. That is to say, the soul is to dedicate itself to Brahma through all its activities. This dedication is the song of the soul, in this is its freedom. Joy reigns when all work becomes the path to the union with Brahma; when the soul ceases to return constantly to its own desires; when in it our self-offering grows more and more intense. Then there is completion, then there is freedom, then, in this world, comes the kingdom of God.

Who is there that, sitting in his corner, would deride this grand self-expression of humanity in action, this incessant self-consecration? Who is there that thinks the union of God and man is to be found in some secluded enjoyment of his own imaginings, away from the sky-towering temple of the greatness of humanity, which the whole of mankind, in sunshine and storm, is toiling to erect through the ages? Who is there that thinks this secluded communion is the highest form of religion?—thou distraught wanderer, thou Sannyasin, drunk in the wine of self-intoxication, dost thou not already hear the progress of the human soul along the highway traversing the wide fields of humanity—the thunder of its progress in the car of its achievements, which is destined to overpass the bounds that prevent its expansion into the universe? The very mountains are cleft asunder and give way before the march of its banners waving triumphantly in the heavens; as the mist before the rising sun, the tangled obscurities of material things vanish at its irresistible approach. Pain, disease, and disorder are at every step receding before its onset; the obstructions of ignorance are being thrust aside; the darkness of blindness is being pierced through; and behold, the promised land of wealth and health, of poetry and art, of knowledge and righteousness is gradually being revealed to view.

Do you in your lethargy desire to say that this car of humanity, which is shaking the very earth with the triumph of its progress along the mighty vistas of history, has no charioteer leading it on to its fulfilment? Who is there who refuses to respond to his call to join in this triumphal progress? Who so foolish as to run away from the gladsome throng and seek him in the listlessness of inaction? Who so steeped in untruth as to dare to call all this untrue—this great world of men, this civilisation of expanding humanity, this eternal effort of man, through depths of sorrow, through heights of gladness, through innumerable impediments within and without, to win victory for his powers? He who can think of this immensity of achievement as an immense fraud, can he truly believe in God who is the truth? He who thinks to reach God by running away from the world, when and where does he expect to meet him?

How far can he fly—can he fly and fly, till he flies into nothingness itself? No, the coward who would fly can nowhere find him. We must be brave enough to be able to say: We are reaching him here in this very spot, now at this very moment. We must be able to assure ourselves that as in our actions we are realising ourselves, so in ourselves we are realising him who is the self of self. We must earn the right to say so unhesitatingly by clearing away with our own effort all obstruction, all disorder, all discords from our path of activity; we must be able to say, "In my work is my joy, and in that joy does the joy of my joy abide."

Whom does the Upanishad call The chief among the knowers of Brahma? 48 He is defined as He whose joy is in Brahma, whose play is in Brahma, the active one. Joy without the play of joy is no joy at all—play without activity is no play. Activity is the play of joy. He whose joy is in Brahma, how can he live in inaction? For must he not by his activity provide that in which the joy of Brahma is to take form and manifest itself? That is why he who knows Brahma, who has his joy in Brahma, must also have all his activity in Brahma—his eating and drinking, his earning of livelihood and his beneficence. Just as the joy of the poet in his poem, of the artist in his art, of the brave man in the output of his courage, of the wise man in his discernment of truths, ever seeks expression in their several activities, so the joy of the knower of Brahma, in the whole of his everyday work, little and big, in truth, in beauty, in orderliness and in beneficence, seeks to give expression to the infinite.

Brahma himself gives expression to his joy in just the same way. By his many-sided activity, which radiates in all directions, does he fulfil the inherent want of his different creatures. That inherent want is he himself, and so he is in so many ways, in so many forms, giving himself. He works, for without working how could he give himself. His joy is ever dedicating itself in the dedication which is his creation.

In this very thing does our own true meaning lie, in this is our likeness to our father. We must also give up ourselves in many-sided variously aimed activity. In the Vedas he is called the giver of himself, the giver of strength. He is not content with giving us himself, but he gives us strength that we may likewise give ourselves. That is why the seer of the Upanishad prays to him who is thus fulfilling our wants, May he grant us the beneficent mind 52, may he fulfil that uttermost want of ours by granting us the beneficent mind.

That is to say, it is not enough he should alone work to remove our want, but he should give us the desire and the strength to work with him in his activity and in the exercise of the goodness. Then, indeed, will our union with him alone be accomplished. The beneficent mind is that which shows us the want (swartha) of another self to be the inherent want (nihitartha) of our own self; that which shows that our joy consists in the varied aiming of our many-sided powers in the work of humanity. When we work under the guidance of this beneficent mind, then our activity is regulated, but does not become mechanical; it is action not goaded on by want, but stimulated by the satisfaction of the soul. Such activity ceases to be a blind imitation of that of the multitude, a cowardly following of the dictates of fashion. Therein we begin to see that He is in the beginning and in the end of the universe 53, and likewise see that of our own work is he the fount and the inspiration, and at the end thereof is he, and therefore that all our activity is pervaded by peace and good and joy.

The Upanishad says: Knowledge, power, and action are of his nature. It is because this naturalness has not yet been born in us that we tend to divide joy from work. Our day of work is not our day of joy—for that we require a holiday; for, miserable that we are, we cannot find our holiday in our work. The river finds its holiday in its onward flow, the fire in its outburst of flame, the scent of the flower in its permeation of the atmosphere; but in our everyday work there is no such holiday for us. It is because we do not let ourselves go, because we do not give ourselves joyously and entirely up to it, that our work overpowers us. — giver of thyself! at the vision of thee as joy let our souls flame up to thee as the fire, flow on to thee as the river, permeate thy being as the fragrance of the flower.

Give us strength to love, to love fully, our life in its joys and sorrows, in its gains and losses, in its rise and fall. Let us have strength enough fully to see and hear thy universe, and to work with full vigour therein. Let us fully live the life thou hast given us, let us bravely take and bravely give. This is our prayer to thee. Let us once for all dislodge from our minds the feeble fancy that would make out thy joy to be a thing apart from action, thin, formless, and unsustained.

Wherever the peasant tills the hard earth, there does thy joy gush out in the green of the corn, wherever man displaces the entangled forest, smooths the stony ground, and clears for himself a homestead, there does thy joy enfold it in orderliness and peace. — worker of the universe! We would pray to thee to let the irresistible current of thy universal energy come like the impetuous south wind of spring, let it come rushing over the vast field of the life of man, let it bring the scent of many flowers, the murmurings of many woodlands, let it make sweet and vocal the lifelessness of our dried-up soul-life. Let our newly awakened powers cry out for unlimited fulfilment in leaf and flower and fruit.

The Realisation of Beauty

Things in which we do not take joy are either a burden upon our minds to be got rid of at any cost; or they are useful, and therefore in temporary and partial relation to us, becoming burdensome when their utility is lost; or they are like wandering vagabonds, loitering for a moment on the outskirts of our recognition, and then passing on. A thing is only completely our own when it is a thing of joy to us. The greater part of this world is to us as if it were nothing. But we cannot allow it to remain so, for thus it belittles our own self. The entire world is given to us, and all our powers have their final meaning in the faith that by their help we are to take possession of our patrimony.

But what is the function of our sense of beauty in this process of the extension of our consciousness? Is it there to separate truth into strong lights and shadows, and bring it before us in its uncompromising distinction of beauty and ugliness? If that were so, then we would have had to admit that this sense of beauty creates a dissension in our universe and sets up a wall of hindrance across the highway of communication that leads from everything to all things.

But that cannot be true. As long as our realisation is incomplete a division necessarily remains between things known and unknown, pleasant and unpleasant. But in spite of the dictum of some philosophers man does not accept any arbitrary and absolute limit to his knowable world. Every day his science is penetrating into the region formerly marked in his map as unexplored or inexplorable. Our sense of beauty is similarly engaged in ever pushing on its conquests. Truth is everywhere, therefore everything is the object of our knowledge. Beauty is omnipresent, therefore everything is capable of giving us joy.

In the early days of his history man took everything as a phenomenon of life. His science of life began by creating a sharp distinction between life and non-life. But as it is proceeding farther and farther the line of demarcation between the animate and inanimate is growing more and more dim. In the beginning of our apprehension these sharp lines of contrast are helpful to us, but as our comprehension becomes clearer they gradually fade away.

The Upanishads have said that all things are created and sustained by an infinite joy. To realise this principle of creation we have to start with a division—the division into the beautiful and the non-beautiful. Then the apprehension of beauty has to come to us with a vigorous blow to awaken our consciousness from its primitive lethargy, and it attains its object by the urgency of the contrast. Therefore our first acquaintance with beauty is in her dress of motley colours, that affects us with its stripes and feathers, nay, with its disfigurements. But as our acquaintance ripens, the apparent discords are resolved into modulations of rhythm. At first we detach beauty from its surroundings, we hold it apart from the rest, but at the end we realise its harmony with all. Then the music of beauty has no more need of exciting us with loud noise; it renounces violence, and appeals to our heart with the truth that it is meekness inherits the earth.

In some stage of our growth, in some period of our history, we try to set up a special cult of beauty, and pare it down to a narrow circuit, so as to make it a matter of pride for a chosen few. Then it breeds in its votaries affections and exaggerations, as it did with the Brahmins in the time of the decadence of Indian civilisation, when the perception of the higher truth fell away and superstitions grew up unchecked.

In the history of aesthetics there also comes an age of emancipation when the recognition of beauty in things great and small become easy, and when we see it more in the unassuming harmony of common objects than in things startling in their singularity. So much so, that we have to go through the stages of reaction when in the representation of beauty we try to avoid everything that is obviously pleasing and that has been crowned by the sanction of convention. We are then tempted in defiance to exaggerate the commonness of commonplace things, thereby making them aggressively uncommon. To restore harmony we create the discords which are a feature of all reactions. We already see in the present age the sign of this aesthetic reaction, which proves that man has at last come to know that it is only the narrowness of perception which sharply divides the field of his aesthetic consciousness into ugliness and beauty. When he has the power to see things detached from self-interest and from the insistent claims of the lust of the senses, then alone can he have the true vision of the beauty that is everywhere. Then only can he see that what is unpleasant to us is not necessarily unbeautiful, but has its beauty in truth.

When we say that beauty is everywhere we do not mean that the word ugliness should be abolished from our language, just as it would be absurd to say that there is no such thing as untruth. Untruth there certainly is, not in the system of the universe, but in our power of comprehension, as its negative element. In the same manner there is ugliness in the distorted expression of beauty in our life and in our art which comes from our imperfect realisation of Truth. To a certain extent we can set our life against the law of truth which is in us and which is in all, and likewise we can give rise to ugliness by going counter to the eternal law of harmony which is everywhere.

Through our sense of truth we realise law in creation, and through our sense of beauty we realise harmony in the universe. When we recognise the law in nature we extend our mastery over physical forces and become powerful; when we recognise the law in our moral nature we attain mastery over self and become free. In like manner the more we comprehend the harmony in the physical world the more our life shares the gladness of creation, and our expression of beauty in art becomes more truly catholic. As we become conscious of the harmony in our soul, our apprehension of the blissfulness of the spirit of the world becomes universal, and the expression of beauty in our life moves in goodness and love towards the infinite. This is the ultimate object of our existence, that we must ever know that "beauty is truth, truth beauty"; we must realise the whole world in love, for love gives it birth, sustains it, and takes it back to its bosom. We must have that perfect emancipation of heart which gives us the power to stand at the innermost centre of things and have the taste of that fullness of disinterested joy which belongs to Brahma.

Music is the purest form of art, and therefore the most direct expression of beauty, with a form and spirit which is one and simple, and least encumbered with anything extraneous. We seem to feel that the manifestation of the infinite in the finite forms of creation is music itself, silent and visible. The evening sky, tirelessly repeating the starry constellations, seems like a child struck with wonder at the mystery of its own first utterance, lisping the same word over and over again, and listening to it in unceasing joy. When in the rainy night of July the darkness is thick upon the meadows and the pattering rain draws veil upon veil over the stillness of the slumbering earth, this monotony of the rain patter seems to be the darkness of sound itself. The gloom of the dim and dense line of trees, the thorny bushes scattered in the bare heath like floating heads of swimmers with bedraggled hair, the smell of the damp grass and the wet earth, the spire of the temple rising above the undefined mass of blackness grouped around the village huts—everything seems like notes rising from the heart of the night, mingling and losing themselves in the one sound of ceaseless rain filling the sky.

Therefore the true poets, they who are seers, seek to express the universe in terms of music.

They rarely use symbols of painting to express the unfolding of forms, the mingling of endless lines and colours that goes on every moment on the canvas of the blue sky.

They have their reason. For the man who paints must have canvas, brush and colour-box. The first touch of his brush is very far from the complete idea. And then when the work is finished the artist is gone, the windowed picture stands alone, the incessant touches of love of the creative hand are withdrawn.

But the singer has everything within him. The notes come out from his very life. They are not materials gathered from outside. His idea and his expression are brother and sister;

very often they are born as twins. In music the heart reveals itself immediately; it suffers not from any barrier of alien material.

Therefore though music has to wait for its completeness like any other art, yet at every step it gives out the beauty of the whole. As the material of expression even words are barriers, for their meaning has to be constructed by thought. But music never has to depend upon any obvious meaning; it expresses what no words can ever express.

What is more, music and the musician are inseparable. When the singer departs, his singing dies with him; it is in eternal union with the life and joy of the master.

This world-song is never for a moment separated from its singer. It is not fashioned from any outward material. It is his joy itself taking never-ending form. It is the great heart sending the tremor of its thrill over the sky.

There is a perfection in each individual strain of this music, which is the revelation of completion in the incomplete. No one of its notes is final, yet each reflects the infinite.

What does it matter if we fail to derive the exact meaning of this great harmony? Is it not like the hand meeting the string and drawing out at once all its tones at the touch? It is the language of beauty, the caress, that comes from the heart of the world straightway reaches our heart.

Last night, in the silence which pervaded the darkness, I stood alone and heard the voice of the singer of eternal melodies. When I went to sleep I closed my eyes with this last thought in my mind, that even when I remain unconscious in slumber the dance of life will still go on in the hushed arena of my sleeping body, keeping step with the stars. The heart will throb, the blood will leap in the veins, and the millions of living atoms of my body will vibrate in tune with the note of the harp-string that thrills at the touch of the master.

The Realisation of the Infinite

The Upanishads say: "Man becomes true if in this life he can apprehend God; if not, it is the greatest calamity for him."

But what is the nature of this attainment of God? It is quite evident that the infinite is not like one object among many, to be definitely classified and kept among our possessions, to be used as an ally specially favouring us in our politics, warfare, money-making, or in social competitions. We cannot put our God in the same list with our summer-houses, motor-cars, or our credit at the bank, as so many people seem to want to do.

We must try to understand the true character of the desire that a man has when his soul longs for his God. Does it consist of his wish to make an addition, however valuable, to his belongings? Emphatically no! It is an endlessly wearisome task, this continual adding to our stores. In fact, when the soul seeks God she seeks her final escape from this incessant gathering and heaping and never coming to an end. It is not an additional object the she seeks, but it is the nityo 'nityanam, the permanent in all that is impermanent, the rasanam rasatamah, the highest abiding joy unifying all enjoyments. Therefore when the Upanishads teach us to realise everything in Brahma, it is not to seek something extra, not to manufacture something new. Know everything that there is in the universe as enveloped by God. Enjoy whatever is given by him and harbour not in your mind the greed for wealth which is not your own.

When you know that whatever there is is filled by him and whatever you have is his gift, then you realise the infinite in the finite, and the giver in the gifts. Then you know that all the facts of the reality have their only meaning in the manifestation of the one truth, and all your possessions have their only significance for you, not in themselves but in the relation they establish with the infinite.

So it cannot be said that we can find Brahma as we find other objects; there is no question of searching from him in one thing in preference to another, in one place instead of somewhere else. We do not have to run to the grocer's shop for our morning light; we open our eyes and there it is; so we need only give ourselves up to find that Brahma is everywhere.

This is the reason why Buddha admonished us to free ourselves from the confinement of the life of the self. If there were nothing else to take its place more positively perfect and satisfying, then such admonition would be absolutely unmeaning. No man can seriously consider the advice, much less have any enthusiasm for it, of surrendering everything one has for gaining nothing whatever.

So our daily worship of God is not really the process of gradual acquisition of him, but the daily process of surrendering ourselves, removing all obstacles to union and extending our consciousness of him in devotion and service, in goodness and in love. The Upanishads say: Be lost altogether in Brahma like an arrow that has completely penetrated its target. Thus to be conscious of being absolutely enveloped by Brahma is not an act of mere concentration of mind. It must be the aim of the whole of our life. In all our thoughts and deeds we must be conscious of the infinite. Let the realisation of this truth become easier every day of our life, that none could live or move if the energy of the all-pervading joy did not fill the sky. In all our actions let us feel that impetus of the infinite energy and be glad.

It may be said that the infinite is beyond our attainment, so it is for us as if it were naught. Yes, if the word attainment implies any idea of possession, then it must be admitted that the infinite is unattainable. But we must keep in mind that the highest enjoyment of man is not in the having but in a getting, which is at the same time not getting. Our physical pleasures leave no margin for the unrealised. They, like the dead satellite of the earth, have but little atmosphere around them. When we take food and satisfy our hunger it is a complete act of possession. So long as the hunger is not satisfied it is a pleasure to eat. For then our enjoyment of eating touches at every point the infinite.

But, when it attains completion, or in other words, when our desire for eating reaches the end of the stage of its non-realisation, it reaches the end of its pleasure. In all our intellectual pleasures the margin is broader, the limit is far off. In all our deeper love getting and non-getting run ever parallel. In one of our Vaishnava lyrics the lover says to his beloved: "I feel as if I have gazed upon the beauty of thy face from my birth, yet my eyes are hungry still: as if I have kept thee pressed to my heart for millions of years, yet my heart is not satisfied."

This makes it clear that it is really the infinite whom we seek in our pleasures. Our desire for being wealthy is not a desire for a particular sum of money but it is indefinite, and the most fleeting of our enjoyments are but the momentary touches of the eternal. The tragedy of human life consists in our vain attempts to stretch the limits of things which can never become unlimited,—to reach the infinite by absurdly adding to the rungs of the ladder of the finite.

It is evident from this that the real desire of our soul is to get beyond all our possessions. Surrounded by things she can touch and feel, she cries, "I am weary of getting; ah, where is he who is never to be got?"

We see everywhere in the history of man that the spirit of renunciation is the deepest reality of the human soul. When the soul says of anything, "I do not want it, for I am above it," she gives utterance to the highest truth that is in her. When a girl's life outgrows her doll, when she realises that in every respect she is more than her doll is, then she throws it away. By the very act of possession we know that we are greater than the things we possess.

It is a perfect misery to be kept bound up with things lesser than ourselves. This it is that Maitreyi felt when her husband gave her his property on the eve of leaving home. She asked him, "Would these material things help one to attain the highest?"— or, in other words, "Are they more than my soul to me?" When her husband answered, "They will make you rich in worldly possessions," she said at once, "then what am I to do with these?" It is only when a man truly realises what his possessions are that he has no more illusions about them; then he knows his soul is far above these things and he becomes free from their bondage. Thus man truly realises his soul by outgrowing his possessions, and man's progress in the path of eternal life is through a series of renunciations.

That we cannot absolutely possess the infinite being is not a mere intellectual proposition. It has to be experienced, and this experience is bliss. The bird, while taking its flight in the sky, experiences at every beat of its wings that the sky is boundless, that its wings can never carry it beyond. Therein lies its joy. In the cage the sky is limited; it may be quite enough for all the purposes of the bird's life, only it is not more than is necessary. The bird cannot rejoice within the limits of the necessary. It must feel that what it has is immeasurably more than it ever can want or comprehend, and then only can it be glad.

Thus our soul must soar in the infinite, and she must feel every moment that in the sense of not being able to come to the end of her attainment is her supreme joy, her final freedom.

Man's abiding happiness is not in getting anything but in giving himself up to what is greater than himself, to ideas which are larger than his individual life, the idea of his country, of humanity, of God. They make it easier for him to part with all that he has, not expecting his life. His existence is miserable and sordid till he finds some great idea which can truly claim his all, which can release him from all attachment to his belongings. Buddha and Jesus, and all our great prophets, represent such great ideas. They hold before us opportunities for surrendering our all. When they bring forth their divine alms-bowl we feel we cannot help giving, and we find that in giving is our truest joy and liberation, for it is uniting ourselves to that extent with the infinite.

Man is not complete; he is yet to be. In what he is he is small, and if we could conceive him stopping there for eternity we should have an idea of the most awful hell that man can imagine. In his to be he is infinite, there is his heaven, his deliverance. His is is occupied every moment with what it can get and have done with; his to be is hungering for something which is more than can be got, which he never can lose because he never has possessed.

The finite pole of our existence has its place in the world of necessity. There man goes about searching for food to live, clothing to get warmth. In this region—the region of nature—it is his function to get things. The natural man is occupied with enlarging his possessions.

But this act of getting is partial. It is limited to man's necessities. We can have a thing only to the extent of our requirements, just as a vessel can contain water only to the extent of its emptiness. Our relation to food is only in feeding, our relation to a house is only in habitation. We call it a benefit when a thing is fitted only to some particular want of ours. Thus to get is always to get partially, and it never can be otherwise. So this craving for acquisition belongs to our finite self.

But that side of our existence whose direction is towards the infinite seeks not wealth, but freedom and joy. There the reign of necessity ceases, and there our function is not to get but to be. To be what? To be one with Brahma. For the region of the infinite is the region of unity. Therefore the Upanishads say: If man apprehends God he becomes true. Here it is becoming, it is not having more. Words do no gather bulk when you know their meaning; they become true by being one with the idea.

Though the West has accepted as its teacher him who boldly proclaimed his oneness with his Father, and who exhorted his followers to be perfect as God, it has never been reconciled to this idea of our unity with the infinite being. It condemns, as a piece of blasphemy, any implication of man's becoming God. This is certainly not the idea that Christ preached, nor perhaps the idea of the Christian mystics, but this seems to be the idea that has become popular in the Christian west.

But the highest wisdom in the East holds that it is not the function of our soul to gain God, to utilise him for any special material purpose. All that we can ever aspire to is to become more and more one with God.

In the region of nature, which is the region of diversity, we grow by acquisition; in the spiritual world, which is the region of unity, we grow by losing ourselves, by uniting. Gaining a thing, as we have said, is by its nature partial, it is limited only to a particular want; but being is complete, it belongs to our wholeness, it springs not from any necessity but from our affinity with the infinite, which is the principle of perfection that we have in our soul.

Yes, we must become Brahma. We must not shrink to avow this. Our existence is meaningless if we never can expect to realise the highest perfection that there is. If we have an aim and yet can never reach it, then it is no aim at all.

But can it then be said that there is no difference between Brahma and our individual soul? Of course the difference is obvious. Call it illusion or ignorance, or whatever name you may give it, it is there. You can offer explanations but you cannot explain it away. Even illusion is true an illusion.

Brahma is Brahma, he is the infinite ideal of perfection. But we are not what we truly are; we are ever to become true, ever to become Brahma. There is the eternal play of love in the relation between this being and the becoming; and in the depth of this mystery is the source of all truth and beauty that sustains the endless march of creation.

In the music of the rushing stream sounds the joyful assurance, "I shall become the sea." It is not a vain assumption; it is true humility, for it is the truth. The river has no other alternative. On both sides of its banks it has numerous fields and forests, villages and towns; it can serve them in various ways, cleanse them and feed them, carry their produce from place to place. But it can have only partial relations with these, and however long it may linger among them it remains separate; it never can become a town or a forest.

But it can and does become the sea. The lesser moving water has its affinity with the great motionless water of the ocean. It moves through the thousand objects on its onward course, and its motion finds its finality when it reaches the sea.

The river can become the sea, but she can never make the sea part and parcel of herself. If, by some chance, she has encircled some broad sheet of water and pretends that she has made the sea a part of herself, we at once know that it is not so, that her current is still seeking rest in the great ocean to which it can never set boundaries.

In the same manner, our soul can only become Brahma as the river can become the sea. Everything else she touches at one of her points, then leaves and moves on, but she never can leave Brahma and move beyond him. Once our soul realises her ultimate object of repose in Brahma, all her movements acquire a purpose. It is this ocean of infinite rest which gives significance to endless activities. It is this perfectness of being that lends to the imperfection of becoming that quality of beauty which finds its expression in all poetry, drama and art.

There must be a complete idea that animates a poem. Every sentence of the poem touches that idea. When the reader realises that pervading idea, as he reads on, then the reading of the poem is full of joy to him. Then every part of the poem becomes radiantly significant by the light of the whole. But if the poem goes on interminably, never expressing the idea of the whole, only throwing off disconnected images, however beautiful, it becomes wearisome and unprofitable in the extreme. The progress of our soul is like a perfect poem. It has an infinite idea which once realised makes all movements full of meaning and joy. But if we detach its movements from that ultimate idea, if we do not see the infinite rest and only see the infinite motion, then existence appears to us a monstrous evil, impetuously rushing towards an unending aimlessness.

I remember in our childhood we had a teacher who used to make us learn by heart the whole book of Sanskrit grammar, which is written in symbols, without explaining their meaning to us. Day after day we went toiling on, but on towards what, we had not the least notion.

So, as regards our lessons, we were in the position of the pessimist who only counts the breathless activities of the world, but cannot see the infinite repose of the perfection whence these activities are gaining their equilibrium every moment in absolute fitness and harmony. We lose all joy in thus contemplating existence, because we miss the truth. We see the gesticulations of the dancer, and we imagine these are directed by a ruthless tyranny of chance, while we are deaf to the eternal music which makes every one of these gestures inevitably spontaneous and beautiful. These motions are ever growing into that music of perfection, becoming one with it, dedicating to that melody at every step the multitudinous forms they go on creating.

And this is the truth of our soul, and this is her joy, that she must ever be growing into Brahma, that all her movements should be modulated by this ultimate idea, and all her creations should be given as offerings to the supreme spirit of perfection.

There is a remarkable saying in the Upanishads: I think not that I know him well, or that I know him, or even that I know him not.

By the process of knowledge we can never know the infinite being. But if he is altogether beyond our reach, then he is absolutely nothing to us. The truth is that we know him not, yet we know him.

This has been explained in another saying of the Upanishads: From Brahma words come back baffled, as well as the mind, but he who knows him by the joy of him is free from all fears.

Knowledge is partial, because our intellect is an instrument, it is only a part of us, it can give us information about things which can be divided and analysed, and whose properties can be classified part by part. But Brahma is perfect, and knowledge which is partial can never be a knowledge of him.

But he can be known by joy, by love. For joy is knowledge in its completeness, it is knowing by our whole being. Intellect sets us apart from the things to be known, but love knows its object by fusion. Such knowledge is immediate and admits no doubt. It is the same as knowing our own selves, only more so.

Therefore, as the Upanishads say, mind can never know Brahma, words can never describe him; he can only be known by our soul, by her joy in him, by her love. Or, in other words, we can only come into relation with him by union—union of our whole being. We must be one with our Father, we must be perfect as he is.

But how can that be? There can be no grade in infinite perfection. We cannot grow more and more into Brahma. He is the absolute one, and there can be no more or less in him.

Indeed, the realisation of the paramatman, the supreme soul, within our antaratman, our inner individual soul, is in a state of absolute completion. We cannot think of it as non-existent and depending on our limited powers for its gradual construction. If our relation with the divine were all a thing of our own making, how should we rely on it as true, and how should it lend us support?

Yes, we must know that within us we have that where space and time cease to rule and where the links of evolution are merged in unity. In that everlasting abode of the ataman, the soul, the revelation of the paramatman, the supreme soul, is already complete. Therefore the Upanishads say: He who knows Brahman, the true, the all-conscious, and the infinite as hidden in the depths of the soul, which is the supreme sky (the inner sky of consciousness), enjoys all objects of desire in union with the all-knowing Brahman.

The union is already accomplished. The paramatman, the supreme soul, has himself chosen this soul of ours as his bride and the marriage has been completed. The solemn mantram has been uttered: Let thy heart be even as my heart is. There is no room in this marriage for evolution to act the part of the master of ceremonies. The eshah, who cannot otherwise be described than as This, the nameless immediate presence, is ever here in our innermost being. "This eshah, or This, is the supreme end of the other this"; 62 "this This is the supreme treasure of the other this"; 63 "this This is the supreme dwelling of the other this"; 64 "this This is the supreme joy of the other this." 65 Because the marriage of supreme love has been accomplished in timeless time.

And now goes on the endless lila, the play of love. He who has been gained in eternity is now being pursued in time and space, in joys and sorrows, in this world and in the worlds beyond. When the soul-bride understands this well, her heart is blissful and at rest. She knows that she, like a river, has attained the ocean of her fulfilment at one end of her being, and at the other end she is ever attaining it; at one end it is eternal rest and completion, at the other it is incessant movement and change. When she knows both ends as inseparably connected, then she knows the world as her own household by the right of knowing the master of the world as her own lord. Then all her services becomes services of love, all the troubles and tribulations of life come to her as trials triumphantly borne to prove the strength of her love, smilingly to win the wager from her lover.

But so long as she remains obstinately in the dark, lifts not her veil, does not recognise her lover, and only knows the world dissociated from him, she serves as a handmaid here, where by right she might reign as a queen; she sways in doubt, and weeps in sorrow and dejection. She passes from starvation to starvation, from trouble to trouble, and from fear to fear.

I can never forget that scrap of a song I once heard in the early dawn in the midst of the din of the crowd that had collected for a festival the night before: "Ferryman, take me across to the other shore!"

In the bustle of all our work there comes out this cry, "Take me across." The carter in India sings while driving his cart, "Take me across." The itinerant grocer deals out his goods to his customers and sings, "Take me across".

What is the meaning of this cry? We feel we have not reached our goal; and we know with all our striving and toiling we do not come to the end, we do not attain our object. Like a child dissatisfied with its dolls, our heart cries, "Not this, not this." But what is that other? Where is the further shore?

Is it something else than what we have? Is it somewhere else than where we are? Is it to take rest from all our works, to be relieved from all the responsibilities of life?

No, in the very heart of our activities we are seeking for our end. We are crying for the across, even where we stand. So, while our lips utter their prayer to be carried away, our busy hands are never idle.

In truth, thou ocean of joy, this shore and the other shore are one and the same in thee. When I call this my own, the other lies estranged; and missing the sense of that completeness which is in me, my heart incessantly cries out for the other. All my this, and that other, are waiting to be completely reconciled in thy love.

This "I" of mine toils hard, day and night, for a home which it knows as its own. Alas, there will be no end of its sufferings so long as it is not able to call this home thine. Till then it will struggle on, and its heart will ever cry, "Ferryman, lead me across." When this home of mine is made thine, that very moment is it taken across, even while its old walls enclose it. This "I" is restless.

It is working for a gain which can never be assimilated with its spirit, which it never can hold and retain. In its efforts to clasp in its own arms that which is for all, it hurts others and is hurt in its turn, and cries, "Lead me across". But as soon as it is able to say, "All my work is thine," everything remains the same, only it is taken across.

Where can I meet thee unless in this mine home made thine? Where can I join thee unless in this my work transformed into thy work? If I leave my home I shall not reach thy home; if I cease my work I can never join thee in thy work. For thou dwellest in me and I in thee. Thou without me or I without thee are nothing.

Therefore, in the midst of our home and our work, the prayer rises, "Lead me across!" For here rolls the sea, and even here lies the other shore waiting to be reached—yes, here is this everlasting present, not distant, not anywhere else.

5

Sadhana as a Tapas

Indian and Classical Greek philosophical traditions both recommend that we structure our lives around the performance of certain kinds of actions as daily and regular habits. Under some circumstances and for some individuals, this means merely doing what comes naturally. For others, it requires varying degrees of self-control. For yet others, adhering to these practices is impossible or unimportant, beyond the scope of their interests or abilities. I want to take issue with one familiar answer to the question of why this is, and to suggest a different one.

Sadhana

The Yoga Sutras (II.29) enjoin us to cultivate the values and habits appropriate to the higher practices of yoga through consistent sadhana, or spiritual practice-the daily performance of very specific kinds of action:

The yamas are restraints on action that govern our relationships with others. They include nonviolence, avoidance of falsehood, abstention from theft, celibacy, and non-possessiveness or detachment.

The niyamas are positive observances that govern our relation to our higher self. They include mental and physical purity, contentment, self-discipline, self-study, and devotion to the sacred.

The asanas are physical postures that cultivate physical and physiological strength, flexibility and balance.

Pranayama consists in exercises that cultivate control of the breath, the strength and endurance of the central nervous system, and so mental and psychological equilibrium. Pratyahara, dharana, dhyana and samadhi are meditation practices that cultivate perceptual and intellectual discrimination, sustained and focused attention, and in-depth self-scrutiny.

Adhering to all of these practices can seem like a lot of work. For this reason they are considered to be forms of tapas, i.e. disciplines or austerities we may choose to impose on our behaviour that, at the beginning, generate heat and energy because our ego-selves resist them. The stronger and more expansive the ego, the harder the work of bringing it into line.

However, we do not escape this work by turning to the Western philosophical tradition. Socrates in the Euthyphro enjoins us to "give [our] first and greatest care to the improvement of [our] souls," (30b1-2); "to set our thoughts on goodness," (31b5-6); to "not allow to grow in [our]selves the habit of dishonesty," (35c6-7); to "make [ourselves] as good and wise as possible." (36c5-6) He warns us that "[i]t is much more honorable and much easier, not to suppress others, but to make [our]selves as good as [we] can." (39d6-8) And in the Crito he advises that "we ought not to repay injustice with injustice or to do harm to any man, no matter what we may have suffered from him." (49c11-d1).

Socrates' counsel is more general than the detailed instructions for sadhana we find in the Yoga Sutras. But the similarities in the kind and content of actions he recommends are clear.

It is tempting to interpret Socrates' recommendations as telling us simply to be good and wise, or to act honorably and truthfully-as though we could easily follow these recommendations through simple acts of will; as though we could immediately become the model of human excellence to which we aspire, merely by wanting to. This impression is reinforced by Socrates' own behaviour, which embodied this model of excellence with ease and grace.

Aristotle, Plato's student, corrects this impression for the rest of us. He says we are to cultivate virtuous traits of character-courage, temperance, generosity, kindness, patience, truthfulness, friendliness, modesty, and so on-by diligently practising them until they become second nature. (1103a15-19; 33-1103b2)

Through systematic repetition of the relevant actions, Aristotle tells us, these actions become habitual character traits. We then reflexively and naturally express them in action, as circumstances call them forth. He says,

It is the way that we behave in our dealings with other people that makes us just or unjust, and the way that we behave in the face of danger, accustoming ourselves to be timid or confident, that makes us brave or cowardly. Similarly with situations involving desires and anger: some people become temperate and patient from one kind of conduct in such situations, others licentious and irritable from another. In a word, then, like activities produce like dispositions. (1103b14-22)

I believe that Aristotle's inspiration for this insight came from the Brihadaranyaka Upanishad, in which Yagnavalkya argues,

As a man acts, so does he become. A man of good deeds becomes good, a man of evil deeds becomes evil. A man becomes pure through pure deeds, impure through impure deeds. (paragraph 232)

Both texts argue that we sculpt our characters and inner selves using the tool of our physical behaviour. Both challenge the Western psychoanalytic assumption that right outward action stems from successful inner self-scrutiny. Both claim that cultivation of character and self progresses in the opposite direction, from outer to inner. Once we have trained ourselves to be fluent and effortless in right action through practice and repetition, we already will have achieved the moral and spiritual character that such action naturally and effortlessly expresses. In the meantime, we may choose to exert ourselves in less ambitious acts of will. If we can now, on this occasion, bring ourselves to behave outwardly in the way a morally and spiritually developed person would behave, we begin to carve the pathways of habit and disposition in which we want our inclinations to travel. We in effect gradually mold ourselves to be the kind of person we aspire to be. In time, Aristotle assures us, the inner qualities of mind and temperament will follow.

So we find in both Indian and Greek philosophical traditions the very strong recommendation to undertake certain physical and mental activities on a regular-indeed even a daily basis; to practice them repeatedly and systematically until they become second nature; in short, to train ourselves in human excellence. Both traditions regard the project of self-cultivation as centrally definitive of a worthwhile human life.

Tapas

I said earlier that all this seems like a lot of work. But appearances, as we know, can deceive. It may be less work than it seems, when one is ready to undertake it; or more work for some people than for others; or more work at some points in one's life than in others. For Socrates it wasn't work at all, but rather his happiness. These practices may require very great self-governance for one individual, or under one set of circumstances. They may be not only effortless but intensely pleasurable under another.

One explanation is inherent in Aristotle's account of habituation. These practices are perhaps the hardest work of all to the extent that one has had no prior experience with them, and they become easier and more effortless with practice. Just as learning to play the piano is most excruciating at the very beginning, when one's fingers are stiff and unwilling and one's repertoire is confined to Hannon and Czerny fingering exercises, similarly holding one's temper or postponing the satisfaction of desire may be virtually unachievable if one has had no prior practice in doing so. The lesson here is that the work of self-cultivation is hardest at the very beginning of the project; and that one must want overridingly to achieve this end-more than one wants, at that moment, to express one's anger or satisfy one's immediate desire-in order to make any headway at all.

But this explanation leaves many questions unanswered. It does not explain why the hard work of self-cultivation, hard as it is at the beginning for all of us, is so much more challenging for some of us than for others. Nor does it explain why, however hard that work is, some of us but not others have the interest or ability to want it badly enough in order to prevail. Why is sadhana of interest to some but not others? Why is it so much harder for some than for others? And among those for whom it is difficult, why do some but not others succeed in continuing to practice it? Just how much of a tapas is sadhana supposed to be?

A different answer to these questions is supplied by familiar versions of certain Hindu doctrines. These claim that lack of interest, difficulties or failures in the project of self-cultivation-like any other personal difficulties or failures-are the result of "bad karma," i.e. that any such present difficulties are the deserved result of one's own prior derelictions, either in this life or an earlier one. This answer thus motivates us to practice the virtues out of fear that any vicious actions we perform will come back to haunt us. It instructs us to accept any difficulties or failures we are presently experiencing as the just retributive consequences of vicious actions we have performed in the past, or in a past life.

And it thus implies that those for whom sadhana is easier are in some mysterious sense morally superior to those for whom it is hard. I take moral issue with the implied use of fear to motivate virtue; with encouraging acceptance of rather than constructive resistance to present personal misfortune; with the reasoning that any such misfortune-particularly to children, animals, and the innocent-is their own fault; and therefore with the illusion of moral hierarchy in a wisdom tradition that implicitly rejects it. But I focus here on the metaethics behind the "bad karma" argument. This argument presupposes two metaethical doctrines of Hinduism: the doctrine of karma and the doctrine of reincarnation.

In its familiar form, the doctrine of karma states that

(1) all actions are causally determined by earlier ones;

(2) all actions have morally significant, causally determined consequences, extending into the indefinite future; and

(3) morally good actions have morally good consequences and morally bad actions have morally bad consequences.

The familiar doctrine of reincarnation states that

(1) an individual is repeatedly reborn in one life after another and one body after another;

(2) the life circumstances in which one is reborn on a particular occasion are determined by the moral quality of one's previous life; and

(3) morally good actions in a previous life determine better life circumstances the next time around and morally bad actions in a previous life determine worse life circumstances the next time around.

The familiar doctrines of karma and reincarnation are thus mutually interdependent: karma supplies the causal and moral continuities of acts and consequences throughout time, while reincarnation supplies the metaphysical and personal continuities of individual identities who are affected by them throughout time. Thus both assume the temporal continuity, through successive lifetime physical embodiments, of a persisting individual ego-self.

Both assume that persisting ego-self as the causal origin of a succession of behaviours and consequences of behaviours that further mold and influence it. And both assume that those behaviours and consequences can be morally evaluated, consistently and objectively over time, independent of context, community, or culture. As stated, these familiar doctrines are vulnerable to many objections I cannot explore here. In what follows I suggest a different interpretation of these doctrines that is consistent with the metaphysics of the Upanishads, but implies a different explanation for why sadhana requires more self-control for some individuals or under some circumstances than others.

The Spiritual Function of Sadhana

These practices fit into the context of a more general moral view, in both Indian and Greek traditions. In both, we undertake these practices, not as ends in themselves, but rather for the express purpose of cultivating the self-of refining our moral, intellectual and spiritual capacities to their fullest expression. This, in turn, serves a further purpose: to achieve knowledge of ultimate reality. The Katha Upanishad states, [W]hen a man has discrimination and his mind is controlled, his senses, like the well-broken horses of a charioteer, lightly obey the rein. (paragraph 55) ...The senses of the wise man obey his mind, his mind obeys his intellect, his intellect obeys his ego, and his ego obeys the Self. (par. 61) ...When all the senses are stilled, when the mind is at rest, when the intellect wavers not-then, say the wise, is reached the highest state.

This calm of the senses and the mind has been defined as yoga. He who attains it is free from delusion. (par. 106-107)

Here we find the probable inspiration for Plato's metaphor in the Phaedrus of the immortal soul as a charioteer who governs the passions in the form of two horses, one obedient and one not. The thought is that in order to grasp knowledge of ultimate reality, we must physically, physiologically, psychologically and spiritually prepare ourselves to receive it. Our body and central nervous system must be conditioned and balanced, our senses alert, our intellect sharp and clear, and our vision impartial and unclouded by undisciplined desires, impulses, or personal bias or preoccupations. This conception of sadhana is familiar in Yoga and Vedanta. But it is implicit in Aristotle's remarks in the Nicomachean Ethics on the contemplative life as requiring self-sufficiency, leisure, freedom from fatigue, and that we ought, so far as possible, to make ourselves immortal, ... to do all that we can to live in conformity with the highest that is in us; for ... this is the true self of the individual. (1177b 20-1178a4)

Similarly, in both traditions, to achieve this knowledge is intensely pleasurable. In Yoga and Vedanta, the pleasure derives from the lived experience of union with ultimate reality. This experience is the final outcome of the practices already described, which cultivate the discernment of underlying unity behind the multiplicity of appearances. Because direct, experiential insight into this underlying unity at the same time transcends the apparent boundaries between the knowing subject and the object known, the experience of union is simultaneously an experience of unconditional love, unrestricted freedom, and undifferentiated bliss. Thus the final outcome of sadhana is a release from the rigors of tapas because it is a release from the limiting constraints of ego-individuation:

> Having fully ascertained and realized the truth of Vedanta, having established themselves in purity of conduct by following the yoga of renunciation, these great ones attain to immortality in this very life; and when their bodies fall away from them at death, they attain to liberation. (Mundaka Upanishad par.56)

In hindsight, we discover that tapas-the experienced friction of working against the resistance of our delinquent impulses-was also the felt resistance of the physical and spiritual bars that imprisoned us within our limited individual identities. Having achieved knowledge of ultimate reality, we thereby achieve a state in which these temporal and material constraints no longer exist. Aristotle's account of the happiness that comes with the life of contemplation is less explicit, but nevertheless consistent with this account. He defines happiness as "an activity of the soul in accordance with or implying a rational principle," (1098a8-9), i.e. virtue; and declares that "virtuous actions must be pleasurable in themselves." (1099a20-21) Contemplative activity, however, is the highest virtue of "the best part of us.

> Whether this is the intellect or something else that we regard as naturally ruling and guiding us, and possessing insight into things noble and divine ...it is the activity of this part, in accordance with the virtue proper to it, that will be perfect happiness. (1177a12-18) ...any man who lives it will do so not as a human being but in virtue of something divine within him, and in proportion as this divine element is superior to composite human nature. (1177b26-28)

Here Aristotle describes contemplation as insight into "things noble and divine," lived and experienced "in virtue of something divine within [us]." What we come to know through contemplation has a divine dimension, and we come to know it in virtue of the divine dimension within ourselves. Both Indian and Greek traditions associate the divine with the unconditioned-that is, with omnipotence, omniscience, and unconditional freedom. Hence I would propose that Aristotelian contemplation, like yogic meditation, is a process that advances us from the conditioned world of individuated appearances to experiential insight into the unconditioned, unified ultimate reality that lies behind it. Next I try to suggest what it is about this ultimate reality that enables us to arrive at it through the yogic practices of sadhana.

The Metaphysics of Sadhana

Obviously I set myself here an impossible task. By definition, what is unconditioned and unlimited is beyond the capacity of individuating words and concepts to capture. That is why the Upanishads refer to ultimate reality using not a descriptive term but rather a proper name, Brahman. Like the name Susan, the term Brahman designates something without purporting to describe it. Unlike a person named Susan, however, the referent of the term Brahman cannot be described, and to try is immediately to fail. Nevertheless the rishis who authored the Upanishads could not resist the temptation to try. They disagreed violently among themselves as to how best to describe Brahman. I like to envision the rishis, each firmly ensconced within the solitude of his or her forest enclave, furiously e-mailing one another back and forth about this topic.

In the Prasna Upanishad, Brahman is associated with the sun, light, prana (or breath), and energy (pars. 6, 8-9, 13, 40-41, and especially 60). In the Mundaka, Brahman is described as willing the universe into existence and engendering its material cause.

This in turn engenders its primal energy, which in turn engenders mind, and so the subtle elements. These in turn engender multiplicity, and thereby the causal determination of the universe (par. 9). The Mundaka also describes Brahman as formless and self-luminous (pars. 19, 29, 38-39), reinforcing the characterization of the Prasna. The Taittiriya Upanishad narrates the way Brahman, [d]esiring that he should become many, that he should make of himself many forms, ... meditated. Meditating, he created all things. Creating all things, he entered into everything. (pars. 32-33)

Later in the Taittiriya, Brahman is described as the "source of all thought and life and action" (par. 67). Similarly, the Aitareya Upanishad opens by declaring that Before creation, all that existed was the Self, the Self alone. Nothing else was. Then the Self thought: "Let me send forth the worlds." (par.1)

Later, the Aitareya characterizes Brahman as pure consciousness (pars. 13, 15).

The Chandogya Upanishad describes the realized form of the Self as light and its thoughts as true (par. 5). It later declares that In the beginning there was Existence alone-One only, without a second. He, the One, thought to himself: Let me be many, let me grow forth. Thus out of himself he projected the universe; and having projected out of himself the universe, he entered into every being. (par. 42)

These descriptions of Brahman have three features in common: First, they provide a first-cause explanation of the creation of the physical universe of name and form. Second, they characterize this first cause as intentional, or object-directed. Third, they further characterize this first cause as self-aware, i.e. as conscious of the nature and consequences of intentional conscious acts. From these three features we can extrapolate an account of the relation between the ultimate reality we may seek to know, and the concrete practices within our familiar world of multiplicity by which we can come to know it. We need only make one assumption that is implicit but not actually stated in the Upanishads. That one extra assumption is that consciousness is identical to energy.

If consciousness is energy, then since energy can condense into matter, an intentional consciousness can causally engender a physical state of affairs. And if energy is conscious, then every materially condensed physical object has some degree of consciousness, however slight. This provides one way of understanding the frequently repeated claim in the Upanishads, that Brahman, or the true Self, subsists not only in every living thing, but indeed deep within every being of any kind.

Under this assumption, ultimate reality-or Brahman-is pure consciousness, and ultimate reality generates the world of name and form in exactly the same way consciousness always engenders multiplicity. Consciousness-or Brahman-is inherently intentional: it is always consciousness of somethin In the limiting case in which there is only one thing, namely consciousness, consciousness is nevertheless conscious of itself-i.e. it is self-conscious. But then there are two things that are Brahman, namely Brahman as conscious subject and Brahman as object of that consciousness. However this bipartite relation, too, implies consciousness that is neither subject nor object but conscious of both. Brahman is now three things: subject, object, and that consciousness which is neither-with the attendant distinctions of name that identify the distinctions in form which that consciousness has created. Each iteration of the act of self-conscious discrimination creates further multiplicity and diversity in the objects of consciousness, at the same time that it further detaches the ultimate Self from the multiplicity of objects its self-awareness has created.

And because-and here is where our extra assumption becomes useful-consciousness is identical to energy, these acts of self-awareness generate intentional objects of consciousness that have physical reality as well. These individuated forms constitute our familiar, causally determined world of multiplicity, and include human beings. So this world, including humanity, is a product of Brahman, is co-extensive with Brahman, is saturated with Brahman, and also is an illusion that conceals the steady, unitary state of consciousness that Brahman is in fact.

Sadhana comprises spiritual practices within the familiar world of multiplicity that enable us to trace this path back in the opposite direction, from "the world of name and form" to "the One without a second" that underlies it. In the Upanishads, individual human consciousness is an extension of the original, unitary consciousness that engenders it. Like that original consciousness, individual human consciousness in turn creates further objects of awareness-then enters into them, then gets lost in them. Identifying with and pursuing the objects of individual consciousness we have created, we lose our connection to the true Self whose objects they are. In different ways, all of the eight limbs of yoga train us in two habits. First, sadhana trains us to observe and control our mental and physical reactions to stimuli. Second, sadhana cultivates the ability to detach our awareness from those reactions: from our perceptions, interpretations, and beliefs; from the emotions and desires we feel in response to them; from the actions our emotions and desires move us to perform; and finally from the fruits of those actions outside us.

Thus sadhana trains us in the habit of self-awareness. Of course we continue to experience the full force of these ego-states, as long as we survive as ego-selves at all. Simultaneously, through sadhana, we learn to regard the ego's antics reflectively-with detachment, amusement and compassion. From this reflective standpoint, the distinctions of name and form that give our ego-states such personal urgency are not all that important. We learn not to take our ego-selves too seriously. Sadhana teaches us to enjoy and applaud the dance without slipping a disk on the dance floor.

As we learn to view our ego-states from the standpoint of self-awareness, we come to identify with that Self in us that views the ego's antics as entertainment. From that standpoint we see that our ego-states are not essential parts of our Self at all. They are creations of self-consciousness we can observe, enjoy, and finally release. To release our ego-states from our consciousness is to release our consciousness from their imprisonment, and so to rejoin the original, unitary consciousness that engendered them. In this sense, sadhana really is our direct pipeline to God.

"Bad Karma" and the Gunas

The Svetasvatara Upanishad describes how [t]he seers, absorbed in contemplation, saw within themselves the ultimate reality, the self-luminous being, the one God, who dwells as the self-conscious power in all creatures. He is One without a second. Deep within all beings he dwells, hidden from sight by the coverings of the gunas-sattva, rajas, and tamas. (par. 4) The gunas are the three kinds of qualities or dispositions that differentiate ultimate reality into discriminable forms-as we just did a moment ago in distinguishing between Brahman as subject, Brahman as object, and Brahman as neither subject nor object. The gunas thus shape all physical and psychological entities and forces in the universe. So we release our ego-states from consciousness by examining, controlling and releasing their qualities and dispositions

In the Bhagavad Gita, the analysis of the three gunas has a distinctly moral and hierarchical inflection. However, as natural cosmic forces, they are in themselves morally neutral. Sattva is the tendency toward weightlessness, dispersion, and clarity. In human beings it is associated with the character traits of serenity, purity and joyfulness. When we are navigating effortlessly through our lives with ease, grace, and sensitivity, we are sattvic. Rajas is the tendency toward forward propulsion, explosive energy or force, and drive.

In human beings it is associated with ambition, desire, and competitiveness. When we feel driven to speed up on the highway so as to outstrip the car that is trying to pass us, we are being rajasic. Tamas is the tendency toward inertia, resistance, and dullness. In human beings it is associated with ignorance, delusion, and stupefaction. We are tamasic after many hours of watching TV, and even more so if we compound our couch potatohood with Big Macs and beer. It may be difficult for us to think about these three tendencies in and of themselves, without making moral judgments about them. But they do not necessarily indicate a person's moral character. Try, for example, to identify the preponderant guna in Aristotle's portrait of the magnanimous man: The magnanimous man is thought to have slow movements, a deep voice, and unhurried speech. For since he takes few things seriously, he is not excitable; and since he counts nothing great, he is not high-strung.

Aristotle's magnanimous man sounds rather tamasic to me. In human beings, the gunas shape our physical, biochemical, psychological, and spiritual constitution. As psychological and spiritual dispositions, the gunas determine the given traits of character we then may attempt to train and mold through sadhana. The particular mix of gunas is different for each of us, and may be different at different points in our lives. All three of them are present in all of us to varying degrees. For all of us, the key to progress in cultivation of our higher self-to upward spiritual mobility, as it were-is rajas. No matter how much tamasic inertia we each must resist, our apportionment of rajas is what drives us to formulate goals and ambitions and ideals for ourselves, and what energizes us to achieve them. Rajas can find expression in passion, persistence, and commitment, as well as in the less admirable traits described in the Bhagavad Gita.

Thus rajas is the force that propels us along the path, from where we began to where we want to go. Where we want to go is determined by our individual priorities and our social conditioning. If we want to go to Brahman, rajas charges up our sadhana to gradually peel away the gunas or mental tendencies of the ego-self, layer by layer, until we reach "the ultimate reality, the self-luminous being, the one God, who dwells as the self-conscious power ... hidden from sight by the coverings of the gunas" within all of us.

Now back to why sadhana is harder for some individuals at some times than for others at other times; and why "bad karma" does not provide an adequate explanation of this. It follows from this account of the gunas that any project of self-improvement-which relies essentially on one's own initiative rather than external incentives-will be more difficult on the face of it, for those of us who have a large proportion of tamas in our personal constitution. It will be even harder if this inertial resistance is compounded by prior self-destructive or self-indulgent habits-whether learned or chosen-that must be overcome.

Furthermore, some individuals may lack sufficient rajas ever to blast through these resistant habits of mind and body. They may be unable to make themselves want cultivation of their higher self, or union with ultimate reality enough to endure the tapas of self-discipline. They may, quite simply, have other priorities. Others who lack these impediments will find the journey easier, and perhaps even pleasurable, because there is a greater proportion of sattva in their personal constitutions.

Moreover, neither science nor logic gives reason to dispute the thesis that there are individuated, non-physical continuities of energy that persist throughout several individual lifetimes. The gunas are psycho-physical forces that determine the manner, kind and quality of all entities that condense out of original unitary consciousness. So they determine not only a person's psychological dispositions of character, but also the person's capacity and inclination to alter or improve that character.

What we do or do not do with our lives now may well entrench some of those dispositions so deeply that they survive the dissolution of the body. They may then gravitate to and condense in newborn physical forms in which they find further expression. Other life habits may erase some of those character traits and replace them with others that are, literally, self-canceling: the disposition to openness, generosity, humility, surrender, or self-sacrifice, for example-dispositions that soften and dissolve the boundaries of the ego-self, and make union with ultimate reality much easier.

However, the transpersonal continuity of individual character traits through several lifetimes-call this the "thin" account of reincarnation-does not imply the transpersonal continuity of an individual ego-self-call this the "thick" account. As we have seen, character traits are dispositions to react to given circumstances with a certain kind of response. If the circumstances are never given, the response never occurs. In this case the latent disposition remains present, but unrealized and unexpressed. The person who has it is no less an individual ego-self for that. Furthermore, two people can have the same character trait-say, generosity-and express it differently because the circumstances that call it forth and the resources available to each are different. Those differences are what define each person's ego-self, not the character trait they share in common.

These traits are therefore necessary conditions of individual identity; but they are not sufficient. Rather, my individual identity is determined by the personal content of my actual experiences: my particular environment, relationships, encounters, and my thoughts and feelings about all of these.

Most of all, my individual identity as an ego-self is determined by the personal content of the memories that I am constantly accumulating and shaping with each passing moment in my life.

I find no texts within the Upanishads that might explain how this particular, personal accumulation of memory-content might endure transpersonally throughout several lifetimes-nor, therefore, any that actually support and elucidate the thick account of reincarnation that virtually all of them avow. But it is precisely this continuity of personal memory-content that identifies me to myself and to others as the individual I am. If this lifelong personal continuity does not endure transpersonally, then I as an ego-self cannot be said to endure transpersonally.

If I as an ego-self do not endure transpersonally, then I cannot be held morally responsible for the past-life moral successes or failures of any impersonal mix of gunas that may have found previous human incarnation. Therefore I cannot be held morally responsible for the impersonal mix of gunas that give shape to my efforts in this one. That mix may make my sadhana easy, but I receive no moral credit for that. Or my mix of gunas may make sadhana hard, or impossible or uninteresting, without my racking up any moral demerits. I cannot be blamed for having these gunas, nor for my actions in a previous life that bequeathed me these gunas. For there was no "me" in a previous life to whom such actions could be ascribed.

Of course I am morally responsible for doing the very best I can-or not-with the mix of gunas I happen to have in this life. If I aspire to ultimate knowledge, I can be praised for devoting every resource of character I have to the project of self-cultivation. And I can be blamed for squandering those resources on self-aggrandizement, or destroying them through self-indulgence, selfishness, or vice. In any such case, the proper subject of moral evaluation is what I do with the natural endowments I happen to have. It is neither morally reasonable nor metaphysically sound to pass moral judgment on those natural endowments themselves.

Hence no individual morally "deserves" the character traits with which she begins her life; and no individual is being rewarded or punished with those character traits in this life for moral successes or failures in a previous one. A person who finds sadhana difficult or impossible is a victim of misfortune. But this does not make his personal difficulty a punishment for past-life moral dereliction. His burden is not "bad karma," but rather bad luck.

On Kalacakra Sadhana and Social Responsibility

Most of us want to help. Some do this by involvement in the peace movement, or in the environmentalist movement, or in the movement to end world hunger. We were probably attracted to Buddhism because of its Bodhisattva ideal, the ideal of putting the welfare of others ahead of our own. Human beings everywhere have this ideal, this noble aspiration, in some form. It may manifest as a sense of social responsibility. In Christian countries we find church groups in every town involved in community service. In Buddhist countries such as Tibet, the Lamas begin their morning meditations with the wish and resolve to benefit others.

In the Kalacakra meditation, or sadhana, like virtually all Buddhist sadhanas, one of the first things you do is generate bodhicitta. You know that the Buddha, the enlightened one, has been able to effectively help millions of living beings. You wish to do this, too. So you generate a resolve to become enlightened like the Buddha, for the sole purpose of effectively benefiting others. The state of mind so generated, in which the welfare of others is more important than your own, sets the tone for all that will follow in the meditation.

Since you see the great need in the world around you, you know you must do something effective quickly. That is why you have chosen the path of tantra, the fast path. The Kalacakra Tantra, like other Buddhist tantras, teaches a meditation technique where you visualize yourself as a particular form of a Buddha. You visualize yourself as having all the qualities of this Buddha. It is a technique of transformation. What distinguishes Kalacakra from other Buddhist tantras is that you not only transform yourself during the meditations, you also help transform the world.

I wrote the small book, Kalacakra Sadhana and Social Responsibility, to call attention to this latter aspect. Many sincere workers for world good today have never paid attention to anything as esoteric-sounding as Kalacakra. The idea of meditating on strange-looking deities seems altogether too impractical in face of pressing world needs in the here and now. Yet I have become convinced that there is nothing more effective that could be done for the world than the practice of the Kalacakra sadhana. I think that when the Dalai Lama uses the phrase, "Kalacakra for world peace," it is more than just a slogan. The Buddhist tradition has had 2,500 years to develop effective means, and Tibetans like the Dalai Lama regard Kalacakra as the pinnacle of these.

My book opens with an account of Vedic recitation. That's right, Vedic recitation, as found in Hindu tradition, not in Buddhist tradition. In India, Vedic recitation has been regarded for thousands of years as what upholds the cosmic order. The sounds comprising the Vedic recitation are thought to order the cosmos and keep it in harmony. The rationale of this is much the same as what modern physics shows us, when sand on a drumhead makes different patterns as different musical notes are sounded. In any case, this idea was universal in ancient Brahmanical India, and, as we may deduce from the Vimala-prabha Kalacakra commentary, in the hidden kingdom of Sambhala.

The Vimala-prabha describes Sambhala as having 35 million Brahma-Rishis, or Vedic sages. The account from this commentary forms the second chapter of my book. At the time of the Buddha, the king of Sambhala is said to have travelled to India to request from him the Kalacakra teachings. The king returned to Sambhala with these teachings. He wished to have the Vedic sages of his kingdom adopt them. How this occurred makes an interesting story. In the end, the sages did adopt the Kalacakra teachings, and Kalacakra became the state religion of Sambhala. There they were preserved for many centuries, until an Indian yogi brought them to India about a thousand years ago. From India they were transferred to Tibet, being translated from Sanskrit into Tibetan, where they have been preserved until our time.

A brief summary of these extraordinary teachings is found in the third chapter of my book. These teachings are secret, in the sense that one is not allowed to discuss their details with those who have not received the Kalacakra initiation. Thus what is in my book is only general statements, but enough to see what the practice entails. The idea was also to somewhat contextualize these teachings, since they are so foreign to us in the West. The context of the Vedic precedents, and the adoption of the Kalacakra teachings by the sages of Sambhala, I think illustrate the primary concern of those involved in these teachings, namely, the welfare of the world.

The idea of secrecy is something we are not accustomed to, especially in our modern world where everything is open. But with Kalacakra, like other Buddhist tantras, it is of very real importance. To use the analogy given by Lama Govinda in his book, The Way of the White Clouds, Tibetans regard the Buddhist tantric teachings much like we in the West regard nuclear reactors. For the safety of everyone, knowledge of and access to them must be carefully restricted. To continue the analogy, receiving a tantric initiation is required for access to the secret tantric teachings, just as receiving security clearance is required for access to the secret specifications of nuclear reactions. An experience of mine may serve to show just how seriously this is taken in Tibetan tradition.

I had first heard of Kalacakra around Christmas of 1974, from Nicholas Roerich's book, Shambhala. His references to the Kalacakra teachings were very inspiring. But of course, almost nothing was available on them at that time in Western languages. In 1977 I began to study Sanskrit, and in early 1979 in Dharamsala, Tibetan. I was delighted to find that the Kalacakra Tantra had earlier been published in the original Sanskrit, along with its Tibetan and Mongolian translations. About 1980 I began reading the Sanskrit Kalacakra Tantra, but it was almost incomprehensible. By then the Institute for Advanced Studies of World Religions had microfilmed a number of Sanskrit manuscripts in Nepal, including the great Kalacakra commentary entitled Vimala-prabha, Immaculate Light. I was able to obtain a microfilm of this manuscript from them. It was a huge help, as were the Tibetan translations; but there were still problems, questions of what the text means.

By the fall of 1980, when I had hardly gotten 20 verses into the Kalacakra Tantra, I took one of these questions to a Tibetan Geshe who was giving public teachings in the U.S.A. He did not answer the question. He said emphatically that I must not attempt to read this book, or even open it, without first receiving the Kalacakra initiation. He said it would be very dangerous to do so. I followed his advice. I put the texts away, until in 1981 I received the Kalacakra initiation from the Dalai Lama in Madison, Wisconsin, the first time he gave it in the West. In this way it was strongly impressed upon me that the Kalacakra initiation gives the necessary permission to study and practice the Kalacakra teachings, and it provides protection for the student and practitioner of these teachings.

Tantric initiations, in keeping with the idea of secrecy, have traditionally always been limited to a few selected pupils. Kalacakra is an exception to this, because many people take the Kalacakra initiation as a blessing rather than as a prerequisite to its study and practice. Many Tibetans believe that the contact with these teachings provided by the Kalacakra initiation will sow the seeds for them to be reborn in Sambhala in the future. So there is a tradition in Tibet of giving large public Kalacakra initiations. For the comparatively few attendees who will actually take up the study and practice of Kalacakra, the initiation also means a commitment. You commit to at least a minimum daily practice from that time on, for the rest of your life.

When the Dalai Lama gave the Kalacakra initiation in the U.S.A. in 1981, there were no materials available in English from which to do any such practice. So he provided a six-session guru-yoga Kalacakra practice in a book that everyone there received. After he gave the Kalacakra initiation in Switzerland in 1985, translations of other Kalacakra sadhanas were also made available to those who requested them, through the kind efforts of Andy Wistreich. This was all truly wonderful, making possible the practice of Kalacakra by those in the West. Yet for me, it made a new problem, that obliged me to mentally put the initiation I had received in 1981 on hold, at least in so far as the daily practice commitment was concerned.

What defines a tantra, and thus distinguishes it from a text that need not be kept secret, is the presence in it of mantras. Mantras are composed of Sanskrit syllables. The recitation of mantras forms an integral part of all tantric sadhana practice. Just as Tibetan Buddhist tradition regards initiation as absolutely indispensable for the practice of tantra, so Indian Brahmanical tradition regards exactitude as absolutely indispensable for the recitation of mantras. They went to what we would regard as great extremes to insure exactitude in the transmission of their mantras, both of the syllables these are composed of, and of their correct pronunciation. I took this tradition just as seriously as I did the Geshe's warning about the necessity of first receiving the initiation. So I could not practice the sadhana until I had ascertained the correct form and pronunciation of its Sanskrit mantras, which were found in varying forms in the Tibetan sadhanas.

Much like we in the West look up to the Tibetans as the source of the precious Buddhist teachings, so the Tibetans have always looked up to the Indians as the source of these precious teachings. The Tibetan Buddhist canon consists of Tibetan translations of the original Sanskrit Buddhist texts from India. The Tibetans' love for these must have rubbed off on me. I still remember the thrill when on my first trip to India in 1978 I found in a bookstore a published reproduction of an ancient Sanskrit manuscript of the Kalacakra Tantra.

By the time my problem about doing the Kalacakra practice arose in the early 1980s, the Nepal-German Manuscript Preservation Project was well underway, filming many thousands of Sanskrit Buddhist manuscripts in Nepal. A friend who was doing a thesis on the first chapter of the Kalacakra texts had gone to Nepal for part of his research. With his help, I was able to obtain in the mid-1980s microfilms of several more Kalacakra manuscripts, including a Sanskrit full-length

Kalacakra sadhana extracted from the Vimala-prabha. These allowed me to eventually ascertain the correct form of all the mantras.

Thus I was finally able to begin my daily practice commitment in 1987, six years after I had received the Kalacakra initiation. Of course, this highly unusual situation was peculiar to my own path. No such problem exists for other Kalacakra practitioners. This is because the great majority of Tibetan Lamas find that the blessings of the transmission lineage override any concerns about the form or pronunciation of the mantras. Indeed, this has proven fully adequate for many centuries. But I love Sanskrit. Even after all these years, the Sanskrit texts have never lost their appeal for me. To me, the most impressive work being done anywhere on the planet is the work of the Rare Buddhist Texts Research Project of the Central Institute of Higher Tibetan Studies in Sarnath.

Here at this institute, in a reversal of the transmission of the Buddhist canon to Tibet a millennium ago, Sanskrit pandits of India are working in collaboration with learned Tibetans to again make the Buddhist canon available in its original Sanskrit. They are utilizing the long lost Sanskrit manuscripts that have now been microfilmed, and are editing these with the help of their Tibetan translations. Many important volumes have already been published, including the great Vimala-prabha Kalacakra commentary. I have utilized this text to prepare an appendix to my book, giving the deities of the Kalacakra mind mandala. All Kalacakra sadhanas, whether written by Indians or Tibetans, must necessarily be based on this primary text. Occasional differences in these sadhanas occur, and this appendix is meant to provide what is now available from the original Sanskrit source.

Bibliography

Akers, Brian Dana : *The Hatha Yoga Pradipika,* Woodstock, YogaVidya, New York, 2002.

Apte, V. M.: *Social and Religious Life in the Grihya Sutras*, Rawat Press, Bombay, 1954.

Avalon, Arthur and Ellen : *Hymns to the Goddess*, Ganesh and Co., Madras, 1964.

Avalon, Arthur: *Hymn to Kali (Karpuradi-Stotra)*, Ganesh and Co., Madras, 1965.

Baba, Pagal : *Temple of the Phallic King: The Mind of India*, Simon and Schuster, New York, 1973.

Basu, Manoranjan : *Tantras: A General Study*, Shrimati Mira Basu, Calcutta, 1976.

Beyer, Stephen : *The Cult of Tara: Magic and Ritual in Tibet*, University of California Press, Berkeley, 1973.

Bose, Ram Chandra, *Brahmoism*, Oxford, New York, 1884.

Chattopadhyaya, Sudhakar: *Reflections on the Tantras*, Motilal Banarsidass, New Delhi, 1978.

Chawdhri, L. R. : *Practicals of Mantras Tantras,* Sagar Publications, New Delhi, 1985.

Collect, S. D.: *The Life and Letter of Raju Rahmmohun Roy*, Kali Ram Press, Calcutta, 1962.

Comfort, Alex: *The Koka Shastra: and other Medieval Indian Writings on Love*, George Allen and Unwin, London, 1964.

Cozort, Daniel : *Highest Yoga Tantra,* Snow Lion Publications, New York, 1986.

Crawford, Cromwell S.: *Ram Mohan Roy: His Era and Ethics*, Acharya Press, New Delhi, 1984.

Datta, V.N.: *Sati: Widow Burning in India*, Manohar, New Delhi, 1990.

De Ropp, S. R. : *Sex Energy: The Sexual Force in Man and Animals*, Corgi Books, London, 1972.

Douglas, Nik and Slinger, Penny: *Sexual Secrets: The Alchemy of Ecstasy*, Destiny Books, New York, 1979.

Dyczkowski, Mark. S. G. : *The Canon of the Shaivagama and the Kubjika Tantras of the Western Kaula Tradition,* State University of New York Press, Albany, 1988.

Eliade, Mircea: *Rites and Symbols of Initiation*, Harper Torchbook, New York, 1965.

Farrow, G. W. and Menon, I. : *The Concealed Essence of the Hevajra Tantra,* Motilal Banarsidass, Delhi, 1992.

Feuerstein, Georg : *The Philosophy of Classical Yoga,* Inner Traditions, Rochester, 1996.

Gambhirananda, Swami: *Brahma Sutra Shamkar Bhasya,* Adavita Ashrama, Calcutta, 1977.

Guenther, Herbert. V.: *Gampopa's Jewel Ornament of Liberation*, Rider and Co., London, 1970.

Haich, Elisabeth : *Sexual Energy and Yoga*, Aurora Press, New York, 1982.

Hopkins, W. E.: *Ethics of India,* Yale University Press, New Haven, 1924.

Jacobs, Hans : *Western Psychotherapy and Hindu Sadhana*, George Allen and Unwin, London, 1961.

Joshi, V.C.: *Rammohun Roy and the Process of Modernization in India*, Saraswati Press, Delhi, 1975.

Karmarkar, R.D.: *Gaudepada Karika*, Bhandarkar Oriental Institute, Poona, 1953.

Kaushalayan, Bhadant Anand: *Swami Vivekananda and the Great Buddha*, Buddha Bhoomi Prakashan, Nagpur 1994.

Kramrisch, Stella: *Manifestations of Shiva*, Philadelphia Museum of Art, Philadelphia, 1981.

Krishna, Gopi : *Kundalini: Path to Higher Consciousness,* Orient Paperbacks, New Delhi, 1976.

Lessing, Ferdinand : *Introduction to the Buddhist Tantric Systems*, Motilal Banarsidass, Delhi, 1993.

Majumdar, A. K.: *Caitanya: His Life and Doctrine*, MacMillan, Bombay, 1969.

Mulin, G. H. : *Meditation on the Lower Tantras*, Library of Tibetan Works and Archives, Dharamsala, 1983.

Munshi, K M.: *Glory that was Gurjaradesa*, Rawat Press, Bombay, 1955.

Narayanananda, Swami : *The Kundalini Shakti*, Rishikesh, 1950.

Natalia V. Isaeva: *Shankara and Indian Philosophy*, SUNY, New York, 1993.

Panikkar, K. M.: *Himdnism and the West*, Panjab University Publication, Chandigarh, 1964.

Payne, E. : *The Shaktas: An Introduction and Comparative Study*, Calcutta, 1933.

Pratyagatmananda, Swami : *Japasutram*, Ganesh and Co., Madras, 1961

Prime, Ranchor: *Hinduism and Ecology*, Motilal Banarsidass, Delhi 1994.

Rajneesh, Bhagwan : *Tantra: The Supreme Understanding*, Chidvilas, Boulder, 1993.

Ranade, R. D.: *Mysticism in Maharashtra*, MacMillan, Delhi, 1933.

Ranganathananda, Swami: *Science and Religion*, Advaita Ashram, Calcutta, 1978.

Rastogi, Navjivan : *The Krama Tantricism of Kashmir*, Motilal Banarsidass, Delhi, 1979.

Sayyambhava, Arya: *Dasa Vaikalika Sutra,* Kastur Chand Lalwani. Delhi, 1973.

Schmidt, Toni : *The Eighty-Five Siddhas*, Stat Etnografiska Museum, Stockholm, 1958.

Singer, June : *Androgyny: Toward a New Theory of Sexuality,* Anchor Press/Doubleday, New York, 1976.

Singh, Kirpal: *Jap Ji: The Message of Guru Nanak*, MacMillan, Delhi, 1964.

Sircar, D. C. : *The Sakta Pithas*, Indological Publishers and Booksellers, Delhi, 1973.

Taylor, A. E.: *Elements Metaphysics*, Methnen & Co., London, 1924.

Trevor Leggett: *Realization of the Supreme Self: the Bhagavad Gita Yogas*, Kegan Paul International, London, 1995.

Van Kooij, K. R. : *Worship of the Goddess According to the Kalikapurana*, E. J. Brill, Leiden, 1972.

Vidhushekhara Bhattacharya: *The Agamasastra of Gaudapada*, Motilal Banarsidass, Delhi, 1989.

Wayman, Alex : *Yoga of the Guhyasamaja Tantra*, Motilal Banarsidass, Delhi, 1977.

Wheeler, Robert Eric Mortimer: *Civilization of the Indus Valley and Beyond*, McGraw-Hill, New York, 1966.

Winternitz, M. : *Notes on the Guhyasamaja Tantra and the Age of the Tantras*, IHQ, Calcutta, 1933.

Woodroffe, Sir John : *The World as Power*, Ganesh and Co., Madras, 1966.

Yogananda, Paramahansa, *Autobiography of a Yogi,* Self-Realization Fellowship, Los Angeles, 1946.

Yogananda, Swami : *Autobiography of a Yogi,* Fellowship, Los Angeles, 1946.

Zimmer, Heinrich: *Myths and Symbols in Indian Art and Civilization*, Joseph Campbell, Delhi, 1946.

Zvelebil, Kamil. V. : *The Poets of the Powers*, Rider and Co., London, 1973.

Index

I

J

K

L

M

S

T

U